The Expositor's Bible
The Book of Revelation
By William Milligan, D.D.
Edited by Anthony Uyl

Devoted Publishing
Woodstock, Ontario, 2017

The Expositor's Bible: The Book of Revelation
By William Milligan, D.D.
Professor of divinity and Biblical criticism in the University of Aberdeen. author of "The Resurrection of our Lord," etc.
Edited by Anthony Uyl
Originally edited by W. Robertson Nicoll, D.D., LL.D.

Hodder & Stoughton, New York, George H. Doran Company

The text of The Expositor's Bible: The Book of Revelation is all in the Public Domain. This edition is published by Devoted Publishing a division of 2165467 Ontario Inc.

What kind of philosophies do you have?
Let us know!

Contact us at: devotedpub@hotmail.com
Visit us on Facebook: @DevotedPublishing
Published in Woodstock, Ontario, Canada 2017.

For bulk educational rates, please contact us at the above email address.

ISBN: 978-1-988297-98-9

Table of Contents

PREFATORY NOTE

In ordinary circumstances one who undertakes to comment upon a book of the New Testament may be justly expected to make every effort to explain each successive clause and each difficult expression of the book on which he writes. My aim in the following Commentary is rather to catch the general import and object of the Revelation of St. John considered as a whole. The latter purpose indeed cannot be attained unless the commentator has himself paid faithful attention to the former; but it is not necessary that the results of these inquiries should in every case be presented to the English reader. To him this book is for the most part a perplexity and enigma, and he would only be embarrassed by a multitude of details. It seemed well, therefore, to treat the book in its sections and paragraphs rather than verse by verse; and this is the course pursued in the following pages. The translation used is for the most part that of the Revised Version. An examination of the words and clauses of the book, conducted upon a plan different from that here adopted, and much more minute in its character, will be found in the Author's Commentary on the Apocalypse, in the Commentary upon the books of the New Testament edited by Professor Schaff and published by Messrs. Clark, Edinburgh. The principles upon which the Author has proceeded have been fully discussed in his Baird Lectures.

The University, Aberdeen, May 1889.

CHAPTER I - THE PROLOGUE

Rev. i.

> *The Revelation of Jesus Christ, which God gave Him to show unto His servants, even the things which must shortly come to pass: and He sent and signified it through His angel unto His servant John; who bare witness of the word of God, and of the testimony of Jesus Christ, even of all things that he saw. Blessed is he that readeth, and they that hear the words of the prophecy, and keep the things which are written therein: for the season is at hand* (i. 1-3).

The first chapter of Revelation introduces us to the whole book, and supplies in great measure the key by which we are to interpret it. The book is not intended to be a mystery in the sense in which we commonly understand that word. It deals indeed with the future, the details of which must always be dark to us; and it does this by means of figures and symbols and modes of speech far removed from the ordinary simplicity of language which marks the New Testament writers. But it is not on that account designed to be unintelligible. The figures and symbols employed in it are used with perfect regularity; its peculiar modes of speech are supposed to be at least not unfamiliar to the reader; and it is taken for granted that he understands them. The writer obviously expects that his meaning, so far from being obscured by his style, will be thereby illustrated, enforced, and brought home to the mind, with greater than ordinary power. The word Revelation by which he describes to us the general character of his work is of itself sufficient to show this. "Revelation" means the uncovering of that which has hitherto been covered, the drawing back of a veil which has hung over a person or thing, the laying bare what has been hitherto concealed; and the book before us is a revelation instead of a mystery.

Again, the book is a revelation of Jesus Christ; not so much a revelation of what Jesus Christ Himself is, as one of which He is the Author and Source. He is the Head of His Church, reigning supreme in His heavenly abode. He is the Eternal Son, the Word without whom was not anything made that was made, and who executes all the purposes of the Father, "the same yesterday, and to-day, and forever." [1] He is at the same time "Head over all things to the Church." [2] He regulates her fortunes. He controls in her behalf the events of history. He fills the cup which He puts into her hand with prosperity or adversity, with joy or sorrow, with victory or defeat. Who else can impart a revelation so true, so weighty, and so precious?

Yet again, the revelation to be now given by Jesus Christ is one which God gave Him, the revelation of the eternal and unchangeable plan of One who turneth the hearts of kings as the rivers of water, who saith and it is done, who commandeth and it stands fast.

Finally, the revelation relates to things that must shortly come to pass, and thus has all the interest of the present, and not merely of a far-distant future.

Such is the general character of that revelation which Jesus Christ sent and signified through His angel unto His servant John. And that Apostle faithfully recorded it for the instruction and comfort of the Church. Like his Divine Master, with whom throughout all this book believers are so closely identified, and who is Himself the Amen, the faithful and true witness, [3] the disciple whom He loved stands forth to bear witness of the word of God thus given him, of the testimony of Jesus thus signified to him, even of all things that he saw. He places himself in thought at the end of the visions he had witnessed, and re-traces for others the elevating pictures which had filled, as he beheld them, his own soul with rapture.

Therefore may he now, ere yet he enters upon his task, pronounce a blessing upon those who shall pay due heed to what he is to say. Does he think of the person by whom the apostolic writings were read aloud in the midst of the Christian congregation? then, Blessed is he that readeth. Does he think of those who listen? then, Blessed are they that hear the words of the prophecy. Or, lastly, does he think not merely of reading and hearing, but of that laying up in the heart to which these were only preparatory? then, Blessed are they that keep the things which are written therein, for the season, the short season in which everything shall be accomplished, is at hand.

The Introduction to the book is over; and it may be well to mark for a moment that tendency to divide his matter into three parts which peculiarly distinguishes St. John, and to which, as supplying an important rule of interpretation, we shall often have occasion to refer. There are obviously three parts in the Introduction,--the Source, the Contents, and the Importance of the revelation: and each of these is again divided into three. Three persons are mentioned when the Source is spoken of,--God, Jesus Christ, and the servants of Jesus; three when the Contents are referred to,--the Word of God, the Testimony of Jesus, and All things that he saw; and three when the Importance of the book is described,--He that readeth, They that hear, and They that keep the things written therein.

> *John to the seven churches which are in Asia: Grace to you, and peace, from Him which is, and which was, and which is to come; and from the seven Spirits which are before His throne; and from Jesus Christ, who is the faithful witness, the firstborn of the dead, and the ruler of the kings of the earth. Unto Him that loveth us, and loosed us from our sins in His blood; and He made us to be a kingdom, to be priests unto His God and Father; to Him be the glory and the dominion for ever and ever. Amen. Behold, He cometh with the clouds; and every eye shall see Him, and they which pierced Him; and all the tribes of the earth shall wail over Him. Even so, Amen. I am the Alpha and the Omega, saith the Lord, God, which is and which was and which is to come, the Almighty* (i. 4-8).

From the Introduction we pass to the Salutation, extending from ver. 4 to ver. 8. Adopting a method different from that of the fourth Gospel, which is also the production of his pen, the writer of Revelation names himself. The difference is easily explained. The fourth Gospel is original not only in its contents but its form. The Apocalypse is moulded after the fashion of the ancient prophets, and of the numerous apocalyptic authors of the time; and it was the practice of both these classes of writers to place their names at the head of what they wrote. The fourth Gospel was also intended to set forth in a purely objective manner the glory of the Eternal Word made flesh, and that too in such a way that the glory exhibited in Him should authenticate itself, independently of human testimony. The Apocalypse needed a voucher from one known and trusted. It came through the mind of a man, and we naturally ask, Who is the man through whom it came? The enquiry is satisfied, and we are told that it comes from John. In telling us this St. John speaks with the authority which belongs to him. By-and-by we shall see him in another light, occupying a position similar to ours, and standing on the same level with us in the covenant of grace. But at this moment he is the Apostle, the Evangelist, the Minister of God, a consecrated priest in the Christian community who is about to pronounce a priestly blessing on the Church. Let the Church bow her head and reverently receive it.

The Salutation is addressed to the seven churches which are in Asia. On this point it is enough to say that by the Asia spoken of we are to understand neither the continent of that name, nor its great western division Asia Minor, but only a single district of the latter, of which Ephesus, where St. John spent the later years of his life and ministry, was the capital. There the aged Apostle tended all those portions of the flock of Christ that he could reach, and all the churches of the neighbourhood were his peculiar care. We know that these were in number more than seven. We know that to no church could the Apostle be indifferent. The conclusion is irresistible, that here, as so often in this book as well as in other parts of Scripture, the number seven is not to be literally understood. Seven churches are selected, the condition of which appeared most suitable to the purpose which the Apostle has in view; and these seven represent the Church of Christ in every country of the world, down to the very end of time. The universal Church spreads itself out beneath his gaze; and before he instructs he blesses it.

The blessing is, Grace to you, and peace; grace first, the Divine grace, in its enlightening, quickening, and beautifying power; and then peace, peace with God and man, peace that in the deep recesses of the heart remains undisturbed by outward trouble, the peace of which it is said by Him who is the Prince of peace, "Peace I leave with you; My peace I give unto you: not as the world giveth give I unto you. Let not your heart be troubled, neither let it be fearful." [4]

The source of the blessing is next indicated,--the Triune God, the three Persons of the glorious Trinity, the Father, the Holy Spirit, and the Son. Probably we should have thought of a different order; but the truth is that it is the Son, as the manifestation of the Godhead, who is mainly in the Apostle's mind. Hence the peculiarity of the first designation, Him which is, and which was, and which is to come, a designation specially applicable to our Lord. Hence also the peculiarity of the second designation, The seven Spirits which are before His throne; not so much the Spirit viewed in His individual personality, in the eternal relations of the Divine existence, as that Spirit in the manifoldness of His operation in the Church, the Spirit of the glorified Redeemer,--not one therefore, but seven. Hence, again, the peculiar designation of Christ, Jesus Christ, who is the faithful witness, the firstborn of the dead, and the ruler of the kings of the earth; not so much the Son in His metaphysical relation to the Godhead, as in attributes connected with His redemptive work. And hence, finally, the fact that when these three Persons have been named, the Seer fills up the remaining verses of his Salutation with thoughts, not of the Trinity, but of Him who has already redeemed us, and who will in due time come to perfect our salvation.

Now, therefore, the Church, reflecting upon all that has been done, is done, and shall be done for her, is able to raise the song of triumphant thanksgiving, Unto Him that loveth us, and loosed us from our sins in His blood, and He made us to be a kingdom, to be priests unto His God and Father; to Him be the glory and the dominion for ever and ever. Amen. In these words the possession of complete redemption is implied. The true reading of the original is not that of our Authorised Version, "Unto Him that washed," but "Unto Him that loosed" us from our sins. We have received not merely the pardon of sin, but deliverance from its power. "Our soul is escaped as a bird out of the snare of the fowler; the snare is broken, and we are escaped." [5] The chains in which Satan held us captive have been snapped asunder and we are free. Again, this loosing has taken place "in" rather than "by" the blood of Christ, for the blood of Christ is living blood, and in that life of His we are enfolded and enwrapped, so that it is not we that live, but Christ that liveth in us. Once more they who are thus spoken of are "a kingdom, priests unto His God and Father," the former being the lower stage, the latter the higher. The word "kingdom" has reference, less to the splendour of royalty than to victory over foes. Christians reign in conquering their spiritual enemies; and then, in possession of the victory that overcometh the world, they enter into the innermost sanctuary of the Most High and dwell in the secret of His Tabernacle. There their great High Priest is one with "His God and Father," and there they also dwell with His Father and their Father, with His God and their God.

The statement of these verses, however, reveals not only what the Christian Church is to which the Apocalypse is addressed; it reveals also what the Lord is from whom the revelation comes. He is indeed the Saviour who died for us, the witness faithful unto death: but He is also the Saviour who rose again, who is the firstborn of the dead, and who has ascended to the right hand of God, where He lives and reigns in glory everlasting. It is the glorified Redeemer from whom the book of His revelation comes; and He has all power committed to Him both in heaven and on earth. More particularly, He is "the ruler of the kings of the earth." This is not a description of such honour as might be given by a crowd of loyal nobles to a beloved prince. It rather gives expression to a power by which "the kings of the earth," the potentates of a sinful world, are subdued and crushed.

Lastly, the Salutation includes the thought that He who is now hidden in heaven from our view, will yet appear in the glory that belongs to Him. He is the Lord who "is to come"; or, as it is expanded in the words immediately following the doxology, Behold, He cometh with the clouds; and every eye shall see Him, and they which pierced Him; and all the tribes of the earth shall wail over Him. Even so, Amen. It is of importance to ask what the glory is in which the glorified Lord is thus spoken of as coming. Is it that of one who shall be the object of admiration to every eye, and who, by the revelation of Himself, shall win all who behold Him to godly penitence and faith? The context forbids such an interpretation. The tribes "of the earth" are like its kings in ver. 5, the tribes of an ungodly world, and the "wailing" is that of chap. xviii. 9, where the same word is used, and where the kings of the earth weep and wail over the fall of guilty Babylon, which they behold burning before their eyes. The tones of that judgment which is to re-echo throughout the book are already heard: "Give the king Thy judgments, O God, and Thy righteousness unto the king's Son. He shall judge the people with righteousness, and Thy poor with judgment"; "Verily there is a reward for the righteous: verily, He is a God that judgeth in the earth." [6]

And now the glorified Redeemer Himself declares what He is: I am the Alpha and the Omega, saith the Lord, God, which is and which was and which is to come, the Almighty. It will be observed that after the word "Lord" we have interposed a comma not found in either the Authorised or the Revised Version. [7] On various other occasions we shall have to do the same, and the call to do so arises partly from the connexion of the thought, partly from St. John's love of that tripartite division of an idea which has been already spoken of. The former does not lead us to the Father; it leads us, on the contrary, to the Son. He it is Who has been described immediately before, and with Him the description which follows is to be occupied. No doubt the thought of God, of the Father, lies immediately behind the words. No doubt also "the Son can do nothing of Himself, but what He seeth the Father doing"; yet "what things soever He doeth, these the Son also doeth in like manner." [8] By the Son the Father acts. In the Son the Father speaks. The Son is the manifestation of the Father. The same Divine attributes, therefore, which are to be seen in the Father, are to be seen in the Son. Let us hear Him as He seals His intimations of coming judgment with the assurance that He is God, who has come who is and who is to come, the Almighty.

I John, your brother and partaker with you in the tribulation and kingdom and patience which are in Jesus, was in the isle that is called Patmos, for the word of God and the testimony of Jesus. I was in the Spirit on the Lord's day, and I heard behind me a great voice, as of a trumpet, saying, What thou seest, write in a book, and send it to the seven churches; unto Ephesus, and unto Smyrna, and unto Pergamum, and unto Thyatira, and unto Sardis, and unto Philadelphia, and unto Laodicea. And I turned to see the voice which spake with me. And having turned, I saw seven golden candlesticks; and in the midst of the candlesticks one like unto a Son of man, clothed with a garment down to the foot, and girt about at the breasts with a golden girdle. And His head and His hair were white as white wool, white as snow; and His eyes were as a flame of fire; and His feet like unto burnished brass, as if it had been refined in a furnace; and His voice as the voice of many waters. And He had in His right hand seven stars: and out of His mouth proceeded a sharp two-edged sword: and His countenance was as the sun shineth in his strength. And when I saw Him, I fell at His feet as one dead. And He laid His right hand upon me, saying, Fear not; I am the first and the last, and the living One; And I became dead, and behold, I am alive for evermore, and I have the keys of death and of Hades. Write therefore the things which thou sawest, and the things which are, and the things which shall come to pass hereafter; the mystery of the stars which thou sawest upon My right hand, and the seven golden candlesticks. The seven stars are the angels of the seven churches; and the seven candlesticks are seven churches (i. 9-20).

After the Introduction and Salutation, the visions of the book begin, the first being the key to all that follow. The circumstances amidst which it was given are described, not merely to satisfy curiosity, or to afford information, but to establish such a connexion between St. John and his readers as shall authenticate and vivify its lessons.

I John, he begins, your brother and partaker with you in the tribulation and kingdom and patience which are in Jesus, was in the isle that is called Patmos, for the word of God and the testimony of Jesus. It is no longer only the Apostle, the authoritative messenger of God, who speaks; it is one who occupies the same ground as other members of the Church, and is bound to them by the strong deep tie of common sorrow. The aged and honoured Evangelist, "the disciple whom Jesus loved," is one with them, bears the same burden, drinks the same cup, and has no higher consolation than they may have. He is their "brother," a brother in adversity, for he is a partaker with them of the "tribulation" that is in Jesus. The reference is to outward suffering and persecution; for the words of the Master were now literally fulfilled: "A servant is not greater than his lord. If they persecuted Me they will also persecute you;" "Yea, the hour cometh, that whosoever killeth you shall think that he offereth service unto God." [9] The scorn, the hatred, the persecution of the world! for such as were exposed to these things was the Apocalypse written, by such was it understood; and if, in later times, it has often failed to make its due impression on the minds of men, it is because it is not intended for those who are at ease in Zion. The more Christians are compelled to feel that the world hates them, and that they cannot be its friends, the greater to them will be the power and beauty of this book. Its revelations, like the stars of the sky, shine most brightly in the cold, dark night.

"Tribulation" is the chief thing spoken of, but the Apostle, with his love of groups of three, accompanies it with other two marks of the Christian's condition in the world,--the "kingdom" and "patience" that are in Jesus. St. John therefore was in tribulation. He had been driven from Ephesus, we know not why, and had been banished to Patmos, a small rocky island of the Ægean Sea. He had been banished for his faith, for his adherence to "the word of God and the testimony of Jesus," the former expression leading our thoughts to the revelation of the Old Testament, the latter to that of the New; the former to those prophets, culminating in the Baptist, of whom the same Apostle who now writes tells us in the beginning of his Gospel, that they "came for witness, that they might bear witness of the light;" [10] the latter to "the true light, even the light which lighteth every man coming into the world." [11] Driven from the society of his friends and "children," we cannot doubt that St. John would be drawn even more closely than was his wont to the bosom of his Lord; would feel that he was still protected by His care; would remember the words uttered by Him in the most sublime and touching moment of His life, "And I am no more in the world, and these are in the world, and I come to Thee. Holy Father, keep them in Thy name which Thou hast given Me"; [12] and would share the blessed experience of knowing that, on every spot of earth however remote, and amidst all trials however heavy, he was in the hands of One who stills the tumults of the people as well as the waves of the sea beating upon the rock-bound coast of Patmos.

Animated by feelings such as these, the Apostle knew that, whatever appearances to the contrary might present themselves, the time now passing over his head was the time of the Lord's rule, and not of man's. No thought could be more inspiring, and it was the preparation in his soul for the scene which followed.

I was in the Spirit on the Lord's day, and I heard behind me a great voice, as of a trumpet, saying, What thou seest, write in a book, and send it to the seven churches; unto Ephesus, and unto Smyrna, and unto Pergamum, and unto Thyatira, and unto Sardis, and unto Philadelphia, and unto Laodicea. The Lord's day here referred to may have been the Sunday, the first day of the Christian week, the day commemorative of that morning when He who had been "crucified through weakness, yet lived through the power of God." [13] If so, there was a peculiar fitness in that vision, now to be granted, of the risen and glorified Redeemer. But it seems doubtful if this is the true interpretation. Proof is wanting that the first day of the week had yet received the name of "The Lord's Day," and it is more in accordance with the prophetic tone of the book before us, to think that by St. John the whole of that brief season which was to pass before the Church should follow her Lord to glory was regarded as "The Lord's Day." Whichever interpretation we adopt, the fact remains that, meditating in his lonely isle upon the glory of his Lord in heaven and the contrasted fortunes of His Church on earth, St. John passed into a state of spiritual ecstasy. Like St. Paul, he was caught up into the third heavens; but, unlike him, he was permitted, and even commanded, to record what he heard and saw. [14]

And I heard behind me, he says, a great voice as of a trumpet, saying, What thou seest, write in a book, and send it to the seven churches; unto Ephesus, and unto Smyrna, and unto Pergamum, and unto Thyatira, and unto Sardis, and unto Philadelphia, and unto Laodicea. We need not dwell now upon these churches. We shall meet them again. They are "the seven churches which are in Asia" already spoken of in ver. 4; and they are to be viewed as representative of the whole Christian Church in all countries of the world, and throughout all time. In their condition they represented to St. John what that Church is, in her Divine origin and human frailty, in her graces and defects, in her zeal and lukewarmness, in her joys and sorrows, in the guardianship of her Lord, and in her final victory after many struggles. Not to Christians in these cities alone is the Apocalypse spoken, but to all Christians in all their circumstances: "He that hath an ear, let him hear." The Apostle heard.

And I turned to see the voice which spake with me. And having turned I saw seven golden candlesticks; and in the midst of the candlesticks one like unto a Son of man. It was a splendid vision which was thus presented to his eyes. The golden candlestick, first of the Tabernacle and then of the Temple, was one of the gorgeous articles of furniture in God's holy house. It was wrought, with its seven branches, after the fashion of an almond tree, the earliest tree of spring to hasten (whence also it was named) into blossom; and, as we learn from the elaborateness and beauty of the workmanship, from the symbolical numbers largely resorted to in its construction, and from the analogy of all the furniture of the Tabernacle, it represented Israel when that people, having offered themselves at the altar, and having been cleansed in the laver of the court, entered as a nation of priests into the special dwelling-place of their heavenly King. Here, therefore, the seven golden candlesticks, or as in ver. 4 the one in seven, represent the Church, as she burns in the secret place of the Most High.

But we are not invited to dwell upon the Church. Something greater attracts the eye,--He who is "like unto a Son of man." The expression of the original is remarkable. It occurs only once in any of the other books of the New Testament, in John v. 27, although there, both in the Authorised and Revised versions, it is unhappily translated "the Son of man." It is the humanness of our Lord's Person more than the Person Himself, or rather it is the Person in His humanness, to which the words of the original direct us. Amidst all the glory that surrounds Him we are to think of Him as man; but what a man!

Clothed with a garment down to the foot, and girt about at the breasts with a golden girdle. And His head and His hair were white as white wool, white as snow; and His eyes were as a flame of fire; and His feet like unto burnished brass as if it had been refined in a furnace; and His voice as the voice of many waters. And He had in His right hand seven stars; and out of His mouth proceeded a sharp two-edged sword: and His countenance was as the sun shineth in His strength. The particulars of the description indicate the official position of the Person spoken of, and the character in which He appears. (1) He is a priest, clothed with the long white garment reaching to the feet that was a distinguishing part of the priestly dress, but at the same time so wearing the girdle at the breasts, not at the waist, as to show that He was a priest engaged in the active service of the sanctuary. (2) He is a king, for, with the exception of the last mentioned particular, all the other features of the description given of Him point to kingly rather than to priestly power, while the prophetic language of Isaiah, as he looks forward to Eliakim the son of Hilkiah, language which we may well suppose to have been now in the Seer's thoughts, leads to the same conclusion: "And I will clothe him with thy robe and strengthen him with thy girdle, and I will commit thy government into his hand." [15] The "Son of man," in short, here brought before us in His heavenly glory, is both Priest and King.

Not only so. It is even of peculiar importance to observe that the attributes with which the Priest-King is clothed are not so much those of tenderness and mercy as those of power and majesty, inspiring the beholder with a sense of awe and with the fear of judgment. Already we have had some traces of this in considering ver. 7: now it comes out in all its force. That hair of a glistering whiteness which, like snow on which the sun is shining, it almost pains the eye to look upon; those eyes penetrating like a flame of fire into the inmost recesses of the heart; those feet which like metal raised to a white heat in a furnace consume in an instant whatever they tread upon in anger; that voice loud and continuous, like the sound of the mighty sea as it booms along the shore; that sword sharp, two-edged, issuing from the mouth, so that no one can escape it when it is drawn to slay; and lastly, that countenance like the sun in the height of a tropical sky, when man and beast cower from the irresistible scorching of his beams,--all are symbolical of judgment. Eager to save, the exalted High Priest is yet also mighty to destroy. "Thou shalt break them with a rod of iron; Thou shalt dash them in pieces like a potter's vessel. Be wise now, therefore, O ye Kings; be instructed, ye judges of the earth. Serve the Lord with fear, and rejoice with trembling. Kiss the Son, lest He be angry, and ye perish from the way, when His wrath is kindled but a little. Blessed are all they that put their trust in Him." [16]

The Apostle felt all this; and, believer as he was in Jesus, convinced of his Master's love, and one who returned that love with the warmest affections of his heart, he was yet overwhelmed with terror. And when I saw Him, he tells us, I fell at His feet as one dead. In circumstances somewhat similar to the present, a somewhat similar effect had been produced upon other saints of God. When Isaiah beheld the glory of the Lord he cried, "Woe is me! for I am undone; because I am a man of unclean lips, and I dwell in the midst of a people of unclean lips; for mine eyes have seen the King, the Lord of hosts." [17] When Ezekiel beheld a vision of the same kind, he tells us that he "fell upon his face." [18] When the angel Gabriel appeared to Daniel in order to explain the vision which had been shown him, the prophet says, "I was afraid, and fell upon my face." [19] Here the effect was greater than in any of these instances, corresponding to the greater glory shown; and the Apostle fell at the feet of the glorified Lord as one "dead." But there is mercy with the Lord that He may be feared; and He laid His right hand upon me, adds St. John, saying, Fear not: and then follows in three parts that full and gracious declaration of what He is, in His eternal pre-existence, in that work on behalf of man which embraced not only His being lifted on high upon the cross, but His Resurrection and Ascension to His Father's throne, and in the consummation of His victory over all the enemies of our salvation,--1. I am the First and the Last, and the Living One; 2. And I became dead, and behold, I am alive for evermore; 3. And I have the keys of death and of Hades.

A few more words are spoken by the glorified Person who thus appeared to St. John, but at this point we may pause for a moment, for the vision is complete. It is the first vision of the book, and it contains the key-note of the whole. As distinguished from the fourth Gospel, in which Jesus clothed as He is with His humanity is yet pre-eminently the Son of God, the Saviour while here retaining His Divinity is yet pre-eminently a Son of man. In other words, He is not merely the Only Begotten who was from eternity in the bosom of the Father: He is also Head over all things to His Church. And He is this as the glorified Redeemer who has finished His work on earth, and now carries it on in heaven. This work too He carries on, not only as a High Priest "touched with the feeling of our infirmities," but as One clothed with judgment. He is a man of war, and to Him the words of the Psalmist may be applied:

"Gird Thy sword upon Thy thigh, O Mighty One,
Thy glory and Thy majesty.
And in Thy majesty ride prosperously,
Because of truth and meekness and righteousness:
And Thy right hand shall teach Thee terrible things.
Thine arrows are sharp;
The peoples fall under Thee;
They are in the heart of the King's enemies." [20]

Yet we cannot separate the body of Christ from the head, who is Son of man as well as Son of God. With the Head the members are one, and they too therefore are here contemplated as engaged in a work of judgment. With their Lord they are opposed by an ungodly world. In it they also struggle, and war, and overcome. The tribulation, and the kingdom and patience "in Jesus," [21] are their lot; but living a resurrection life and escaped from the power of death and Hades, salvation has been in principle made theirs, and they have only to wait for the full manifestation of that Lord with whom, when He is manifested, they also shall be manifested in glory. [22]

Thus we are taught what to expect in the book of Revelation. It will record the conflict of Christ and His people with the evil that is in the world, and their victory over it. It will tell of struggle with sin and Satan, but of sin vanquished and Satan bruised beneath their feet. It will be the story of the Church as she journeys through the wilderness to the land of promise, encountering many foes, but more than conqueror through Him that loved her, and often raising to heaven her song of praise, "Sing unto the Lord, for He hath triumphed gloriously, the horse and his rider He hath cast into the sea." [23]

Now then we are prepared to listen to the closing words of the glorious Person who had revealed Himself to St. John, as He repeats His injunction to him to write, and gives him some explanation of what he had seen: Write, therefore, the things which thou sawest, and the things which are, and the things which shall come to pass hereafter; the mystery of the seven stars which thou sawest upon My right hand, and the seven golden candlesticks. The seven stars are the angels of the seven churches; and the seven candlesticks are seven churches. The golden candlesticks and the stars, the churches and the angels of the churches, will immediately meet us when we proceed to the next two chapters of the book. Meanwhile it is enough to know that we are about to enter upon the fortunes of that Church of the Lord Jesus Christ in the world which embraces within it the execution of the final purposes of the Almighty, and the accomplishment of His plans for the perfection and happiness of His whole creation.

Footnotes:

1. John v. 19; Heb. xiii. 8.
2. Eph. i. 22.
3. Chap. iii. 14.
4. John xiv. 27.
5. Psalm cxxiv. 7.
6. Psalm lxxii. 1, 2; lviii. 11.
7. Compare the Greek text of Westcott and Hort.
8. John v. 19.
9. John xv. 20; xvi. 2.
10. John i. 7.
11. John i. 9.
12. John xvii. 11.
13. 2 Cor. xiii. 4.
14. Compare 2 Cor. xii. 4.
15. Isa. xxii. 21; comp. also ver. 22 with Rev. iii. 7.
16. Psalm ii. 9-12.
17. Isa. vi. 5.
18. Ezek. i. 28.
19. Dan. viii. 17.
20. Psalm xlv. 3-5.
21. Ver. 9.
22. Col. iii. 4.
23. Exod. xv. 1.

CHAPTER II – THE CHURCH ON THE FIELD OF HISTORY

Rev. ii., iii.

To the angel of the church in Ephesus write; These things saith He that holdeth the seven stars in His right hand, He that walketh in the midst of the seven golden candlesticks: I know thy works, and thy toil and patience, and that thou canst not bear evil men, and didst try them which call themselves apostles, and they are not, and didst find them false; and thou hast patience and didst bear for My name's sake, and hast not grown weary. But I have this against thee, that thou didst leave thy first love. Remember therefore from whence thou art fallen, and repent, and do the first works; or else I come to thee, and will move thy candlestick out of its place, except thou repent. But this thou hast, that thou hatest the works of the Nicolaitans, which I also hate. He that hath an ear, let him hear what the Spirit saith to the churches. To him that overcometh, to him will I give to eat of the tree of life, which is in the Paradise of God. And to the angel of the church in Smyrna write; These things saith the first and the last, which became dead, and lived again: I know thy tribulation, and thy poverty (but thou art rich), and the blasphemy of them which say they are Jews, and they are not, but are a synagogue of Satan. Fear not the things which thou art about to suffer: behold, the devil is about to cast some of you into prison, that ye may be tried; and ye shall have tribulation ten days. Be thou faithful unto death, and I will give thee the crown of life. He that hath an ear, let him hear what the Spirit saith to the churches. He that overcometh shall not be hurt of the second death. And to the angel of the church in Pergamum write; These things saith He that hath the sharp two-edged sword: I know where thou dwellest, even where Satan's throne is: and thou holdest fast My name, and didst not deny My faith, even in the days of Antipas My witness, My faithful one, who was killed among you, where Satan dwelleth. But I have a few things against thee, because thou hast there some that hold the teaching of Balaam, who taught Balak to cast a stumbling-block before the children of Israel, to eat things sacrificed to idols and to commit fornication. So hast thou also some that hold the teaching of the Nicolaitans in like manner. Repent therefore; or else I come to thee quickly, and I will make war against them with the sword of My mouth. He that hath an ear, let him hear what the Spirit saith to the churches. To him that overcometh, to him will I give of the hidden manna, and I will give him a white stone, and upon the stone a new name written, which no one knoweth but he that receiveth it. And to the angel of the church in Thyatira write; These things saith the Son of God, who hath His eyes like a flame of fire, and his feet are like unto burnished brass: I know thy works, and thy love and faith and ministry and patience, and that thy last works are more than the first. But I have this against thee, that thou sufferest thy wife Jezebel, which calleth herself a prophetess; and she teacheth and seduceth My servants to commit fornication, and to eat things sacrificed to idols. And I gave her time that she should repent; and she willeth not to repent of her fornication. Behold, I do cast her into a bed, and them that commit adultery with her into great tribulation, except they repent of her works. And I will kill her children with death; and all the churches shall know that I am He which searcheth the reins and hearts: and I will give unto each one of you according to your works. But to you I say, to the rest that are in Thyatira, as many as have not this teaching, which know not the deep things of Satan, as they say; I cast upon you none other burden. Howbeit that which ye have, hold fast till I come. And he that overcometh, and he that keepeth My works unto the end, to him will I give authority over the nations: and as a shepherd he shall tend them with a sceptre of iron, as the vessels of the potter are they broken to shivers; as I also have received of My Father: and I will give him the morning star. He that hath an ear, let him hear what the Spirit saith to the churches. And to the angel of the church in Sardis write; These things saith He that hath the seven Spirits of God, and the seven stars: I know thy works, that thou hast a name that thou livest, and thou art dead. Be thou watchful, and stablish the things that remain, which were ready to die: for I have found no works of thine fulfilled before My God. Remember therefore how thou hast received and didst hear; and keep it, and repent. If therefore thou shalt not watch, I will come as a thief, and thou shalt not know what hour I will come upon thee. But thou hast a few names in Sardis which did not defile their garments: and they shall walk with Me in white; for they are worthy. He that overcometh shall thus be arrayed in white garments; and I will in no wise blot his name out of the book of life, and I will confess his name before My Father, and before His angels. He that hath an ear, let him hear what the Spirit *saith to the churches. And to the angel of the church in Philadelphia write; These things saith He that is holy, He that is true, He that hath the key of David, He that openeth, and none shall shut, and that shutteth, and none openeth: I know thy works (behold, I have set before thee a door opened, which none can shut), that thou hast a little power, and didst keep My word, and didst not deny My name. Behold, I give of the synagogue of Satan, of them which say they are Jews, and they are not, but do lie; behold, I will make them to come and worship before thy feet, and to know that I have loved thee. Because thou didst keep the word of My patience, I also will keep thee from the hour of trial, that hour which is to come upon the whole inhabited earth, to try them that dwell upon the earth. I come quickly; hold fast that which thou hast, that no one take thy crown. He that overcometh, I will make him a pillar in the temple of My God, and he shall come no more forth: and I will write upon him the name of My God, and the name of the city of My God, the new Jerusalem, which cometh down out of heaven from My God, and Mine own new name. He that hath an ear, let him hear what the Spirit saith to the churches. And to the angel of the church in Laodicea write; These things saith the Amen, the faithful and true Witness, the Beginning of the creation of God: I know thy works, that thou art neither cold nor hot: I would thou wert cold or hot. So because thou art lukewarm, and neither hot nor cold, I will spew thee out of My mouth. Because thou sayest, I am rich, and have gotten riches, and have need of nothing; and knowest not that thou art the wretched one, and miserable and poor and blind and naked: I counsel thee to buy of Me gold refined by fire, that thou mayest become rich; and white garments, that thou mayest clothe thyself, and that the shame of thy nakedness be not made manifest, and eyesalve to anoint thine eyes, that thou mayest see. As many as I love, I reprove and chasten: be zealous therefore, and repent. Behold, I stand at the door and knock: if any man hear My voice and open the door, I will come in to him, and will sup with him, and he with Me. He that overcometh, I will give to him to sit down with Me in My throne, as I also overcame, and sat down with My Father in His throne. He that hath an ear, let him hear what the Spirit saith to the churches* (ii., iii.).

The fortunes of the Church are to be traced in the Revelation of St. John; and the first thing necessary therefore is that we shall learn what the Church is. To accomplish this is the leading aim of the second and third chapters of the book. An object precisely similar appears to determine the arrangement of the fourth Gospel. The Introduction or Prologue of that Gospel is found in chap. i. 1-18; and there can be no doubt that we meet there, in brief and compendious form, the ideas afterwards illustrated and enforced by its selection of incidents from the life of Jesus. After the Prologue follows a section, extending from chap. i. 19 to chap. ii. 11, in which it is obvious that that struggle of Jesus with the world, together with His victory over it, which it is the chief purpose of the Evangelist to relate, has not yet begun. The question thus arises, What is the aim of that section? and the answer is, that it is to set forth the Redeemer with whom the Gospel is to be occupied as He enters upon the field of history. Thus also here. The first chapter of Revelation is the Introduction or Prologue of the book, containing the ideas to be afterwards illustrated in the history of the Church. The struggle of the Church with the world does not yet begin, nor will it begin until we come to chap. vi. In the meantime we are to see in chaps. ii. and iii. that Body of Christ the struggle and victory of which are to engage our thoughts.

These chapters consist of seven epistles addressed to the churches of the seven cities of Asia named in chap. i. 11, and now written to in the same order, beginning with Ephesus and ending with Laodicea. Each epistle contains much that is peculiar to it, but we shall fail to understand the picture presented by the two chapters as a whole if we look only at the individual parts. General considerations, therefore, regarding the seven epistles first demand our notice.

Each epistle, it will be observed, is addressed to the "angel" of the church named. The object of this commentary, as explained in the prefatory note, renders an examination of the meaning of the word "angel" here used a point of subordinate importance. A few remarks, however, can hardly be avoided. The favourite interpretations of the term are two: that the "angels of the churches" are either the guardian angels to whom they were severally committed, or their bishops or chief pastors. Both interpretations may be unhesitatingly rejected. For as to the first, there is a total absence of proof that it was either a Jewish or an early Christian idea that each Christian community had its guardian angel; and as to the second, if there was, as there seems to have been, in the synagogues of the Jews, an official known as the "angel" or "messenger," he occupied an altogether inferior position, and possessed none of the authoritative control here ascribed to the several "angels" mentioned. Besides this, both interpretations are set aside by the single consideration that, keeping in view what has been said of the number seven in its relation to the number one, the seven angels, like the seven churches, must be capable of being regarded as a unity. But this cannot be the case with seven guardian angels, for such a universal guardianship can be predicated of the Lord Jesus Christ, the great Head of the Church, alone. Nor can seven bishops or chief pastors be reasonably resolved into one universal bishop or the moderator of one universal presbytery. The true idea seems to be that the "angels" of the churches are a symbolical representation in which the active, as distinguished from the passive, life of the Church finds expression. To St. John every person, every thing, has its angel. God proclaims and executes His will by angels. [24] He addresses even the Son by an angel. [25] The Son acts and reveals His truth by an angel. [26] The waters have an angel. [27] Fire has an angel. [28] The winds have an angel. [29] The abyss has an angel. [30] On all these occasions the "angel" is interposed when the persons or things spoken of are represented as coming out of themselves and as taking their part in intercourse or in action. In like manner the "angels of the churches" are the churches themselves, with this mark of distinction only,-- that, when they are thus spoken of, they are viewed not merely as in possession of inward vigour, but as exercising it towards things without.

The interpretation now given is confirmed by the fact that the "angels," as appears from the words of chap. i. 20, "The seven stars are the angels of the seven churches," are not different from the "stars," for it is the province of the star, instead of hiding itself in some secret chamber, to shine, and from its place in the firmament to shed light upon the earth. The uniformity of treatment, too, which must be claimed for the number seven when used both with the churches and the stars, is thus rendered possible; for if the former may represent the universal Church in what she is, the latter will represent the same Church in what she does. Thus, then, in the seven "golden candlesticks" and in the seven "stars" or "angels" we have a double picture of the Church; and each of the two figures employed points to a different aspect of her being. It is possible also that the double designation may have been chosen in conformity with a rule, often observed in the Apocalypse, which leads the writer to speak of the same thing, first under an emblem taken from Judaism, and then under one from the wider sphere of the great Gentile Church. The "golden candlestick" burning in the secret of God's Tabernacle gives the former, the "star" shining in the firmament the latter.

Such then being the case, the seven epistles being addressed to the seven churches, and not to any individual in each, the following particulars with regard to them ought to be kept in view:--

1. They are intended to set before us a picture of the universal Church. At first sight indeed it may seem as if they were only to be looked at individually and separately. The different churches are addressed by name. In what is said of each there is nothing out of keeping with what we may easily suppose to have been its condition at the time. There is as much reason to believe that each epistle contains an actual historical picture as there is to believe this in the case of the epistles of St. Paul to Rome, or Corinth, or Ephesus, or Philippi. Any other supposition would convey a false idea of the principles upon which the Apocalypse is framed, would destroy the reality of the Apostle's writing, and would compel us to think that his words must have been unintelligible to those for whom, whatever their further application, they were primarily designed. The question, however, is not thus exhausted; for it is perfectly possible that both certain churches and certain particulars in their state may have been selected rather than others, because they afforded the best typical representation of the universal Church. Several reasons may satisfy us that this was actually done.

· (1) We have good ground for believing that, besides these seven churches of Asia, there were other churches in existence in the same district at the time when the Apostle wrote. One of the early fathers speaks of churches at Magnesia and Tralles. It is also possible that there were churches at Colossæ and Hierapolis, although these cities had suffered from an earthquake shortly after the days of St. Paul. Yet St. John addressed himself not to seven, but to "the seven churches which are in Asia," as if there were no more churches in the province. [31] More, however, there certainly were; and he cannot therefore have intended to address them all. He makes a selection, without saying that he does so; and it is a natural supposition that his selection is designed to represent the universal Church.

(2) Importance must be attached to the number seven. Every reader of the book of Revelation is familiar with the singular part played by that number in its structure, and with the fact that (unless chap. xvii. 9 be an exception) it never means that numeral alone. It is the number of unity in diversity, of unity in that manifoldness of operation which alone entitles it to the name of unity. Such expressions, therefore, as the "seven Spirits of God" or the "seven eyes of the Lamb," are evidently symbolical. The same idea must be carried through all the notices of the number, unless there be something in the context clearly leading to a different conclusion. Nothing of that kind exists here. Were these two chapters indeed out of harmony with the rest of the book, or had they little or no relation to it, it might be urged that they were simply historical, and that no deeper meaning was to be sought in them than that lying on the surface. We have already seen, however, that their connexion with the other chapters is of the closest kind; and we cannot therefore avoid bringing them under the scope of the same principles of interpretation as are elsewhere applicable. Their number--seven--must thus be regarded as typical of unity, and the seven churches as representative of the one universal Church.

(3) The nature of the call to the hearers of each epistle to give heed to the words addressed to them leads to the same conclusion. Had each epistle been designed only for those to whom it was immediately sent, that call would probably have been addressed to them alone. Instead of this it is couched in the most general form: He that hath an ear, let him hear what the Spirit saith to the churches.

(4) The character in which the Saviour speaks to each of the seven churches is always taken from the vision of the Son of man beheld by St. John in the first chapter of his book. It is true that in the case of one or two of the particulars mentioned this is not at once apparent; but in that of by far the larger

number it is so clear that we are entitled to infer the existence of some secret link of connexion in the mind of the sacred writer even when it may not be distinctly perceptible to us. The descriptions, too, of the epistles are no doubt fuller and more elaborate than those of the vision; but this circumstance is easily accounted for when we remember that the seven different delineations of our Lord contained in the second and third chapters are in the first chapter combined in one. Keeping these considerations in view, the main point is incontestable that the germ of the epistolary description is to be found in every case in the preliminary vision.

Thus to the first church--that of Ephesus--Jesus introduces Himself as He that holdeth the seven stars in His right hand, He that walketh in the midst of the seven golden candlesticks [32] ; and the description is evidently that of chap. i. 12, 13, 16, where the Seer beheld "seven golden candlesticks; and in the midst of the candlesticks one like unto a Son of man; and He had in His right hand seven stars." To the second--the church of Smyrna--Jesus introduces Himself with the words, These things saith the first and the last, which became dead, and lived again [33] ; and the description is taken from chap. i. 17, 18: "I am the first and the last, and the Living One; and I became dead, and behold, I am alive for evermore." To the third--the church of Pergamum--the introduction is, These things saith He that hath a sharp two-edged sword [34] ; and the original of the description is found in chap. i. 16: and out of His mouth proceeded a sharp two-edged sword. To the fourth--the church of Thyatira--the Saviour begins, These things saith the Son of God, who hath His eyes like a flame of fire, and His feet are like unto burnished brass [35] ; and we see the source whence the words are drawn when we read in chap. i. 14, 15, "And His eyes were as a flame of fire; and His feet like unto burnished brass, as if it had been refined in a furnace." Of the latter part of the salutation to the fifth church--that of Sardis--which runs, These things saith He that hath the seven Spirits of God, and the seven stars, [36] it is unnecessary to speak; but the first part is more difficult to trace. Comparing chap. v. 6 and chap. iv. 5, we learn that the seven Spirits of God are the possession of the Redeemer, and that they are symbolized by seven lamps burning before the throne of God. Turning now to chap. i., we find the Seer speaking in ver. 4 of "the seven Spirits which are before the throne," those very spirits which in chap. v. 6 he tells us that the Redeemer "hath." This latter thought therefore he is accustomed to associate with them; and though in chap. i. 4 he does not expressly say that the seven Spirits there referred to are the possession of Jesus, this view of them is obviously a part of his general conception of the matter. In chap. i. 4, therefore, the source of the words addressed to Sardis is to be found. To the sixth church--that of Philadelphia--it is said, These things saith He that is holy, He that is true, He that hath the key of David, He that openeth, and none shall shut, and that shutteth, and none openeth [37] ; and we can have no difficulty in recognising the germ of the extended description in chap. i. 14, 18, where we are told that Jesus Christ, in token of His holiness, hath "His head and His hair white as white wool, white as snow," and that He hath "the keys of death and of Hades." Lastly, we have the introductory address to the seventh church-- that of Laodicea--These things saith the Amen, the faithful and true Witness, the beginning of the creation of God [38] ; and the origin of it is to be seen in chap. i. 5, where we are told of "Jesus Christ, who is the faithful Witness, and the first-born of the dead, and the Ruler of the kings of the earth." Each salutation of the seven epistles is thus part of the description of the Son of man in the first chapter of the book; and it is a legitimate inference that the contents of the epistles are, like the salutations, only portions of one whole.

(5) Many expressions are to be met with in the seven epistles which find their explanation only in those later chapters of the book where a reference to the Church universal cannot be denied. The tree of life of the first epistle meets us again, more fully spoken of, in the description of the new Jerusalem. [39] The second death mentioned in the second epistle is not explained till judgment upon the Church's enemies is complete. [40] The writing upon believers of the new name, promised in the third epistle, is almost unintelligible until we behold the hundred and forty-four thousand upon Mount Zion. [41] The authority over the nations, and more especially the gift of the morning star, referred to in the fourth epistle, cannot be comprehended until we are introduced to the vision of the thousand years and the last utterances of the glorified Redeemer. [42] The white garments of the fifth epistle can hardly be rightly understood until we see the white-robed company standing before the throne and before the Lamb. [43] The mention in the sixth epistle of the city of My God, the new Jerusalem, which cometh down out of heaven from My God, remains a mystery until we actually witness her descent. [44] And, finally, the sitting in Christ's throne of the seventh epistle is only elucidated by the reign of the thousand years with Him. [45]

(6) It is worthy of notice that the descriptions of our Lord given in the first and last epistles have a wider application than to the churches of Ephesus and Laodicea, to which they are immediately addressed, thus making it evident that, while each of these epistles has its own place in the series, it is at the same time treated as the first or last member of a group which is to be regarded as a whole.

To the church of Ephesus the Saviour describes Himself as He that holdeth the seven stars in His right hand, He that walketh in the midst of the seven golden candlesticks [46] ; and the description has no more reference to Ephesus than to any other of the churches named. In like manner to the church of

Laodicea He describes Himself as the Amen, the Witness faithful and true, the Beginning of the creation of God. [47] The first of these appellations is no doubt derived from Isa. lxv. 16, where we have twice repeated in the same verse the formula "God Amen;" and the meaning of the name as applied to Jesus is, not that all the Divine promises shall be accomplished by Him, but that He is Himself the fulfilment of every promise made by the Almighty to His people. The second appellation reminds us of John xviii. 37, where Jesus replies to Pilate's question in the words, "To this end have I been born, and to this end am I come into the world, that I should bear witness unto the truth." His whole mission is summed up by Him in the idea of "witnessing." He is the perfect, the true, the real Witness to eternal truth in its deepest sense, in its widest and most comprehensive range. The third appellation, again, cannot be limited to the thought of the mere material creation, as if equivalent to the statement that by the Word were all things made. It would thus fail to correspond with the two appellations preceding it, which undoubtedly apply to the work of redemption, while at the same time the addition of the words "of God" would be meaningless or perplexing. Let us add to this that in chap. i. 5, immediately after Jesus has been called the "faithful Witness," He is described as the "first-begotten of the dead," and we shall not be able to resist the conviction that the words before us refer primarily to the new creation, the Christian Church, that redeemed humanity which has its true life in Christ. It may not indeed be necessary to exclude the thought of the material universe; but, in so far as it is alluded to, it is only as redeemed, in its ideal condition of rest and glory, when the new Jerusalem has come down out of heaven, and when the Church's enemies have been cast into the lake of fire. [48] The three appellations, it will be observed, have thus a general rather than a special aspect; and the salutation containing them is to be distinguished from the salutations of the other epistles, all of which, with the exception of the last, exhibit the closest possible connexion with the contents of the epistles to which they respectively belong. It is no mere fancy, therefore, when we say that we have in this a proof that the first and last epistles are not simply members of a continuous series, the last of which may leave the first far behind, but that they are binding terms which gather up all the members of the series and group them into one.

(7) It ought to be noticed that all the cities to which the seven epistles are addressed were situated beyond the boundaries of the Holy Land, and that the Christian Church in each was certainly composed, at least in large measure, of Gentile converts. These churches cannot therefore represent the Jewish Church alone, but must embody that wider idea of the Christian Church which was brought in when the middle wall of partition between Jews and Gentiles was broken down, and when both were reconciled in one body by the Cross, becoming one Church in the Son and in the Father. Were we dealing with the Jewish-Christian Church, we should unquestionably find it located in Jerusalem or in some of the cities of Palestine. When we are taken to heathen soil, and to churches known to have been at least for the most part Gentile, it is a proof that we have before us that great Gentile Church in the very conception of which lies the thought of universality.

(8) The view now taken is confirmed by the general nature of the Apocalypse. That book is symbolical. It begins with a symbolical representation in the first chapter. Symbolism, by the admission of all, is resumed in the fourth chapter, and is continued from that point to the end. Now it is certainly possible that between these two groups of symbols a passage only strictly historical might be introduced. But if there be reason on independent grounds to think that here also we have facts used at least to a certain extent to serve a higher than a simply historic thought, it cannot fail to be allowed that the general unity of the book is thus preserved, and that a completeness is lent to it which we are entitled to expect, but which would be otherwise wanting.

The seven churches then of chaps. ii. and iii. are thus intended to represent the one universal Church. The Seer selects such particular churches of Asia and such special features of their condition as afford the best illustration of that state of God's kingdom in the world which is to be the great subject of his prophetic words. He is to keep in view throughout all his revelation certain aspects of the Church in herself and in her relation to the world. But these aspects were not merely in the bosom of the future. Still less are they an ideal picture drawn from the resources of the writer's own imagination. To his enlightened eye, looking abroad over that part of the world in which his lot was cast, they were also present, one in one church, another in another. St. John therefore groups them together. They are "the things which are," and they are types of "the things which shall come to pass hereafter." [49]

The universalism of the Apocalypse is from the first apparent.

2. A second characteristic of the epistles addressed to the seven churches demands our notice, for these epistles are clearly divisible into two portions, the first consisting of the first three, the second of the other four. Every inquirer admits the fact, the proof resting upon the difference of place assigned in the two portions to the call, He that hath an ear, let him hear what the Spirit saith to the churches. In the first three this call comes in as a central part of the epistle, immediately before the promise to him that overcometh [50] ; in the last four it closes the epistle. [51] There is a still more interesting difference, though the Authorised English Version conceals it from view. According to the best attested readings of the original, the second and third epistles--those to Smyrna and Pergamum--omit the words, found in all the others, I know thy works. The circumstance is at least remarkable, and it seems to admit of only one

explanation. In the mind of the writer the first three epistles were so closely associated together--more closely perhaps than even the seven or the last four--that these words occurring in the first epistle were thought by him to extend their influence over the second and third, much in the same way as the description of the exalted Lord in the same epistle sent its voice forward, and that in the last epistle its voice backward, through the rest. At all events, it is impossible not to see that the first three epistles and likewise the last four, to whatever extent they form parts of one whole, constitute in each case a special unity. What, we have now to ask, is the ground of the distinction? In what light is the Church viewed in each of the two portions spoken of?

There are two aspects of the Church which may be said to pervade the whole Apocalypse: first, as she is in herself, in her own true nature; and secondly, as she is engaged in, and affected by, a struggle with the world. The distinction between the two may be traced in the grouping of which we speak. The first three epistles lead us to the thought of the Church in the former, the remaining four to the thought of her in the latter, aspect. In the first three she is the pure bride of Christ; in the last four she has yielded to the influences of the world, and the faithful remnant within her is separated from her professing but unfaithful members.

The numbers into which the two portions of the seven epistles are distributed illustrate this. Three is the number of the Divine; four, as appears from many passages of this book, is the number of the world. The simple fact that we have a group of three as distinguished from one of four epistles is sufficient to lead to the impression that, in one way or another the thought of the Divine is more closely associated with the former, and the thought of the world with the latter.

This impression is confirmed when we look at the contents of the epistles. Let us take the first three, and we shall find that in not one of them is a contrast drawn between the whole Church and any faithful remnant within her borders, that in not one of them is the Church represented as yielding to the influences of the world. No doubt she has evil in her midst; and evil always springs from the world, not from God. But she is not yet conscious of the sin by which she is surrounded. She has not yet begun to traffic with the world, to accommodate herself to it, or to lust after what it bestows. The great charge against the church in Ephesus is that she has left her first love. [52] She has passed out of the bright and joyous feelings which marked the time of her espousals to the heavenly Bridegroom. But from sin the Church as she actually exists in the world can never be wholly free; and, so far in particular as the Nicolaitans are concerned, she shares in Ephesus the feelings of her Lord, and views them with the hatred which they deserve. No reproach is directed against the church in Smyrna. She is rather the object of her Lord's perfect confidence; and He is only preparing trial for her in correspondence with the law by which He trains His people: "Every branch that beareth fruit, He cleanseth it, that it may bear more fruit." [53] Remarks of a similar kind apply to the church in Pergamum. There is no charge against the church there that she is allowing the world to gain dominion over her. She has certainly persons in her midst who hold the teaching of the Nicolaitans, but they are few in number; they are no more than "some," [54] and she lends them no countenance. On the contrary, though dwelling in the place where Satan has his throne, she has remained true to her Lord, and has been purified in the fires of persecution then raging even unto death. In none of the three cases is the church perfect, but in none is she really faithless to her trust. She is in danger; she needs to be perfected by suffering [55] ; by suffering she is perfected: but she knows that he who will be the friend of the world is the enemy of God, and the enemies of God are her enemies.

When we turn to the second group of the seven epistles, we at once breathe a different atmosphere; and the contrast is rendered more striking by the fact that in the first of the four we have the very sins spoken of which have already twice crossed our path in the epistles to Ephesus and to Pergamum. According to the best critical reading of chap. ii. 20, the charge against Thyatira is, "Thou sufferest" (Thou lettest alone; thou toleratest) "thy wife Jezebel." Jezebel was a heathen princess, the first heathen queen who had been married by a king of the northern kingdom of Israel. She was therefore peculiarly fitted to represent the influences of the world; and the charge against Thyatira is thus that, in the persons not of a few only, but of her united membership, she tolerated the world, with its heathen thoughts and practices. She knew it to be the world that it was; but notwithstanding this she was content to be at peace, or even to ally herself, with it. The church in Sardis is not less blameable. There are a few names in her that have not defiled their garments; but the church as a whole has deeply sinned. She has reproduced the Pharisaic type with which the Gospels have made us acquainted, substituting the outward for the inward in religion, and then yielding to the sins of the flesh to which she has thus given the supremacy. The church in Philadelphia, like that in Smyrna, is not blamed, and it is well that there should be one church even in the midst of the world of which this can be said; yet even Philadelphia has only a little power, [56] while the exhortation, Hold fast that which thou hast, [57] appears to indicate that she has been losing much. Lastly, no one can mistake the willing identification of herself with the world on the part of the church in Laodicea. She says that she is rich, that she has gotten riches, that she has need of nothing. [58] Her members are well-to-do and in easy circumstances, and they have found so much comfort in their worldly goods that they have become blind to the fact that man needs something better and higher for his portion. In all these four churches, in short, we have an entirely different relation between the Church and the world from that set before us in the first three. There is not simply danger of decay within, and the need of trial with the benefit resulting from it. There is actual conflict with the world; sometimes, it may be, a victory over it, at other times a yielding to its influences and an adoption of its spirit. In the first three churches all, or all with few exceptions, are on the side of Christ; in the last four the "remnant" alone is true to Him.

Attention to the promises to him that overcometh in the different epistles seems to confirm what has been said. There is a marked contrast between the tone of these promises as they are given in the two groups of epistles; and even where a certain amount of similarity exists, the promises in the second group will be found to be fuller and richer than in the first. At Ephesus, at Smyrna, and at Pergamum "he that overcometh" is rewarded much, as one still in a simple and childlike state would be. The first promise made to him is that he shall eat of the tree of life, which is in the Paradise of God [59] ; the second, that he shall not be hurt of the second death [60] ; the third, that he shall eat of the hidden manna, and be like the high-priest in the innermost recesses of the sanctuary. [61] All is quiet. The appeal of Him who promises is to the gentler susceptibilities of the soul. The privileges and enjoyments spoken of are adapted to the condition of those who have not yet experienced the struggle of life.

When we turn to the second group of epistles there is a different tone. We enter upon rewards conceived in bolder and more manly figures. The first promise now is, He that overcometh, and he that keepeth My works unto the end, to him will I give authority over the nations: and as a shepherd he shall tend them with a sceptre of iron; as the vessels of the potter are they broken to shivers. [62] This is the reward of victory after well-fought fields. The warrior thus crowned must have braved the strife and won with difficulty. The second promise is not less marked in its character. He that overcometh shall not simply, as in the case of Smyrna, receive the reward of not being "hurt of the second death;" he shall be arrayed in white garments, and Jesus will confess his name before His Father, and before His angels. [63] The third promise is at least a large extension of that given to Pergamum, for of him that now overcometh it is said, I will make him a pillar in the temple of My God, and he shall come no more forth--that is, shall come no more forth to a struggle with the world similar to that in which he has been engaged--and I will write upon him the name of My God, and the name of the city of My God, the new Jerusalem, which cometh down out of heaven from My God, and Mine own new name. [64] Finally, the fourth promise is the noblest of all: He that overcometh, I will give to him to sit down with Me in My throne, as I also overcame, and sat down with My Father in His throne. [65] All the promises of the second group of epistles are clearly distinguished in tone and spirit from those of the first group. They presuppose a fiercer struggle, a hotter conflict; and they are therefore full of a more glorious reward.

Such seems to be the relation to one another of the two groups into which the seven epistles naturally divide themselves. In the first group the Church has stood firm against the world. She is full of toil and endurance; in her poverty she is rich; and the troubles of the future she does not fear. She holds fast the name of Christ, and openly confesses Him. Seeds of evil are indeed within her, which will too soon develop themselves; but she has the Divine life within her in as much perfection as can be expected amidst the infirmities of our present state. She walks with God and hears His voice in her earthly paradise. In the second group the evil seed sown by the enemy has sprung up. The Church tolerates the sins that are around her, makes her league with the world, and yields to its influence. She rallies indeed at times to her new and higher life, but she finally submits to the world and is satisfied with its goods. There are many faithful ones, it is true, in her midst. As in the Jewish Church there was a "remnant according to the election of grace," so in her there are those who listen to the Saviour's voice and follow Him. Yet they are the smaller portion of her members, and they shall eventually come forth out of her. It is the same sad story which has marked all the previous dispensations of the Almighty with His people, and which will continue to be repeated until the Second Coming of the Lord. That story culminates in this book of the Revelation of St. John, when the bride, allying herself with the world, becomes a harlot, and when the Seer hears "another voice out of heaven, saying, Come forth, My people, out of her, that ye have no fellowship with her sins, and that ye receive not of her plagues." [66]

We have considered the epistles contained in these chapters as a unity representative of the universal Church in the two main aspects of her condition in the world; but before leaving them it will be well to look at them individually, and to mark the peculiar condition of each Church addressed.

1. The first epistle is that to Ephesus, the central or metropolitan city of the district to which all the seven churches belonged, and with which the almost unanimous voice of antiquity associates the later years of the pastorate of St. John himself. Hence, in part at least, as we have already seen, the general nature of the salutation with which the glorified Lord presents Himself to that church. He does not merely hold its star in His right hand, nor does He merely walk in the midst of it alone. He holdeth the seven stars in His right hand. He walketh in the midst of the seven golden candlesticks. He is present in every part of His Church on earth. To every part of it He says, "Lo, I am with you alway, even unto the consummation of the age." [67]

The church at Ephesus is faithful as a whole. I know, is the language of her Lord to her, thy works, and thy toil and patience, and that thou canst not bear evil men, and didst try them which call themselves apostles, and they are not, and didst find them false; and thou hast patience and didst bear for My name's sake, and hast not grown weary. The tribute is a noble one. The church is not only working, but toiling, in her Master's service; she is firm amidst trial, whether from within or from without; she views with abhorrence all workers of iniquity; she tries, only in order to reject, those pretended messengers of Christ who would have preached another gospel than that the power of which she knew. Amidst all the speciousness of their claims, she had "found" them false. Then she turned again to her steadfast endurance until it became a settled principle in her life, and it could be said to her, with the strong force of the word in the writings of St. John, that she "had" it. The spirit of all this, too, had been found in the "name" of Jesus, the revelation of the love and grace of God given her in Him. Finally, she had not grown weary. Seven marks of faithfulness appear to be mentioned; and, if so, the fourth--her judgment of false teachers--occupies the central position. Nor does it seem fanciful to say this when we notice that of all the seven points the fourth is the only one returned to, and that in a more specific form, at a later point in the epistle: But this thou hast, that thou hatest the works of the Nicolaitans, which I also hate. In other words, doctrinal faithfulness was the peculiar distinction of the Ephesian church. She knew that the revelation of God in Christ must be kept pure, or toil would lose its spring, patience its encouragement, shrinking from evil men its intensity, and perseverance its support. Therefore she valued the doctrinal truth which had been committed to her, and held fast the "form of sound words" which she had received, for the sake of the life to which it led.

Amidst all this the church at Ephesus was not wholly what she ought to have been. I have this against thee, had to be said to her, that thou didst leave thy first love; and she needed words of exhortation and warning: Remember therefore from whence thou art fallen, and repent, and do the first works; or else I come to thee, and will move thy candlestick out of its place, except thou repent. The church had declined from the bright and joyous feelings of her first condition. Might her very zeal for the purity of Christian doctrine have had anything to do with this? It is not impossible. Eager defence of truth against error, notwithstanding its importance, is apt to shift the centre of the soul's inner life. The strifes of theologians and the cry "First purity, then peace," translated into "Purity without peace," have been in every age the scandal and the weakness of the Church. Well might even David speak of it as one of the most signal instances of God's goodness to them that fear Him, "Thou shalt keep them secretly in a pavilion from the strife of tongues;" [68] and never, alas! have tongues been sharper or more contentious than in the maintenance of the faith. There is something without which even zeal for truth may be but a scorching and devouring flame; and that is the "first love," the love ever fresh and tender for Him who first loved us, the love which teaches us to win and not to alienate, to raise and not to crush, those who may only be mistaken in their views, and are not determined enemies of God.

Possessed of this spirit, we shall overcome; and the first love will meet its first reward. To him that overcometh, says the Lord, recalling the blessedness of Eden, will I give to eat of the tree of life, which is in the Paradise of God.

2. The second epistle is that to Smyrna, a rich, prosperous, and dissolute city, and largely inhabited by Jews bitterly opposed to Christ and Christianity. Here therefore persecution of those leading the pure and holy life of the Gospel might be peculiarly expected, as indeed it also peculiarly appeared. The church at Smyrna thus becomes the type of a suffering church, the representative of that condition of things foretold in the words of Christ, and constantly fulfilled in the history of His people, "A servant is not greater than his lord. If they have persecuted Me, they will also persecute you." [69]

It will be observed that at Smyrna the church is still faithful, and that against her no word of reproach is uttered. Hence the aspect under which the Redeemer presents Himself to that church is purely animating and consolatory, the same as that which, in the introductory vision in chap. i., followed the action of the Lord when He laid His right hand upon the Apostle, who had fallen to the ground as dead, and when He said to him, "Fear not." [70] So now: These things saith the first and the last, which became dead, and lived again. Death and resurrection are the two great divisions of the work of Christ on our behalf, and the Gospel is summed up in them. Just as St. Paul wrote to the Corinthians when he would remind them of the substance of his preaching in their midst, "For I declared unto you first of all that which also I received, how that Christ died for our sins according to the Scriptures; and that He was buried, and that He hath been raised on the third day according to the Scriptures," [71] in like manner here the same two facts include all the truth which Smyrna held fast, and with which come the life that conquers sin and the joy that triumphs over sorrow.

The state of the church is then described: I know thy tribulation, and thy poverty (but thou art rich), and the blasphemy of them which say they are Jews, and they are not, but are a synagogue of Satan. Tribulation, persecution, the blasphemy of men calling themselves the only people of God and denying to Christians any portion in His covenant, are alone alluded to, though the church is at the same time cheered with the remark that if she had no share in worldly wealth and splendour, she was rich. "God had chosen them that were poor as to the world to be rich in faith, and heirs of the kingdom which He promised to them that love Him." [72]

The church then was in the midst of suffering. Was not that enough; and shall she not be told that her sufferings were drawing to an end, that the night of weeping was gone by, and that the morning of joy was about to dawn? So we might think; but God's thoughts are not as our thoughts, nor His ways as our ways, and we are like children bathing on the shore,

> *Buried a wave beneath;*
> *The second wave succeeds before*
> *We have had time to breathe.*

How often does it happen in the Christian's experience that one burden is laid upon another, and that one wave succeeds another, till he seems left desolate and alone upon the earth. Yet even then he has no assurance that his sufferings are at a close. The consolation afforded to him is, not that there shall be a short campaign, but only that, whether long or short, he shall be more than conqueror through Him that loved him. Thus our Lord does not now say to His church at Smyrna, Fear none of those things that thou art suffering, but Fear not the things which thou art about to suffer: behold, the devil is about to cast some of you into prison, that ye may be tried; and ye shall have tribulation ten days. It is hardly necessary to say to any intelligent reader of the Apocalypse that the "ten days" here spoken of are neither ten literal days, nor ten years, nor ten successive persecutions of indefinite length. In conformity with the symbolical use of numbers in this book, "ten days" expresses no more than a time which, though troubled, shall be definite and short, a time which may be otherwise denoted by the language of St. Peter when he says of believers that "now for a little while they have been put to grief in manifold temptations." [73] Encompassed by affliction, therefore, those who are thus tried have only to be faithful unto death, or to the last extremity of martyrdom. He who died and lived again will bestow upon them the crown of life, the crown of the kingdom, incorruptible, undefiled, and unfading. He that overcometh shall not be hurt of the second death.

3. The third epistle is that to Pergamum, a city at the time devoted to the worship of Æsculapius, the god of medicine, and in particular largely engaged with those parts of medical science which are occupied with inquiries into the springs of life. That the wickedness of the city was both greater and more widespread than was common even in the dark days of heathenism is borne witness to by the fact that the first words addressed to it by Him that hath the sharp two-edged sword were these: I know where thou dwellest, even where Satan's throne is. The word "throne" (not, as in the Authorised Version, "seat") is intentionally selected by the Seer; and its use affords an illustration of one of his principles of style, the remembrance of which is not unfrequently of value in interpreting his book. Everywhere it is his wont to see over against the good its mocking counterpart of evil, over against the light a corresponding darkness. Thus because God occupies a throne Satan does the same; and inasmuch as in Pergamum sin was marked by a refinement of greater than ordinary depth, Satan might be said to have his "throne" there. This circumstance, combined with the promise to the Church contained in the seventeenth verse, To him that overcometh, to him will I give of the hidden manna, and I will give him a white stone, and upon the stone a new name written, which no one knoweth but he that receiveth it, may help us to understand the main thought of this epistle as distinguished from the others. We have seen reason to believe that there was some secret mystery of evil in the city; and, contrasted with this, we have now the promise of a secret mystery of life to the faithful church. The Church then in the secret of her Divine preservation is here before us. She lives a life the springs of which no one sees, a life that is hid with Christ in God.

It will be observed, accordingly, that, whatever may be said against the condition of the city, nothing is said against the church within it. There is no hint that she has yielded to the influences of the world. She has certainly evil-doers in her midst; but these, though in her, are not of her: and the Christianity of the great majority of her members remains sound and sweet. Let us listen to the words of commendation: And thou holdest fast My name, and didst not deny My faith, even in the days of Antipas My witness, My faithful one, who was killed among you, where Satan dwelleth. But I have a few things against thee, because thou hast there some that hold the teaching of Balaam, who taught Balak to cast a stumbling-block before the children of Israel, to eat things sacrificed to idols, and to commit fornication. So hast thou also some that hold the teaching of the Nicolaitans in like manner. Repent therefore; or else I come to thee quickly, and I will make war against them with the sword of My mouth. Those who are described in these words as "holding the teaching of Balaam" and those who are here called "the Nicolaitans" are the same, denoted in the first instance by a description taken from the history of Balaam in the Old Testament, and in the second by a word formed in Greek after the fashion of Balaam's name in Hebrew. That the church in her corporate capacity had not yielded to the sinfulness referred to is manifest from this, that they who had done so are described as "some," and that in the threatening of the sixteenth verse it is not said, I will war against "thee," but I will war against "them." The sin therefore found in the bosom of the church was not, as we shall find it to have been at Thyatira, with her consent. She failed, not because she encouraged it, but because she did not take more vigorous steps for its extinction. She did not sufficiently realize the fact that she was a part of the Body of Christ, and that, if one member suffer, all the members suffer with it. Believers in her community were too easily satisfied with working out their own salvation, and thought too little of presenting the whole church "as a pure virgin to Christ." [74] Therefore it was that, even amidst much faithfulness, they needed to repent, to feel more deeply than they did that "a little leaven leaveneth the whole lump," [75] and that in the Church of the Lord Jesus we are to a large extent responsible, not only for our own, but for our neighbours', sins. By keeping up the Christian tone of the whole Church the tone of each member of the Church is heightened.

We thus reach the close of the first three epistles "to the churches;" and we see that, while each is accommodated to the particular circumstances of the Christian community to which it is sent, the three taken together present to us the three leading considerations upon which, when we think of Christ's Church in this world, we naturally dwell. First, she is in the main true to her Divine Master, even when compelled to confess that she has left her first love. Secondly, she is exposed for her further cleansing to many trials. Lastly, she is sustained by the unseen influences of Divine love and grace. She eats of the hidden manna. She has within her breastplate a white, glistering stone, upon which is inscribed the new name which no man knoweth saving he that receiveth it. She dwells, like the high-priest of old at the moment of his greatest dignity and honour, in the secret place of the Most High. She abides under the shadow of the Almighty. As a child she has entered into the garden of the Lord; and yet, in all the simplicity of her childhood, she is both king and priest.

Such is the Church of Christ in Ephesus, Smyrna, and Pergamum. Happy days of innocence and bliss! We may well linger over them for a little. Too soon will they pass away, and too soon will the Church's conflict with the world and her yielding to it begin.

4. With the fourth epistle we enter upon the second group of epistles, where the Church is brought before us less as she is in herself, than as she fails to maintain her true position in the world, and as that separation between a faithful remnant and the whole body which meets us at every step of her history, throughout both the Old Testament and the New, begins to show itself. Now therefore there is a change of tone.

The first of the four, the fourth in the series of seven, is that to Thyatira; and to the church there the Lord presents Himself in all the penetrating power of those eyes that as a flame of fire search the inmost recesses of the heart, and in all the resistless might of those feet that are as "pillars of fire:" [76] These things saith the Son of God, who hath His eyes like a flame of fire, and His feet are like unto burnished brass.

The commendation of the church follows, what is good being noted before defects are spoken of: I know thy works, and thy love and faith and ministry and patience, and that thy last works are more than the first. The commendation is great. There was not only grace, but growth in grace, not only work, but work in Christ's cause abounding more and more. Yet there was also failure. To understand this it is necessary, as already noticed, to adopt the translation of the Revised Version, founded on the more correct reading of the later critical editions of the Greek. Even in that version, too, the translation, given in the margin, of one important expression has to be substituted for that of the text. Keeping this in view, the Saviour thus addresses Thyatira: But I have this against thee, that thou sufferest (that thou toleratest, that thou lettest alone) thy wife Jezebel, which calleth herself a prophetess; and she teacheth and seduceth My servants to commit fornication, and to eat things sacrificed to idols. And I gave her time that she should repent; and she willeth not to repent of her fornication. Behold, I do cast her into a bed, and them that commit adultery with her into great tribulation, except they repent of her works. And I will kill her children with death; and all the churches shall know that I am He which searcheth the reins and hearts: and I will give unto each one of you according to your works. In these words "Jezebel" is clearly a symbolical name. It is impossible to think that the "angel" of the church was the chief pastor, and that the woman named Jezebel, spoken of as she is, was his wife. We have before us the notorious Jezebel of Old Testament history. Her story is so familiar to every one that it is unnecessary to dwell on it; and we need only further call attention to the fact that the sentence in which her name is mentioned is complete in itself. The sin of the church at Thyatira was that she "suffered" her. In other words, the church tolerated in her midst the evil of which Ahab's wife was so striking a representative. She knew the world to be what it was; but, instead of making a determined effort to resist it, she yielded to its influences. She repeated the sin of the Corinthian Church: "It is actually reported that there is fornication among you.... And ye are puffed up, and did not rather mourn, that he that had done this deed might be taken away from among you." [77] The world, in short, was in the church, and was tolerated there. Of the threatened punishment, the "bed" of tribulation and sorrow instead of that of guilty pleasure, nothing need be said. It is of more consequence to observe the change in the manner of address which meets us after that punishment has been described: But to you I say, to the rest that are in Thyatira, as many as have not this teaching, which know not the deep things of Satan, as they say; I cast upon you none other burden. Howbeit that which ye have, hold fast till I come. For the first time in these epistles we meet with those who are spoken of as "the rest," the remnant, who are to be carefully distinguished from the great body of the Church's professing members. The world has penetrated into the Church; the Church has become conformed to the world: and the hour is rapidly approaching when the true disciples of Jesus will no longer find within her the shelter which she has hitherto afforded them, and when they will have to "come forth out of her" in her degenerate condition. [78] It is a striking feature of these apocalyptic visions, which has been too much missed by commentators. We shall meet it again and again as we proceed. In the meantime it is enough to say that the moment of withdrawal has not yet come. The faithful "rest," who had rejected the false teaching and shunned the sinful life, are to continue where they were; and the Lord will cast upon them none other burden. Well for them that they had such a promise! Their burden of suffering was heavy enough already. Hard to contend with under any circumstances, suffering rises nearer to the height of the sufferings of Christ when the Christian is "wounded," not by open foes, but "in the house of his friends." "It was not an enemy that reproached me; then I could have borne it: neither was it he that hated me that did magnify himself against me; then I would have hid myself from him: but it was thou, a man mine equal, my companion, and my familiar friend. We took sweet counsel together; we walked in the house of God with the throng." [79]

The trial was great; so also is the consolation: And he that overcometh, and he that keepeth My works unto the end, to him will I give authority over the nations: and as a shepherd he shall tend them with a sceptre of iron, as the vessels of the potter are they broken to shivers; as I also have received of My Father: and I will give him the morning star. It was a heathen element that clouded the sky of the church at Thyatira. That element, nay the nations out of which it springs, shall be crushed beneath the iron sceptre of the King who shall "reign in Mount Zion, and in Jerusalem, and before His ancients gloriously." [80] The clouds shall disappear; and Jesus, "the bright, the morning star," [81] having given Himself to His people, He and they together shall shine with its clear but peaceful light when it appears in the heavens, the harbinger of day.

5. The fifth epistle is that to Sardis, and in the superscription He who sends it describes Himself as One that hath the seven Spirits of God, and the seven stars. Both expressions have already met us, the former in chap. i. 4, the latter in chap. ii. 1. A different word from that used in the address to Ephesus is indeed used here to indicate the relation of the Lord to these stars or angels of the churches. There the glorified Lord "holdeth the seven stars in His right hand;" here He "hath" them. Like every other change, even of the slightest kind, in this book, the difference is instructive. To "hold" them is to hold them fast for their protection; to "have" them is to have them for a possession, to have them not only outwardly and in name, but inwardly and in reality, as His own. Thus Christ "hath" the Holy Spirit, who in all His varied and sevenfold influences is, as He proceedeth from the Father and the Son, not only God's, but His. Thus also Christ "hath" the seven stars or churches, here spoken of in immediate connexion with the Spirit, and therefore viewed chiefly in that spirituality of feeling and of life which ought to be the great mark distinguishing them from the world. It was the mark in which Sardis failed. Let her take heed to Him with whom she has to do.

I know, are the words addressed to her, thy works, that thou hast a name that thou livest, and thou art dead. Be thou watchful, and stablish the things that remain, which were ready to die: for I have found no works of thine fulfilled before My God. Remember therefore how thou hast received and didst hear; and keep it, and repent. If therefore thou shalt not watch, I will come as a thief, and thou shalt not know what hour I will come upon thee. The world had been tolerated in Thyatira, the first of the last four churches; in Sardis, the second, it is more than tolerated. Sardis has substituted the outward for the inward. She has been proud of her external ordinances, and has thought more of them than of living in the Spirit and walking in the Spirit. True piety has declined; and, as a natural consequence, sins of the flesh, alluded to in the immediately following words of the epistle, have asserted their supremacy. More even than this, Sardis had a name that she lived while she was dead. She was renowned among men. The world looked, and beheld with admiration what was to it the splendour of her worship; it listened, and heard with enthusiasm the music of her praise. And the church was pleased that it should be so. Not in humility, lowliness, and deeds of self-sacrificing love did she seek her "name," but in what the world would have been equally delighted with though the inspiring soul of it all had been folly or sin. A stronghold had been established by the world in Sardis.

Yet there also the Good Shepherd had His little flock, and there again we meet them. But thou hast a few names in Sardis which did not defile their garments. These were to Sardis what "the rest" were to Thyatira. They were the "gleanings left in Israel, as the shaking of an olive tree, two or three berries in the top of the uppermost bough, four or five in the outmost branches of a fruitful tree." [82] They were the "new wine found in the cluster, and one saith, Destroy it not; for a blessing is in it." [83] To them therefore great promises are given: They shall walk with Me in white; for they are worthy. He that overcometh shall thus be arrayed in white garments; and I will in no wise blot his name out of the book of life, and I will confess his name before My Father, and before His angels. It is the glorified Lord who, as the High-priest of His Church, "walketh" in the midst of the golden candlesticks; and, as priests, these shall walk with Him in a similar glory. Upon earth they were despised, but beyond the earth they shall be openly acknowledged and vindicated. They shall be arrayed in those garments of glistering purity which were with difficulty kept white in the world, but which in the world to come Divine favour shall keep free from every stain.

6. The sixth epistle is to Philadelphia; and the remarkable circumstance connected with this church is that, though spoken of as having but "a little power," it is not seriously blamed. In this respect it resembles the church at Smyrna in the first group of these seven epistles. What has mainly to be noticed, however, is that it is not simply, like that at Smyrna, a suffering church. It has been engaged in an earnest and hot struggle with the world, as the superscription, the commendation, and the promises of the epistle combine to testify.

The superscription is, These things saith He that is holy, He that is true, He that hath the key of David, He that openeth, and none shall shut, and that shutteth, and none openeth. The figure is taken from the Old Testament; and both there and here the context shows us that it is neither the key of knowledge, nor the key of discipline, nor the key of the treasures of the kingdom that is spoken of, but the key of power to open the Lord's house as a sure refuge from all evil, and to preserve safe for ever those who are admitted to it. "I will call My servant Eliakim the son of Hilkiah," says the Almighty by His prophet, "and I will clothe him with thy robe, and strengthen him with thy girdle, and I will commit thy government into his hand: and he shall be a father to the inhabitants of Jerusalem, and to the house of Judah. And the key of the house of David will I lay upon his shoulder; and he shall open, and none shall shut; and he shall shut, and none shall open." [84] Whoever be our adversaries, we know that in the hollow of the Lord's hand we are safe.

The commendation of the epistle tells the same tale: I know thy works (behold, I have set before thee a door opened, which none can shut), that thou hast a little power, and didst keep My word, and didst not deny My name. The Church had "a little power," and she had shown this in the struggle.

So also with the promises: Behold, I give of the synagogue of Satan, of them which say they are Jews, and they are not, but do lie; behold, I will make them to come and worship before thy feet, and to know that I have loved thee. Because thou didst keep the word of My patience, I also will keep thee from the hour of trial, that hour which is to come upon the whole inhabited earth, to try them that dwell upon the earth. I come quickly: hold fast that which thou hast, that no one take thy crown. He that overcometh, I will make him a pillar in the temple of My God, and he shall no more come forth: and I will write upon him the name of My God, and the name of the city of My God, the new Jerusalem, which cometh down out of heaven from My God, and Mine own new name. How fierce the struggle of Philadelphia had been with the world we learn from these words, in which the enemies of the Church--"Jews" they call themselves, the people of God, but "they are not"--are brought before us like vanquished nations at her feet, as she sits in the heavenly places, paying homage to her against whom they had so long, but vainly, struggled. It is impossible not to see the difference between this church and that at Smyrna. No doubt there had been "blasphemy of them which say they are Jews" in the latter case, but worse trials were only spoken of as about to come. Here the trials have come, and the church has risen triumphantly above them. Therefore will the Lord admit her to His heavenly mansions, and will make her a pillar in His Father's house, whence she shall come forth no more. He Himself "went forth" from His Father that He might be the Captain of our salvation and might die on our behalf. He returned to His Father, and never again "comes forth" as He came in the days of His flesh. Having died once, He dieth no more; and they who have borne His cross shall wear, when victors in His cause, His crown of victory.

7. The seventh epistle is to Laodicea, and here there can be no doubt that we have the picture of a church in which the power of the world carries almost all before it. The church is addressed by Him who describes Himself as the Amen, the faithful and true Witness, the Beginning of the creation of God, upon which immediately follows a charge as to her condition in which there is no redeeming point. Only later do we see that there is hope. I know thy works, that thou art neither cold nor hot: I would thou wert cold or hot. So because thou art lukewarm, and neither hot nor cold, I will spew thee out of My mouth. Because thou sayest, I am rich, and have gotten riches, and have need of nothing; and knowest not that thou art the wretched one, and miserable and poor and blind and naked: I counsel thee to buy of Me gold refined by fire, that thou mayest become rich; and white garments, that thou mayest clothe thyself, and that the shame of thy nakedness be not made manifest; and eyesalve to anoint thine eyes, that thou mayest see. As many as I love, I reprove and chasten: be zealous therefore, and repent. To interpret the boasting of the church given in these words as if it referred to spiritual rather than material riches is entirely to mistake the meaning. Worldly wealth is in the writer's view. The members of the church generally have aimed at riches, and have gotten them. Possession of riches has also been followed by its usual effects. The seen and the temporal have usurped in their minds the place of the unseen and the eternal. Perhaps they have even regarded their worldly prosperity as a token of the Divine favour, and are soothing themselves with the reflection that they have made the best of both worlds, when they have really sacrificed everything to one world, and that the lower of the two. The last picture of the Church is the saddest of all.

Yet is Laodicea not altogether without hope. Behold, says He whose every word is truth, I stand at the door and knock: if any man hear My voice and open the door, I will come in to him, and will sup with him, and he with Me. Even in Laodicea there are some who, inasmuch as they have fought the hardest battle, shall be welcomed to the highest reward. He that overcometh, I will give to him to sit down with Me in My throne, as I also overcame, and sat down with My Father in His throne. Beyond that neither hope nor imagination can rise.

The epistles to the seven churches are over. They present the Church to us as she appears on the field of history. They set before us the leading characteristics of her condition partly as she was in "Asia" at the moment when the Apostle wrote, partly as she shall be throughout all time and on the widest, as well as the narrowest, scale. These characteristics may be shortly summed up as--in the first group of three, love to the Redeemer, yet love liable, and even beginning, to grow cold; persecution and trials of many kinds; preservation by the secret grace of God and in the hidden life: in the second group of four, yielding on the part of the majority to sins associated with unchristian doctrine; formalism in religion; weakness in the midst of trial, even though not accompanied by faithlessness; and lukewarmness, springing from a preference of the things of time to those of eternity. To these characteristics, however, have to be added, as more or less accompanying them, many of the active graces of the Christian life: labour, and patience, and faith, and charity, and works, whatever makes the Christian Church a light in the world and the object of her Lord's care and watchfulness. In reading the seven epistles, we behold a lively picture of the Church of Christ in her graces and in her failings, in her strength and in her weakness, in her joys and in her sorrows, in her falls under the influence of temptation and in her returns to the path of duty. The characteristics thus spoken of are not peculiar to any particular age, but may mark her at one time less, at another more, at one time individually, at another in combination. Taken as a whole, they present her to us in her Divine ideal marred by human blemishes; we are prepared to acknowledge the necessity, the wisdom, and the mercy of the trials that await her; and we learn to anticipate with gladness her final and glorious deliverance.

One brief concluding remark ought to be made. The epistles now considered ought to be sufficient in themselves to show that the Apocalypse is not a series of visions intended only to illustrate one or two ideas which had taken a strong hold of the Apostle's mind, or one or two great principles of the Divine government in general. St. John starts from the realities around him as much as any writer of the New Testament. It is true that he sees in them eternal principles at work, and that he rises to the thought of ideal good and of ideal evil; but he is not on that account less true to fact, less impressed by fact. On the contrary, his very depth of insight into the meaning of the facts makes him what he is. He who would write a philosophy of history is not less, but more, dependent upon the facts of history than he to whom a fact is valuable simply in its individual and isolated form. It is the present therefore that stirs the writer of this book, but stirs him the more because he beholds in it principles and issues connected with Him who was, and is, and is to come, the covenant-keeping God, the Judge of men, the unchangeable I am.

Hence also the mistake sometimes made of thinking that the purpose of unfolding the principles of the Divine government could not be a sufficient motive to St. John to write. [85] Every cruelty to the saints of God which he witnessed, every cry of oppression which he heard, supplied a motive. We may not feel these things now, but the iron of them entered into the soul of the disciple whom Jesus loved. We need more prophets like him to make it ring in the ears of selfish wealth and of ease indifferent to the ills festering around it, "For the spoiling of the poor, for the sighing of the needy, now will I arise, saith the Lord." [86]

Footnotes:

24. Chaps. vii. 2; viii. 2; xiv. 6, 8, 9; xv. 1, 6.
25. Chap. xiv. 15.
26. Chaps. i. 1; xx. 1; xxii. 6.
27. Chap. xvi. 5.
28. Chap. xiv. 18.
29. Chap. vii. 1.
30. Chap. ix. 11.
31. Chap. i. 4.
32. Chap. ii. 1.
33. Chap. ii. 8.
34. Chap. ii. 12.
35. Chap. ii. 18.
36. Chap. iii. 1.
37. Chap. iii. 7.
38. Chap. iii. 14.

39. Chaps. ii. 7; xxii. 2, 14.
40. Chaps. ii. 11; xx. 14.
41. Chaps. ii. 17; xiv. 1.
42. Chaps. ii. 26, 28; xx. 4, 5; xxii. 16.
43. Chaps. iii. 5; vii. 9, 14.
44. Chaps. iii. 12; xxi. 2, 10.
45. Chaps. iii. 21; xx. 4. Comp. Trench, The Seven Epistles, p. 37.
46. Chap. ii. 1.
47. Chap. iii. 14.
48. Comp. Rom. viii. 21, 22; James i. 18.
49. Chap. i. 19.
50. Chap. ii. 7, 11, 17.
51] Chaps. ii. 29; iii. 6, 13, 22.
52. Chap. ii. 4.
53. John xv. 2.
54. Chap. ii. 14, 15.
55. Comp. Heb. ii. 10.
56. Chap. iii. 8.
57. Chap. iii. 11.
58. Chap. iii. 17.
59. Chap. ii. 7.
60. Chap. ii. 11.
61. Chap. ii. 17.
62. Chap. ii. 26, 27.
63. Chap. iii. 5.
64. Chap. iii. 12.
65. Chap. iii. 21.
66. Chap. xviii. 4.
67. Matt. xxviii. 20.
68. Ps. xxxi. 20.
69. John xv. 20.
70. Chap. i. 17.
71. 1 Cor. xv. 3, 4.
72. James ii. 5.
73. 1 Pet. i. 6.
74. 2 Cor. xi. 2.
75. 1 Cor. v. 6.
76. Chap. x. 1.
77. 1 Cor. v. 1, 2.
78. Comp. chap. xviii. 4.
79. Ps. lv. 12-14.
80. Isa. xxiv. 23.
81. Chap. xxii. 16.
82. Isa. xvii. 6.
83. Isa. lxv. 8.
84. Isa. xxii. 21, 22.
85. Dods, Introduction to New Testament, p. 244.
86. Ps. xii. 5.

CHAPTER III - ANTICIPATIONS OF THE CHURCH'S VICTORY

Rev. iv., v.

We have seen in considering the first chapter of the Apocalypse that the book as a whole is to be occupied with the Church's struggle in the world; and in the second and third chapters the Church herself has been placed before us as she occupies her position upon the field of history. But the struggle has not yet begun, nor will it begin until we reach the sixth chapter. Chaps. iv. and v. are therefore still to be regarded as in a certain measure introductory. They form a separate--the third--section of the book; and the first questions that meet us in connexion with them are, What is their relation to the main purpose of the author? What is their leading conception? and Why are they placed where they are?

In answering these questions, we are aided by the strictly parallel structure of the fourth Gospel. The Prologue of that book, contained in chap. i. 1-18, suggests the object which the writer has in view. The next section--chap. i. 19-ii. 11--places before us the Redeemer whose glory he is to describe. The struggle of the Son of God with the world does not begin till we come to chap. v. Between chap. ii. 12 and chap. iv. 54 there is thus a considerable interval, in which we have the cleansing of the Temple and the victory of Jesus over the unbelief of the Jew Nicodemus, the Samaritan woman, and the king's officer of Galilee, who was probably a Gentile. In this intervening space the leading thought seems to be that of victory, not indeed of victory in the struggle, but of victory which prepares us for it, and fills the mind with hope before it begins. In like manner the two chapters upon which we are about to enter are occupied with songs of victory. Catching their spirit, we shall boldly accompany the Church into the struggle which follows, and shall be animated by a joyful confidence that, whatever her outward fortunes, He that is with her is more than they that be with her enemies. [87]

While such is the general conception of the third and fourth chapters viewed as one, we have further to ask whether, subordinate to their united purpose, there is not a difference between them. Such a difference there appears to be; and words of our Lord in the fourth Gospel, spoken upon an occasion which had deeply impressed itself upon the mind of the Evangelist, may help us to determine what it is. In the fourteenth chapter of that Gospel Jesus encourages His Apostles as He sends them forth to fight His battle in the world. "Let not," He says, "your heart be troubled: believe in God, believe also in Me." The section of the Apocalypse upon which we are about to enter embraces a similar thought in both its parts. Chap. iv. conveys to the Church the assurance that He who is the ultimate source of all existence is on her side; chap. v. that she may depend upon Christ and His redeeming work. The two chapters taken together are a cry to the Church from her glorified Head, before she enters into the tribulation that awaits her, "Let not your heart be troubled: believe in God, believe also in Me."

After these things I saw and, behold, a door opened in heaven, and the first voice which I heard, a voice as of a trumpet speaking with me, one saying, Come up hither, and I will show thee the things which must come to pass hereafter. Straightway I was in the Spirit: and, behold, there was a throne set in heaven, and One sitting upon the throne; and He that sat was to look upon like a jasper stone and a sardius; and there was a rainbow round about the throne, like an emerald to look upon. And round about the throne were four-and-twenty thrones: and upon the thrones I saw four-and-twenty elders sitting, arrayed in white garments, and on their heads crowns of gold. And out of the throne proceed lightnings and voices and thunders. And there were seven lamps of fire burning before the throne, which are the seven Spirits of God (iv. 1-5).

The first voice here spoken of is the voice of chap. i. 10: "And I heard behind me a great voice, as of a trumpet;" and it is well to remember that that voice introduced the vision of a Son of man who, while both King and Priest, was King and Priest in judgment. It is impossible to doubt that the sound of the same voice is intended to indicate the same thing here, and that the King whom we are about to behold is One who has "prepared His throne for judgment." [88]

The Seer is introduced to a scene which we first recognise as the glorious audience-chamber of a great King. Everything as yet speaks of royalty, and of royal majesty, power, and judgment. The jasper stone as we learn from a later passage of this book, in which it is said to be "clear as crystal," [89] was of a bright, sparkling whiteness; and it fitly represents the holiness of Him of whom the seraphim in Isaiah cry one to another, "Holy, holy, holy, is the Lord of hosts," [90] and who in this very chapter is celebrated by the unresting cherubim with the words, "Holy, holy, holy, is the Lord, God, the Almighty, which was and which is and which is to come." The sardius, again, was of a fiery red colour, and can denote nothing but the terror of the Almighty's wrath. Out of the throne also--not merely out of the atmosphere surrounding it, but out of the throne itself--proceed lightnings and voices and thunders, always throughout the Apocalypse emblems of judgment; while the use of the word burn in other parts of the same book, and the fact that what the Seer beheld was not so much lamps as torches, leads to the belief that these torches as they burned before the throne sent out a blazing and fierce rather than a calm and soft light. It is true that the rainbow round about the throne points to the Divine covenant of grace and promise, and that its emerald greenness, absorbing, or at least throwing into the shade, its other and varied hues, tells with peculiar force of something on which the eye loves, and does not fear, to rest. But the mercy of God does not extinguish His righteousness and judgment. Different as such qualities may seem to be, they are combined in Him with whom the Church and the world have to do. In the New Testament not less than in the Old the Almighty reveals Himself in the awakening terrors of His wrath as well as in the winning gentleness of His love. St. Peter speaks of our Lord as not only the chief corner-stone laid in Zion, elect, precious, so that he that believeth on Him shall not be put to shame, but as a stone of stumbling and rock of offence; [91] and when the writer of the Epistle to the Hebrews gives us his loftiest description of the privileges of the Christian Church, he closes it with the words, "Wherefore, receiving a kingdom that cannot be shaken, let us have grace, whereby we may offer service well-pleasing to God with reverence and awe: for our God is a consuming fire." [92] So also here. Would we conceive of God aright, even after we have been brought into the full enjoyment of all the riches of His grace and love, we must think of Him as represented by the jasper and the sardius as well as by the emerald.

The four-and-twenty elders occupying thrones (not seats) around the throne are to be regarded as representatives of the glorified Church; and the number, twice twelve, seems to be obtained by combining the number of the patriarchs of the Old Testament with that of the Apostles of the New.

The description of the heavenly scene is now continued:--

And before the throne, as it were a glassy sea like unto crystal and in the midst of the throne, and round about the throne, four living creatures full of eyes before and behind. And the first creature was like a lion, and the second creature like a calf, and the third creature had a face as of a man, and the fourth creature was like a flying eagle. And the four living creatures, having each one of them six wings, are full of eyes round about and within; and they have no rest day and night, saying, Holy, holy, holy, is the Lord, God, the Almighty, which was and which is and which is to come (iv. 6-8).

Up to this point we have been beholding a royal court; in the words now quoted the priestly element comes in. The glassy sea naturally leads the thoughts to the great brazen laver known as the brazen sea which stood in the court of Solomon's temple between the altar and the sanctuary, and at which the priests cleansed themselves before entering upon the discharge of their duties within the precincts of God's holy house. The resemblance is not indeed exact; and were it not for what follows, there might be little upon which to rest this supposition. We know, however, from many examples, that the Seer uses the figures of the Old Testament with great freedom; and as the Temple source of the living creatures next introduced to us cannot be mistaken, it becomes the more probable that the brazen sea of the same building, whatever be the actual meaning of the figure--a point that will meet us afterwards--suggests the "glassy sea."

When we turn to the "living creatures," there can be no doubt whatever that we are in the midst of Temple imagery. These are the cherubim, two of which, fashioned in gold, were placed above the mercy-seat in the holy of holies, so that, inasmuch as that mercy-seat was regarded as peculiarly the throne of God, Israel was invited to think of its King as "sitting between the cherubim." [93] These figures, however, were not confined to that particular spot, nor were they fashioned only in that particular way, for the curtain and the veil which formed the sides of the Most Holy Place were wrought with cherubim of cunning work, [94] so that one entering that sacred spot was surrounded by them. In the midst of the cherubim spoken of in these verses we are thus in the midst of Temple figures and of priestly thoughts. It is impossible here to trace the history of the cherubim throughout the Bible; and we must be content with referring to two points connected with them, of importance for the interpretation of this book: the representative nature of the figures and the aspect under which we are to see them. [95]

As to the first of these, the human element in the cherubim is at once intelligible. It can be nothing but man; while the fact that they occupy so large a position in the most sacred division of the Tabernacle is sufficient to prove that man, so represented, is thought of as redeemed and brought to the highest stage of spiritual perfection. The other elements referred to certainly do not indicate either new qualities added to humanity, or an intensification of those already possessed by it, as if we might cherish the prospect of a time when the physical qualities of man shall equal in their strength those of the animals around him, when he shall possess the might of the lion, the power of the ox, and the swiftness of the eagle. They represent rather the different departments of nature as these are distributed into the animate and inanimate creation. Taking the "living creatures" together in all their parts, they are thus an emblem of man, associated on the one hand with the material creation, on the other with the various tribes of animals by which it is inhabited, but all redeemed, transfigured, perfected, delivered from the bondage of corruption, and brought into "the liberty of the glory of the children of God." [96] They have a still wider and more comprehensive meaning than the "twenty-four elders," the latter setting before us only the Church, but the former all creation, glorified.

The second point above mentioned--the aspect worn by the living creatures--demands also a few remarks, for the view commonly entertained upon it seems to be erroneous. Misled by the mention of the calf, which is supposed to be the ox, and not the bull-calf, interpreters have allowed the mode in which they understood this particular to rule their interpretation of the others. It has been regarded as the emblem of endurance and of patient labour rather than of power and rage; while, following the same line of thought, the eagle has been treated as the king of birds soaring in the blue vault of heaven rather than as hastening (like the vulture) to his prey. [97] The whole conception of the cherubim has thus been modified and shaped in the minds of men under a form altogether different from that in which it is really presented to us in Scripture. The cherubim of the Old Testament and the "living creatures" of the New are supposed to represent "majesty and peerless strength," "patient and productive industry," and "soaring energy and nimbleness of action." In reality they rather represent qualities that strike terror into the hearts of men and suggest the idea of an irresistibly destructive force. With this view all that is elsewhere said of them corresponds. They are not simply spoken of as partakers of the favour of God. They are instruments in the execution of His wrath. When our first parents were driven from the garden of Eden, they were placed "at the east of the garden," along with "a flaming sword which turned every way, to keep the way of the tree of life." [98] When we are introduced to them in Ezekiel, it is said that "their appearance was like burning coals of fire, like the appearance of torches: it went up and down among the living creatures; and the fire was bright, and out of the fire went forth lightning. And the living creatures ran and returned as the appearance of a flash of lightning." [99] Similar associations are connected with them throughout the Apocalypse. The opening of each of the first four seals, the four that deal with judgments upon the earth, is immediately followed by a voice, "as it were the noise of thunder," from one of the four living creatures, saying, Come. [100] One of them gives to the seven angels "seven golden bowls full of the wrath of God." [101] And after the destruction of Babylon, when her smoke is ascending up for ever and ever, and the voice of much people in heaven calls for praise to Him who hath avenged the blood of His servants at her hand, they "fall down and worship God that sitteth on the throne, saying, Amen; Hallelujah." [102] There can be little doubt, then, as to the meaning of these four living creatures. They are sharers of the Almighty's holiness, and of that holiness in its more awful form, as a holiness that cannot look on sin but with abhorrence. They are the vicegerents of His kingdom. They are assessors by His side. Their aspect is not that of the sweetness associated with the word "cherub," but that of sternness, indignant power, and judgment. Thus also it is that in the Tabernacle they looked toward the mercy-seat. [103] By what they saw there they were restrained from executing wrath upon the guilty. That mercy-seat, sprinkled with the blood of atonement, told them of pardon and of a new life for the sinner. Their sternness was softened; mercy rejoiced over judgment; and the storm-wind upon which God flew swiftly, when "He rode upon a cherub, and did fly," [104] sank into a calm.

The Seer has beheld the audience-chamber of the Godhead in itself. He has seen also the Divine Being who is there clothed with majesty, and those who wait upon Him. He next passes to another thought:--

And when the living creatures shall give glory and honour and thanks to Him that sitteth on the throne, to Him that liveth for ever and ever, the four-and-twenty elders shall fall down before Him that sitteth on the throne, and shall worship Him that liveth for ever and ever, and shall cast their crowns before the throne, saying, Worthy art Thou, our Lord and our God, to receive the glory and the honour and the power: for Thou didst create all things, and because of Thy will they were, and were created (iv. 9-11).

In his beautiful comments upon the Revelation Isaac Williams says, "The four living creatures, or the Church of the redeemed, give thanksgiving to God for their redemption; and then the twenty-four elders fall down and attribute all glory to God alone, inasmuch as prophets, Apostles, and all the ministering priesthood, rejoicing in the salvation of the elect, attribute it not to their own instrumentality, but to God." [105] In thus interpreting the passage, however, that commentator can hardly be regarded as correct. It is true that the living creatures are the representatives of redeemed creation, and the twenty-four elders representatives of the glorified Church. But in the song of praise here put into their mouths they have not yet advanced to the thought of salvation. That is reserved for the next chapter. Here they think of creation, with all its wonders; of the heavens which declare God's glory, and the firmament which shows forth His handiwork; of sun, and moon, and stars in their manifold and resplendent glories; of the mountains and the valleys; of the rivers and the fountains of waters; of the rich exuberance of vegetable life, which covers the earth with a gorgeous carpet of every hue; and of all those animals upon its surface which "run races in their mirth:" and for them they praise. To God all creatures owe their origin. In Him they live, and move, and have their being. Because of His will they were--let the reading be considered and remembered: "were," not "are"--because of His will they were in His idea from eternity; and when the appointed moment came, they were created. Wherefore let them praise. We are reminded of the Psalms of the Old Testament, though it is ours to put into their words a still deeper and richer meaning than they possessed when first uttered by the Psalmist:--

> *Praise ye the Lord.*
> *Praise ye the Lord from the heavens:*
> *Praise Him in the heights.*
> *Praise ye Him, all His angels:*
> *Praise ye Him, all His host.*
> *Praise ye Him, sun and moon*
> *Praise Him, all ye stars of light.*
> *Praise Him, ye heavens of heavens,*
> *And ye waters that be above the heavens.*
> *Let them praise the name of the Lord:*
> *For He commanded, and they were created*
> *He hath also established them for ever and ever:*
> *He hath made a decree which shall not pass away.*
> *Praise the Lord from the earth,*
> *Ye dragons, and all deeps:*
> *Fire, and hail; snow, and vapour;*
> *Stormy wind fulfilling His word:*
> *Mountains, and all hills;*
> *Fruitful trees, and all cedars:*
> *Beasts, and all cattle;*
> *Creeping things, and flying fowl:*
> *Kings of the earth, and all peoples;*
> *Princes, and all judges of the earth:*
> *Both young men, and maidens;*
> *Old men, and children:*
> *Let them praise the name of the Lord:*
> *For His name alone is exalted;*
> *His glory is above the earth and heaven.* [106]

Such then in chap. iv. is the call addressed by the Seer to the Church before she enters upon her struggle, a call similar to that of Jesus to His disciples, "Believe in God."

The fifth chapter continues the same general subject, but with a reference to Christ the Redeemer rather than God the Creator:--

> *And I saw in the right hand of Him that sat on the throne a roll of a book written within and on the back, close sealed with seven seals. And I saw a strong angel proclaiming with a great voice, Who is worthy to open the roll, and to loose the seals thereof? And no one in the heaven, or on the earth, or under the earth, was able to open the roll, or to look thereon. And I wept much, because no one was found worthy to open the roll, or to look thereon. And one of the elders saith unto me, Weep not: behold, the Lion that is of the tribe of Judah, the Root of David, hath overcome to open the roll, and the seven seals thereof* (v. 1-5).

We can easily form to ourselves a correct idea of the outward form of the symbol resorted to in these words. The same symbol is used by the prophet Ezekiel, and in circumstances in some respects precisely analogous to those of the Seer. Ezekiel had just beheld his first vision of the cherubim. "And when I looked," he says, "behold, an hand was put forth unto me; and, lo, a roll of a book was therein; and He spread it before me; and it was written within and without." [107] In both cases it is not a "book," but a roll, like the sacred rolls of the synagogue, that is presented to the prophet's eye, the difference being that in the Apocalypse we read of the roll being close sealed with seven seals. This addition is due to the higher, more sublime, and more momentous nature of the mysteries contained in it. That it is written within and on the back, so that there is no space for further writing, shows that it contains the whole counsel of God with regard to the subject of which it treats. It is the word of Him who is the Alpha and the Omega, the first and the last; and the seven seals are so fastened to the roll that one of them may be broken at a time, and no more of the contents disclosed than belonged to that particular seal. What also the contents of the roll are we learn from the contents of the seals as they are successively disclosed in the following chapters. As yet the Seer does not know them. He knows only that they are of the deepest interest and importance; and he looks anxiously around to see if any one can be found who may break the seals and unfold their mysteries. No such person can be discovered either in heaven, or on the earth, or under the earth. No one will even dare to look upon the roll; and the sorrow of the Seer was so deepened by this circumstance that he wept much.

At that moment one of the elders, the representatives of the glorified Church, advanced to cheer him with the tidings that what he so much desired shall be accomplished. One who had had a battle to fight and a victory to win had overcome, not only to look upon the roll, but to open it and to loose the seven seals thereof, so as to make its contents known. This was the Lion that is of the tribe of Judah, the Root of David. The description is taken partly from the law and partly from the prophets, for is not this "He of whom Moses in the law, and the prophets, did write"? [108] ; the former in the blessings pronounced by the dying patriarch Jacob upon his son Judah: "Judah is a lion's whelp: from the prey, my son, thou art gone up: he stooped down, he couched as a lion, and as a lioness; who shall rouse him up?" [109] ; the latter in such words as those of Isaiah, "And there shall come forth a shoot out of the stock of Jesse, and a Branch out of his roots shall bear fruit;" [110] while, in the language alike of the prophet and of the Seer, the words set forth the Messiah, not as the root out of which David sprang, but as a shoot which, springing from him, was to grow up into a strong and stately tree. In Him the conquering might of David, the man of war, and of Judah, "chosen to be the ruler," [111] comes forth with all the freshness of a new youth. He is "the mystery which hath been hid from all ages and generations, but now hath been manifested to the saints." [112] In Him "the darkness is passing away, and the true light already shineth." [113] "After two days will He revive us: on the third day He will raise us up, and we shall live before Him. And let us know, let us follow on to know, the Lord: His going forth is sure as the morning; and He shall come unto us as the rain, as the latter rain that watereth the earth." [114] Thus then was it now. Like Daniel of old, the Seer had wept in order that he might understand the vision; and the elder said to him, Weep not.

The eagerly desired explanation follows:--

And I saw in the midst of the throne and of the four living creatures, and in the midst of the elders, a Lamb standing as though it had been slaughtered, having seven horns and seven eyes, which are the seven Spirits of God sent forth into all the earth. And He came, and He hath taken it out of the right hand of Him that sat on the throne (v. 6, 7).

A strange and unlooked-for spectacle is presented to the Seer. He had been told of a lion; and he beholds a lamb, nay not only a lamb, the emblem of patience and of innocence, but, as we learn from the use of the word slaughtered (not "slain," as in both the Authorised and Revised Versions), a lamb for sacrifice, and that had been sacrificed. Nor can we doubt for a moment, when we call to mind the Gospel of St. John and its many points of analogy with the Apocalypse, what particular lamb it was. It was the Paschal Lamb, the Lamb beheld in our Lord by the Baptist when, pointing to Jesus as He walked, he said to his disciples, "Behold the Lamb of God," [115] and again beheld by the writer of the fourth Gospel on the Cross, when in the fact that the soldiers broke not the legs of Jesus, as they broke those of the malefactors hanging on either side of Him, he traced the fulfilment of the Scripture, "A bone of Him shall not be broken." [116] This therefore was the true Lamb "that taketh away the sin of the world," the Lamb that gives us His flesh to eat, so that in Him we may have eternal life. [117]

The Lamb has seven horns, the emblem of perfected strength, and seven eyes, which are explained to be the Spirit of God, sent forth in all His penetrating and searching power, so that none even in the very ends of the earth can escape His knowledge. Further the Lamb is standing as though it had been slaughtered, and there never has been a moment's hesitation as to the interpretation of the figure. The words "as though" do not mean that the slaughtering had been only in appearance. It had been real. The Saviour, pierced with cruel wounds, "bowed His head" on Calvary, "and gave up His spirit." [118] "The first and the last and the Living One became dead," [119] and had been laid in the tomb in the garden. But He had risen from that tomb on the third morning; and, "behold, He is alive for evermore." [120] He had ascended to the right hand of the Majesty on high; and there He "stands," living and acting in all the plenitude of endless and incorruptible life.

One thing more has to be noticed: that this Lamb is the central figure of the scene before us, in the midst of the throne and of the living creatures, and of the elders. To Him all the works of God, both in creation and redemption, turn. To Him the old covenant led; and the prophets who were raised up under it searched "what time or what manner of time the Spirit of Christ which was in them did point unto, when it testified beforehand the sufferings of Christ, and the glories that should follow them." [121] From Him the new covenant flowed, and those who under it are called to the knowledge of the truth recognise in Him their "all and in all." [122] The Lamb slaughtered, raised from the grave, ascended, being the impersonation of that Divine love which is the essence of the Divine nature, is the visible centre of the universe. He is "the image of the invisible God, the First-born of all creation: for in Him were all things created, in the heavens and upon the earth, things visible and things invisible, whether thrones, or dominions, or principalities, or powers: all things have been created through Him, and unto Him: and He is before all things, and in Him all things consist. And He is the Head of the Body, the Church: who is the Beginning, the First-born from the dead; that in all things He might have the pre-eminence. For it was the good pleasure of the Father that in Him should all the fulness dwell; and through Him to reconcile all things unto Himself, having made peace through the blood of His cross; through Him, I say, whether things upon the earth, or things in the heavens." [123]

Such is the Lamb; and He now comes, and hath taken the roll out of the right hand of Him that sat on the throne. Let us note the words "hath taken." It is not "took." St. John sees the Lamb not only take the roll, but keep it. It is His,--His as the Son, in whom dwelleth all the fulness of the Godhead bodily; His by right of the victory He has won; His as the First-born of all creation and the Head of the Church. It is His to keep, and to unfold, and to execute, "who is over all, God blessed for ever. Amen." [124]

Therefore is He worthy of all praise, and to Him all praise is given:--

And when He had taken the book, the four living creatures and the four-and-twenty elders fell down before the Lamb, having each one a harp, and golden bowls full of incense, which are the prayers of the saints. And they sang a new song, saying, Worthy art Thou to take the book, and to open the seals thereof: for Thou wast slain, and didst purchase unto God with Thy blood men of every tribe, and tongue, and people, and nation; and madest them to be unto our God a kingdom and priests: and they reign over the earth (v. 8-10).

It is not necessary to dwell upon the figures that are here employed, the harp, as connected with the Temple service, being the natural emblem of praise, and the bowls full of incense the emblem of prayer. But it is of importance to observe the universality of the praises and the prayers referred to, for as the language used here of these men of every tribe, and tongue, and people, and nation, when they are said to have been made a kingdom and priests unto our God, is the same as that of chap. i. 6, we seem entitled to conclude that, even from its very earliest verses, the Apocalypse has the universal Church in view.

The song sung by this great multitude, including even the representatives of nature, now "delivered from the bondage of corruption into the liberty of the glory of the children of God," [125] is wholly different from that of chap. iv. It is a new song, for it is the song of the "new creation;" and its burden, it will be observed, is not creation, but redemption by the blood of the Lamb, a redemption through which all partaking of it are raised to a higher glory and a fairer beauty than that enjoyed and exhibited before sin had as yet entered into the world, and when God saw that all that He had made was good.

The song was sung, but no sooner was it sung than it awoke a responsive strain from multitudes of which we have not yet heard:--

And I saw, and I heard a voice of many angels round about the throne and the living creatures and the elders: and the number was ten thousands of ten thousands, and thousands of thousands; saying with a great voice, Worthy is the Lamb that hath been slain to receive the power, and riches, and wisdom, and might, and honour, and glory, and blessing (v. 11, 12).

These are the angels, who are not within the throne, but round about the throne and the four living creatures and the twenty-four elders. Their place is not so near the throne, so near the Lamb. "For not unto angels did He subject the inhabited earth to come, whereof we speak." [126] He subjected it to man, to Him first of all who, having taken upon Him our human nature, and in that nature conquered, was "crowned with glory and honour," but then also to the members of His Body, who shall in due time be exalted to a similar dignity and shall reign over the earth. Yet angels rejoice with man and with creation redeemed and purified. They "desire to look into" [127] these things: "There is joy in the presence of the angels of God over one sinner that repenteth." [128] He who was God manifested in flesh "appeared" after His resurrection "to angels;" [129] and, although they have not been purchased with the blood of the slaughtered Lamb, their hearts are filled with livelier ecstasy and their voices swell out into louder praise while the "manifold wisdom of God is made known" to them in their heavenly places. [130]

Even this is not all. There is a third stage in the ascending scale, a third circle formed for the widening song:--

And everything which is in the heaven, and on the earth, and under the earth, and on the sea, and all things that are in them, heard I saying, Unto Him that sitteth on the throne, and unto the Lamb, be the blessing, and the honour, and the glory, and the dominion, for ever and ever (v. 13).

What a sublime conception have we here before us! The whole universe, from its remotest star to the things around us and beneath our feet, is one,--one in feeling, in emotion, in expression; one in heart and voice. Nothing is said of evil. Nor is it thought of. It is in the hands of God, who will work out His sovereign purposes in His own good time and way. We have only to listen to the universal harmony, and to see that it move us to corresponding praise.

It did so now:--

And the four living creatures said, Amen. And the elders fell down and worshipped (v. 14).

The redeemed creation is once more singled out for special mention. At chap. iv, 8, 10, they began the song; now we return to them that they may close it. All creation, man included, cries, Amen. The glorified Church has her heart too full to speak. She can only fall down and worship.

The distinction between chap. iv. and chap. v. must now be obvious, even while it is allowed that the same general thought is at the bottom of both chapters. In the one the Church when about to enter on her struggle has the call addressed to her: "Believe in God." In the other that call is followed up by the glorified Redeemer: "Believe also in Me."

Having listened to the call, there is no enemy that she need fear, and no trial from which she need shrink. She is already more than conqueror through Him that loved her. As we enter into the spirit of these chapters we cry,--

"God is our refuge and strength,
A very present help in trouble.
Therefore will we not fear, though the earth do change,
And though the mountains be moved in the heart of the seas;
Though the waters thereof roar and be troubled,
Though the mountains shake with the swelling thereof.
There is a river, the streams whereof make glad the city of God,
The holy place of the tabernacles of the Most High.
God is in the midst of her; she shall not be moved:
God shall help her, and that right early.
The nations raged, the kingdoms were moved:
He uttered His voice, the earth melted.
The Lord of hosts is with us;
The God of Jacob is our refuge." [131]

Footnotes:

87. Comp. 2 Chron. xxxii. 7, 8.
88. Ps. ix. 7.
89. Chap. xxi. 11.
90. Isa. vi. 3.
91. 1 Pet. ii. 6, 8.
92. Heb. xii. 28, 29.
93. Ps. xcix. 1.
94. Exod. xxvi. 1.
95. Comp. Bible Educator, vol. iii., p. 290, where the writer has discussed this subject at some length.
96. Rom. viii. 21.
97. Job ix. 26.
98. Gen. iii. 24.
99. Ezek. i. 13, 14.
100. Chap. vi. 1, 3, 5, 7.
101. Chap. xv. 7.
102. Chap. xix. 4.
103. Exod. xxv. 20.
104. Ps. xviii. 10.

105. The Apocalypse, with Notes and Reflections, p. 69.

106. Ps. cxlviii. 1-3.

107. Ezek. ii. 9, 10.

108. John i. 45.

109. Gen. xlix. 9.

110. Isa. xi. 1.

111. 1 Chron. xxviii. 4.

112. Col. i. 26.

113. 1 John ii. 8.

114. Hos. vi. 2, 3.

115. John i. 36.

116. John xix. 36.

117. The point now spoken of has been doubted. A full discussion of it by the present writer will be found in The Expositor for July and August, 1877.

118. John xix. 30.

119. Chap. i. 18.

120. Chap. i. 18.

121. 1 Pet. i. 11

122. Col. iii. 11.

123. Col. i. 15-20.

124. Rom. ix. 5.

125. Rom. viii. 21.

126. Heb. ii. 5.

127. 1 Pet. i. 12.

128. Luke xv. 10.

129. 1 Tim. iii. 16.

130. Eph. iii. 10.

131. Ps. xlvi. 1-7.

CHAPTER IV – THE SEALED ROLL OPENED

Rev. vi.

With the sixth chapter of the Apocalypse the main action of the book may be said properly to begin. Three sections of the seven into which it is divided have already passed under our notice. The fourth section, extending from chap. vi. 1 to chap. xviii. 24, is intended to bring before us the struggle of the Church, the judgment of God upon her enemies, and her final victory. No detail of historical events in which these things are fulfilled need be looked for. We are to be directed rather to the sources whence the trials spring, and to the principles by which the victory is gained. At this point in the unfolding of the visions it is generally thought that there is a pause, an interval of quietness however brief, and a hush of expectation on the part both of the Seer himself and of all the heavenly witnesses of the wondrous drama. But there seems to be no foundation for such an impression in the text; and it is more in keeping alike with the language of this particular passage and with the general probabilities of the case to imagine that the "lightnings and voices and thunders," spoken of in chap. iv. 5 as proceeding out of the throne, continue to re-echo over the scene, filling the hearts of the spectators with that sense of awe which they are naturally fitted to awaken. We have to meet the Lord in judgment. We are to behold the Lamb as "the Lion of the tribe of Judah;" and when He so appears, "the mountains flow down at His presence." [132]

The Lamb then, who had, in the previous chapter, taken the book out of the hand of Him that sat upon the throne, is now to open it, part by part, seal by seal:--

And I saw when the Lamb opened one of the seven seals, and I heard one of the four living creatures saying as with a voice of thunder, Come (vi. 1).

Particular attention ought to be paid to the fact that the true reading of the last clause of this verse is not, as in the Authorised Version, "Come and see," but simply, as in the Revised Version, Come. The call is not addressed to the Seer, but to the Lord Himself; and it is uttered by one of the four living creatures spoken of in chap. iv. 6, who are "in the midst of the throne and round about the throne," and who in ver. 8 of the same chapter are the first to raise the song from which they never rest, saying, "Holy, holy, holy, is the Lord, God, the Almighty, which was and which is and which is to come." The word Come therefore embodies the longing of redeemed creation that the Lord, for the completion of whose work it waits, will take to Him His great power and reign. Not so much for the perfecting of its own happiness, or for deliverance from the various troubles by which it is as yet beset, and not so much for the manifestation of its Lord in His abounding mercy to His own, does the creation delivered from the bondage of corruption wait, as for the moment when Christ shall appear in awful majesty, King of kings and Lord of lords, when He shall banish for ever from the earth the sin by which it is polluted, and when He shall establish, from the rising of the sun to the going down of the same, His glorious kingdom of righteousness, and peace, and joy in the Holy Ghost.

This prospect is inseparably associated with the Second Coming of Him who is now concealed from our view; and therefore the cry of the whole waiting creation, whether animate or inanimate, to its Lord is Come. The cry, too, and that not only in the case of the first living creature, but (according to a rule of interpretation of which in this book we shall often have to make use) in the case of the three that follow, is uttered with a voice of thunder; and thunder is always an accompaniment and symbol of the Divine judgments.

No sooner is the cry heard than it is answered:--

And I saw, and behold a white horse: and he that sat thereon had a bow; and there was given unto him a crown: and he came forth conquering, and to conquer (vi. 2).

Few figures of the Apocalypse have occasioned more trouble to interpreters than that contained in these words. On the one hand, the particulars seem unmistakeably to point to the Lord Himself; but, on the other hand, if the first rider be the glorified Redeemer, it is difficult to establish that harmonious parallelism with the following riders which appears to be required by the well-ordered arrangement of the visions of this book. Yet it is clearly impossible to regard the first rider as merely a symbol of war, for the second rider would then convey the same lesson as the first; nor is there anything in the text to establish a distinction, frequently resorted to, by which the first rider is thought to denote foreign, and the second civil, war. Every attempt also to separate the white horse of this vision from that of the vision at chap. xix. 11 fails, and must fail. Probably it is enough to say that not one of the four riders is a person. Each is rather a cause, a manifestation of certain truths connected with the kingdom of Christ when that kingdom is seen to be, in its own nature, the judgment of the world. Even war, famine, and death and Hades, which follow, are not literally these things. They are simply used, as scourges of mankind, to give general expression to the judgments of God. Thus also under the first rider the cause rather than the person of Christ is introduced to us, in the earliest stage of its victorious progress, and with the promise of its future triumph. The various points of the description hardly need to be explained. The colour of the horse is white, for throughout these visions that colour is always the symbol of heavenly purity. The rider has a crown given him, a crown of royalty. He has in his hand a bow, the instrument of war by which he scatters his enemies like stubble. [133] Finally, he comes forth conquering and to conquer, for his victorious march knows no interruption, and at last leaves no foe unvanquished. In the first rider we have thus the cause of Christ in its essence, as that cause of light which, having already drawn to it the sons of light, has become darkness to the sons of darkness. By the opening of the first Seal we learn that this cause is in the world, that this kingdom is in the midst of us, and that they who oppose it shall be overwhelmed with defeat.

The interpretation now given of the first rider as one who rides forth to judgment on a sinful world is confirmed by what is said of the three that follow him. In them too we have judgment, and judgment only, while the three judgments spoken of--war, famine, and death--are precisely those with which the prophets in the Old Testament and the Saviour Himself in the New have familiarised our thoughts. [134] They are not to be literally understood. Like all else in the visions of St. John, they are used symbolically; and each of them expresses in a general form the calamities and woes, the misfortunes and sorrows, brought by sinful men upon themselves through rejection of their rightful King.

The second Seal is now broken, and the second rider follows:--

And when He opened the second seal, I heard the second living creature saying, Come. And another horse came forth, a red horse: and to him that sat thereon it was given to take peace from the earth, and that they should slaughter one another: and there was given unto him a great sword (vi. 3, 4).

The second horse is red, the colour of blood, for it is the horse of war: and slaughter follows it as its rider passes over the earth; that is, not over the earth in general, but over the ungodly. Two things in this vision are particularly worthy of notice. In the first place, the war spoken of is not between the righteous and the wicked, but among the wicked alone. The wicked slaughter one another. All persons engaged in these internecine conflicts have cast aside the offers of the Prince of peace; and, at enmity with Him who is the only true foundation of human brotherhood, they are also at enmity among themselves. Of the righteous nothing is yet said. We are left to infer that they are safe in their dwellings, in peaceable habitations, and in quiet resting-places. [135] By-and-by we shall learn that they are not only safe, but surrounded with joy and plenty. In the second place, the original word translated "slay" both in the Authorised and Revised Versions deserves attention. It is a sacrificial term, the same as that found in chap. v. 6, where we read of the "slaughtered Lamb;" and here therefore, as there, it ought to be rendered, not "slay," but "slaughter." The instant we so translate, the whole picture rises before our view in a light entirely different from that in which we commonly regard it. What judgment, nay what irony of judgment, is there in the ways of God when He visits sinners with the terrors of His wrath! The very fate which men shrink from accepting in the form of a blessing overtakes them in the form of a curse. They think to save their life, and they lose it. They seek to avoid that sacrifice of themselves which, made in Christ, lies at the root of the true accomplishment of human destiny; and they are constrained to substitute for it a sacrifice of an altogether different kind: they sacrifice, they slaughter, one another.

The third Seal is now broken, and the third rider follows:--

And when He opened the third seal, I heard the third living creature saying, Come. And I saw, and behold a black horse; and he that sat thereon had a balance in his hand. And I heard as it were a voice in the midst of the four living creatures, saying, A measure of wheat for a penny (or a silver penny), and three measures of barley for a penny; and the oil and the wine hurt thou not (vi. 5, 6).

The third living creature cries as the two before it had done; and a third horse comes forth, the colour of which is black, the colour of gloom and mourning and lamentation. Nor can there be any doubt that this condition of things is produced by scarcity, for the figure of the balance and of measuring bread by weight is on different occasions employed in the Old Testament to express the idea of famine. Thus among the threatenings denounced upon Israel should it prove faithless to God's covenant we read, "And when I have broken the staff of your bread, ten women shall bake your bread in one oven, and they shall deliver you your bread again by weight: and ye shall eat, and not be satisfied." [136] And so also when Ezekiel would describe the miseries of the coming siege of Jerusalem he exclaims, "Moreover He said unto me, Son of man, behold, I will break the staff of bread in Jerusalem: and they shall eat bread by weight, and with care; and they shall drink water by measure, and with astonishment: that they may want bread and water, and be astonied one with another, and consume away for their iniquity." [137] To give out corn by weight instead of measure was thus an emblem of scarcity. The particulars of the scarcity here described are obscured to the English reader by the unfortunate translation, both in this passage and elsewhere, and in the Revised as well as the Authorised Version, of the Greek denarius by the English penny. That coin was of the value of fully eightpence of our money, and was the recognised payment of a labourer's full day's work. [138] In ordinary circumstances it was sufficient to purchase eight of the small "measures" now referred to, so that when it could buy one "measure" only, the quantity needed by a single man for his own daily food, it is implied that wheat had risen eight times in price, and that all that could be purchased by means of a whole day's toil would suffice for no more than one individual's sustenance, leaving nothing for his other wants and the wants of his family. No doubt three measures of barley could be purchased for the same sum, but barley was a coarser grain, and to be dependent upon it was in itself a proof that there was famine in the land. Again, as in the previous judgment, the words of the figure are not to be literally understood. What we have before us is not famine in its strict sense, but the judgment of God under the form of famine; and this second judgment is climactic to the first. Men say to themselves that they will live at peace with one another, and sow, and reap, and plant vineyards, and eat the fruit thereof. But in doing this they are mastered by the power of selfishness; the too eager pursuit of earthly interests defeats its end; and, under the influence of deeper and more mysterious laws than the mere political economist can discover, fields that might have been covered with golden harvests lie desolate and bare.

Nothing has yet been said of the last clause of this judgment: The oil and the wine hurt thou not. The words are generally regarded as a limitation of the severity of the famine previously described, and as a promise that even in judging God will not execute all His wrath. The interpretation can hardly be accepted. Not only does it weaken the force of the threatening, but the meaning thus given to the figure is entirely out of place. Oil and wine were for the mansions of the rich not for the habitations of the poor, for the feast and not for the supply of the common wants of life. Nor would a sufferer from famine have found in them a substitute for bread. The meaning of the words therefore must be looked for in a wholly different direction. "Thou preparest a table before me," says the Psalmist, "in the presence of mine enemies: Thou anointest my head with oil; my cup runneth over." [139] This is the table the supply of which is now alluded to. It is prepared for the righteous in the midst of the struggles of the world, and in the presence of their enemies. Oil is there in abundance to anoint the heads of the happy guests, and their cups are so filled with plenty that they run over. In the words under consideration, accordingly, we have no limitation of the effects of famine. The "wine" and the "oil" alluded to express not so much what is simply required for life as the plenty and the joy of life; and, thus interpreted, they are a figure of the care with which God watches over His own people and supplies all their wants. While His judgments are abroad in the earth they are protected in the hollow of His hand. He has taken them into His banqueting house, and His banner over them is love. The world may be hungry, but they are fed. As the children of Israel had light in their dwellings while the land of Egypt lay in darkness, so while the world famishes the followers of Jesus have all and more than all that they require. They have "life, and that abundantly." [140] Thus we learn the condition of the children of God during the trials spoken of in these visions. Under the second Seal we could only infer from the general analogy of this book that they were safe. Now we know that they are not only safe, but that they are enriched with every blessing. They have oil that makes the face of man to shine, and bread that strengtheneth his heart. [141]

The fourth Seal is now broken, and the fourth rider follows:--

And when He opened the fourth seal, I heard the voice of the fourth living creature saying, Come. And I saw, and behold a pale horse: and he that sat upon him, his name was Death; and Hades followed with him. And there was given unto them authority over the fourth part of the earth, to kill with sword, and with famine, and with death, and by the wild beasts of the earth (vi. 7, 8).

The colour of the fourth horse is pale; it has the livid colour of a corpse, corresponding to its rider, whose name, Death, is in this case given. Hades followed with him, not after him, thus showing that a gloomy and dark region beyond the grave is his inseparable attendant, and that it too is an instrument of God's wrath. In chap. i. 18 these two dire companions had also been associated with one another; and it is important to notice the combination, as the fact will afterwards throw light upon one of the most difficult visions of the book. "Death" is not neutral death, that separation between soul and body which awaits every individual of the human family until the Saviour comes. It is death in the deeper meaning which it so often bears in Scripture, and especially in the writings of St. John,--death as judgment. In like manner Hades is not the neutral grave where the rich and the poor meet together, where the wicked cease from troubling, and where the weary are at rest. It is the region occupied by those who have not found life in Christ; and, not less than death, it is judgment. "Death" and "Hades" then are the culminating judgments of God upon the earth, that is, upon the wicked; and they execute their mission in a fourfold manner: by the sword, and famine, and death, and the wild beasts of the earth. The world, the symbolical number of which is four, instead of blessing such as submit themselves to its sway, turns round upon them with all the powers at its command and kills them. The wicked "are sunk down in the pit that they made: in the net which they hid is their own foot taken." [142]

It is not easy to say why authority is given death and Hades over no more than the fourth part of the earth, when we might rather have expected that their dominion would be extended over the whole. The question may be asked whether it is possible so to understand the Seer as to connect a "fourth part" of the earth, not with all the instruments together, but with each separate instrument of judgment afterwards named--one fourth to be killed with the sword, a second with famine, a third with death, and a fourth by wild beasts. Should such an idea be regarded as untenable, the probability is that a fourth part is mentioned in order to make room for the climactic rise to a "third part" afterwards met under the trumpet judgments.

The end of the first four Seals has now been reached, and at this point there is an obvious break in the hitherto harmonious progress of the visions. No fifth rider appears when the fifth Seal is broken, and we pass from the material into the spiritual, from the visible into the invisible, world. That the transition is not accidental, but deliberately made, appears from this, that the very same principle of division marks the series of the trumpets at chap. ix. 1, and of the bowls at chap. xvi. 10. We have thus the number seven divided into its two parts four and three, while in chaps. ii. and iii. we had it divided into three and four. The difference is easily accounted for, three being the number of God, or the Divine, and therefore taking precedence when we are concerned with the existence of the Church, four being the number of the world, and therefore coming first when judgment on the world is described. It is of more consequence, however, to note the fact than to explain it, for it helps in no small degree to illustrate that artificial structure of the Apocalypse which is so completely at variance with the supposition that it describes in its successive paragraphs the successive historical events of the Christian age.

Passing then into a different region of thought, the fifth Seal is now broken:--

And when He opened the fifth seal, I saw underneath the altar the souls of them that had been slaughtered for the word of God, and for the testimony which they held: and they cried with a great voice, saying, How long, O Master, the holy and true, dost Thou not judge and avenge our blood on them that dwell on the earth? And there was given them to each one a white robe; and it was said unto them, that they should rest yet for a little time, until their fellow-servants also and their brethren, which should be killed even as they were, should be fulfilled (vi. 9-11).

The vision contained in these words is unquestionably a crucial one for the interpretation of the Apocalypse, and it will be necessary to dwell upon it for a little. The minor details may be easily disposed of. By the consent of all commentators of note, the altar referred to is the brazen altar of sacrifice, which stood in the outer court both of the Tabernacle and the Temple; the souls, or lives, seen under it are probably seen under the form of blood, for the blood was the life: and the law of Moses commanded that when animals were sacrificed the blood should be poured out "at the bottom of the altar of burnt-offering, which is before the tabernacle of the congregation;" [143] while the little time mentioned in ver. 11 can mean nothing else than the interval between the moment when the souls were spoken to and that when the killing of their brethren should be brought to a close.

The main question to be answered is, Whom do these "souls" represent? Are they Christian martyrs, suffering perhaps at the hands of the Jews before the fall of Jerusalem, perhaps at the hands of the world to the end of time? Or are they the martyrs of the Old Testament dispensation, Jewish martyrs, who had lived and died in faith? Both suppositions have been entertained, though the former has been, and still is, that almost universally adopted. Yet there can be little doubt that the latter is correct, and that several important particulars of the passage demand its acceptance.

1. Let us observe how these martyrs are designated. They had been slain for the word of God, and for the testimony which they held. But that is not the full expression of Christian testimony. As we read in many other passages of the book before us, Christians have "the testimony of Jesus." [144] The addition needed to bring out the Christian character of the testimony referred to is wanting here. No doubt the saints of old looked forward to the coming of the Christ; but the testimony "of Jesus" is the testimony pertaining to Him as a Saviour come, in all the glory of His person and in all the completeness of His work. It is a testimony embracing a full knowledge of the Messiah, and the inference is natural and legitimate that it is not ascribed to the souls under the altar, because they neither had nor could have possessed it.

2. The cry of these "souls" is worthy of notice, How long, O Master, the holy and the true, where the word "Master," applied also in Acts iv. 24 and Jude 4 [145] to God as distinguished from Christ, corresponds better to the spirit of the Old than of the New Testament dispensation.

3. The time at which the martyrs had been killed belongs not to the present or the future, but to the past. Like all the other Seals, the fifth is opened at the very beginning of the Christian era; and no sooner is it opened than the souls are seen. It is true that the Seer might be supposed to transport himself forward into the future, and, at some point of Christian history more or less distant, to console Christian martyrs who had already fallen with the assurance that they had only to wait a little time, until such as were to be their later companions in martyrdom should have shared their fate. But such a supposition is inconsistent with the fact that St. John in the Apocalypse always thinks of the Christian age as one hardly capable of being divided; while, as we shall immediately see more clearly, it would make it impossible to explain the consolation afforded by the bestowal of the white robe.

4. The altar under which the blood is seen may help to confirm this conclusion, for that blood is not preserved in the inner sanctuary, in that "heaven" which is the ideal home of all the disciples of Jesus: it lies beneath the altar of the outer court.

5. The main argument, however, in favour of the view now contended for, is to be found in the act by which these souls were comforted: And there was given them to each one a white robe. The white robe, then, they had not obtained before; and yet that robe belongs during his life on earth to every follower of Christ. Nothing is more frequently spoken of in these visions than the "white robe" of the redeemed, and it is obviously theirs from the first moment when they are united to their Lord. It is the robe of the priesthood, and at their very entrance upon true spiritual life they are priests in Him. It is the robe with which the faithful remnant in Sardis had been arrayed before they are introduced to us, for they had not "defiled" it; and the emphasis in the promise there given, "They shall walk with Me in white," appears to lie upon its first rather than its second clause. [146] Again, the promise to every one in that church that "overcometh" is that he "shall be arrayed in white garments;" [147] and it is beyond dispute that the promises of the seven epistles belong to the victory of faith gained in this world, not less than to the perfected reward of victory in the world to come. In like manner the Laodicean church is exhorted to buy of her Lord "white garments" that she may be clothed, as well as "gold" that she may be enriched, and "eyesalve" that she may see [148] ; and, as the two latter purchases refer to her present state, so also must the former. When, too, the Lord is united in marriage to His Church, it is said that "it was given unto her that she should array herself in fine linen, bright and pure;" and that fine linen is immediately explained to be "the righteous acts of the saints." [149]

Putting all these passages together, we are distinctly taught that in the language of the Apocalypse the "white robe" denotes that perfect righteousness of Christ, both external and internal, which is bestowed upon the believer from the moment when he is by faith made one with Jesus. It is that more perfect justification of which St. Paul spoke at Antioch in Pisidia when he said to the Jews, "By Him every one that believeth is justified from all things, from which ye could not be justified by the law of Moses." [150] It had been longed for by the saints of the Old Testament, but had never been fully bestowed upon them until Jesus came. David had prayed for it: "Purge me with hyssop, and I shall be clean: wash me, and I shall be whiter than snow;" [151] Isaiah had anticipated it when he looked forward to the acceptable year of the Lord: "I will greatly rejoice in the Lord, my soul shall be joyful in my God; for He hath clothed me with the garments of salvation, He hath covered me with the robe of righteousness, as a bridegroom decketh himself with ornaments, and as a bride adorneth herself with her jewels;" [152] and Ezekiel had celebrated it as the chief blessing of Gospel times: "Then will I sprinkle clean water upon you, and ye shall be clean: from all your filthiness, and from all your idols, will I cleanse you.... And ye shall be My people, and I will be your God. I will also save you from all your uncleannesses." [153] But while thus prayed for, anticipated, and greeted from afar, the fulness of blessing belonging to the New Testament had not been actually received under the Old. "He that is but little in the kingdom of heaven is greater than John." [154] As we are taught in the Epistle to the Hebrews, even Abel, Enoch, Noah, Abraham, Isaac, Jacob, Moses, and all those heroes of faith who had subdued kingdoms, wrought righteousness, obtained promises, stopped the mouths of lions, quenched the power of fire, escaped the edge of the sword, from weakness were made strong, waxed mighty in war, turned to flight armies of aliens--even "these all, having had witness borne to them through their faith, received not the promise: God having provided some better thing concerning us, that apart from us they should not be made perfect." [155] At death they were not made perfect. They passed rather into a holy rest where they waited until, like Abraham, who had "rejoiced that he should see Christ's day," they "saw it and were glad." [156] Then the "white robe" was given them. They were raised to the level of that Church which, now that Jesus had come, rejoiced in Him with "a joy unspeakable and glorified." [157]

These considerations appear sufficient to decide the point. The souls under the altar of the fifth Seal are the saints, not of Christianity, but of Judaism. It is true that all of them had not been literally "slaughtered." But it is a peculiarity of this book, of which further proof will be afforded as we proceed, that it regards all true followers of Christ as martyrs. Christ was Himself a Martyr; His disciples "follow" Him: they are martyrs. Christ's Church is a martyr Church. She dies in her Master's service, and for the world's good.

One point more ought to be noticed before we leave this Seal. The language of these souls under the altar is apt to offend when they apparently cry for vengeance upon their murderers: How long dost Thou not avenge? Yet it is enough to say that so to interpret their cry is to do injustice to the whole spirit of this book Strictly speaking, in fact, they do not themselves cry. It is their blood that cries; it is the wrong done to them that demands reparation. In so far as they may be supposed to cry, they have in view, not their enemies as persons, but the evil that is in them, and that manifests itself through them. At first it may seem difficult to draw the distinction; but if we pause over the matter for a little, the difficulty will disappear. Never do we pity the sinner more, or feel for him with a keener sympathy, than when we are most indignant at sin and most earnest in prayer and effort for its destruction. The more anxious we are for the latter, the more must we compassionate the man who is enveloped in sin's fatal toils. When we long therefore for the hour at which sin shall be overtaken by the just judgment of God, we long only for the establishment of that righteous and holy kingdom which is inseparably bound up with the glory of God and the happiness of the world.

For this kingdom then the saints of the Old Testament, together with all their "brethren" under the New Testament, who like them are faithful unto death, now wait; and the opening of the sixth Seal tells us that it is at hand:--

And I saw when He opened the sixth seal, and there was a great earthquake; and the sun became black as sackcloth of hair, and the whole moon became as blood; and the stars of the heaven fell unto the earth, as a fig tree casteth her unripe figs, when she is shaken of a great wind. And the heaven was removed as a scroll when it is rolled up; and every mountain and island were moved out of their places. And the kings of the earth, and the princes, and the chief captains, and the rich, and the strong, and every bondman and free man, hid themselves in the caves and in the rocks of the mountains; and they say to the mountains and to the rocks, Fall on us, and hide us from the face of Him that sitteth on the throne, and from the wrath of the Lamb: for the great day of their wrath is come; and who is able to stand? (vi. 12-17).

The description is marked by almost unparalleled magnificence and sublimity, and any attempt to dwell upon details could only injure the general effect. The real question to be answered is, To what does it apply? Is it a picture of the destruction of Jerusalem or of the final Judgment? Or may it even represent every great calamity by which a sinful world is overtaken? In each of these senses, and in each of them with a certain degree of truth, has the passage been understood. Each is a part of the great thought which it embraces. The error of interpreters has consisted in confining the whole, or even the primary, sense to any one of them. The true reference of the passage appears to be to the Christian dispensation, especially on its side of judgment. That dispensation had often been spoken of by the prophets in a precisely similar way; and the whole description of these verses, alive with the rich glow of the Eastern imagination, is taken partly from their language, and partly from the language of our Lord in the more prophetic and impassioned moments of His life.

Thus it was that Joel had announced the purpose of God: "And I will show wonders in the heavens and the earth, blood, and fire, and pillars of smoke. The sun shall be turned into darkness, and the moon into blood, before the great and the terrible day of the Lord come," and again, "The sun and the moon shall be darkened, and the stars shall withdraw their shining;" [158] while, apart altogether from the immediately preceding and following words, which prove the interpretation above given to be correct, this announcement of Joel was declared by St. Peter on the day of Pentecost to apply to the introduction of that kingdom of Christ which, in the gift of tongues, was at that moment exhibited in power. [159] In like manner we read in the prophet Haggai, "For thus saith the Lord of hosts; Yet once, it is a little while, and I will shake the heavens, and the earth, and the sea, and the dry land; and I will shake all nations." [160] While, again, without our needing to dwell on the connexion in which the words occur, we find the writer of the Epistle to the Hebrews applying the prophecy to the circumstances of those to whom he wrote at a time when they had heard the voice that speaketh from heaven, and had received the kingdom that cannot be moved. [161] The prophet Malachi also, whose words have been interpreted for us by our Lord Himself, describes the day of Him whom the Baptist was to precede and to introduce as the day that "burneth as a furnace," as "the great and terrible day of the Lord." [162] This aspect, too, of any great era in the history of a land or of a people had always been presented by the voice of prophecy in language from which the words before us are obviously taken. Thus it was that when Isaiah described the coming of a time at which the mountain of the Lord's house shall be established in the top of the mountains and shall be exalted above the hills, and all nations shall flow into it, he mentions, among its other characteristics, "And they shall go into the holes of the rocks, and into the caves of the earth, for fear of the Lord, and for the glory of His majesty, when He ariseth to shake terribly the earth."

[163] When the same prophet details the burden of Babylon which he saw, he exclaims, "Behold, the day of the Lord cometh, cruel both with wrath and fierce anger to make the land a desolation, and to destroy the sinners thereof out of it. For the stars of heaven and the constellations thereof shall not give their light: the sun shall be darkened in his going forth, and the moon shall not cause her light to shine;" [164] and again, when he widens his view from Babylon to a guilty world, "For the Lord hath indignation against all the nations, and fury against all their hosts.... And all the host of heaven shall be dissolved, and the heavens shall be rolled together as a scroll: and all their host shall fade away, as the leaf falleth from off the vine, and as a fading fig from the fig tree." [165] Many other passages of a similar kind might be quoted from the Old Testament; but, without quoting further from that source, it may be enough to call to mind that when our Lord delivered His discourse upon the last things He adopted a precisely similar strain: "Immediately after the tribulation of those days shall the sun be darkened, and the moon shall not give her light, and the stars shall fall from heaven, and the powers of the heavens shall be shaken." [166]

Highly coloured, therefore, as the language used under the sixth Seal may appear to us, to the Jew, animated by the spirit of the Old Testament, it was simply that in which he had been accustomed to express his expectation of any new dispensation of the Almighty, of any striking crisis in the history of the world. Whenever he thought of the Judge of all the earth as manifesting Himself in a greater than ordinary degree, and as manifesting Himself in that truth and righteousness which was the glorious distinction of His character, he took advantage of such figures as we have now before us. To the fall of Jerusalem therefore, to every great crisis in human history, and to the close of all, they may be fittingly applied. In the eloquent language of Dr. Vaughan, "These words are wonderful in all senses, not least in this sense: that they are manifold in their accomplishment. Wherever there is a little flock in a waste wilderness; wherever there is a Church in a world; wherever there is a power of unbelief, ungodliness, and violence, throwing itself upon Christ's faith and Christ's people and seeking to overbear, and to demolish, and to destroy; whether that power be the power of Jewish bigotry and fanaticism, as in the days of the first disciples; or of pagan Rome, with its idolatries and its cruelties, as in the days of St. John and of the Revelation; or of papal Rome, with its lying wonders and its antichristian assumptions, in ages later still; or of open and rampant atheism, as in the days of the first French Revolution; or of a subtler and more insidious infidelity, like that which is threatening now to deceive, if it were possible, the very elect; wherever and whatever this power may be--and it has had a thousand forms, and may be destined yet to assume a thousand more--then, in each successive century, the words of Christ to His first disciples adapt themselves afresh to the circumstances of His struggling servants; warn them of danger, exhort them to patience, arouse them to hope, assure them of victory; tell of a near end for the individual and for the generation; tell also of a far end, not for ever to be postponed, for time itself and for the world; predict a destruction which shall befall each enemy of the truth, and predict a destruction which shall befall the enemy himself whom each in turn has represented and served; explain the meaning of tribulation, show whence it comes, and point to its swallowing up in glory; reveal the moving hand above, and disclose, from behind the cloud which conceals it, the clear definite purpose and the unchanging loving will. Thus understood, each separate downfall of evil becomes a prophecy of the next and of the last; and the partial fulfilment of our Lord's words in the destruction of Jerusalem, or of St. John's words in the downfall of idolatry and the dismemberment of Rome, becomes itself in turn a new warrant for the Church's expectation of the Second Advent and of the day of judgment." [167]

While, however, the truth of these words may be allowed, it is still necessary to urge that the primary application of the language of the sixth Seal is to no one of such events in particular, but to something which includes them all. In other words, it applies to the Christian dispensation, viewed in its beginning, its progress, and its end, viewed in all those issues which it produces in the world, but especially on the side of judgment.

Nor ought such dark and terrible figures to startle us, as if they could not be suitably applied to a dispensation of mercy, of grace that we cannot fathom, of love that passeth knowledge. The Christian dispensation is not effeminary. If it tells of abounding compassion for the sinner, it tells also of fire, and hail, and vapour of smoke for the sin. If it speaks at one time in a gentle voice, it speaks at another in a voice of thunder; and, when the latter is rightly listened to, the air is cleared as by the whirlwind.

Although, therefore, the language of the prophets and of this passage may at first sight appear to be marked by far too great a measure both of strength and of severity to make it applicable to the Gospel age, it is in reality neither too strong nor too severe. It is at variance only with the verdict of that superficial glance which is satisfied with looking at phenomena in their outward and temporary aspect, and which declines to penetrate into the heart of things. So long as man is content with such a spirit, he is naturally enough unstirred by any powerful emotion; and he can only say that words of prophetic fire are words of exaggeration and of false enthusiasm. But no sooner does he catch that spirit of the Bible which brings him into contact with eternal verities than his tone changes. He can no longer rest upon the surface. He can no longer dismiss the thought of mighty issues at stake around him with the reflection that "all the world's a stage, and all the men and women on it only players." When from the shore he looks out upon the mass of waters stretching before him, he thinks not merely of the light waves rippling at his feet and losing themselves in the sand, but of the unfathomed depths of the ocean from which they come, and of those mysterious movements of it which they indicate. He sees sights, he hears sounds, which the common eye does not see, and the common ear does not hear. The slightest motion of the soil speaks to him of earthquakes; the handful of snow loosened from the mountain-side, of avalanches; the simplest utterance of awe, of a cry that the mountains and the hills are falling. The great does not become to him little; but the little becomes great. There is thus no exaggeration in the strength or even in the severity of prophetic figures. The prophet has passed from the world of shadows, flitting past him and disappearing, into the world of realities, Divine, unchangeable, and everlasting.

Footnotes:

132. Isa. lxiv. 1.
133. Isa. xli. 2.
134. Ezek. vi. 11; Matt. xxiv. 6-8.
135. Isa. xxxii. 18.
136. Lev. xxvi. 26.
137. Ezek. iv. 16, 17.
138. Comp. Matt. xx. 2.
139. Ps. xxiii. 5.
140. John x. 10.
141. Ps. civ. 15.
142. Ps. ix. 15.
143. Lev. iv. 7.
144. Comp. chaps. i. 2, 9; xi. 7; xii. 11, 17; xix. 10.
145. Margin of Revised Version.
146. Chap. iii. 4.
147. Chap. iii. 5.
148. Chap. iii. 18.
149. Chap. xix. 8.
150. Acts xiii. 39.
151. Ps. li. 7.
152. Isa. lxi. 10.
153. Ezek. xxxvi. 25-29.
154. Matt. xi. 11.
155. Heb. xi. 39, 40.
156. John viii. 56.
157. 1 Pet. i. 8 (R.V., margin).
158. Joel ii. 30, 31; iii. 15.
159. Acts ii. 16-21.
160. Haggai ii. 6, 7.
161. Heb. xii. 25-29.
162. Mal. iv. 1, 5; Mark ix. 11-13.
163. Isa. ii. 19.
164. Isa. xiii. 9, 10.
165. Isa. xxxiv. 2, 4.
166. Matt. xxiv. 29.
167. Lectures on the Revelation, p. 170.

CHAPTER V - CONSOLATORY VISIONS

Rev. vii.

Six of the seven Seals have been opened by the "Lamb," who is likewise the "Lion of the tribe of Judah." They have dealt, in brief but pregnant sentences, with the whole history of the Church and of the world throughout the Christian age. No details of history have indeed been spoken of, no particular wars, or famines, or pestilences, or slaughters, or preservations of the saints. Everything has been described in the most general terms. We have been invited to think only of the principles of the Divine government, but of these as the most sublime and, according to our own state of mind, the most alarming or the most consolatory principles that can engage the attention of men. God, has been the burden of the six Seals, is King over all the earth. Why do the heathen rage, and the people imagine a vain thing? Why do they exalt themselves against the sovereign Ruler of the universe, who said to the Son of His love, when He made Him Head over all things for His Church, "Thou art My Son; this day have I begotten Thee;" "Rule Thou in the midst of Thine enemies"? [168] Listening to the voice of these Seals, we know that the world, with all its might, shall prevail neither against the Head nor against the members of the Body. Even when apparently successful it shall fight a losing battle. Even when apparently defeated Christ and they who are one with Him shall march to victory.

We are not to imagine that the Seals of chap. vi. follow one another in chronological succession, or that each of them belongs to a definite date. The Seer does not look forward to age succeeding age or century century. To him the whole period between the first and the second coming of Christ is but "a little time," and whatever is to happen in it "must shortly come to pass." In truth he can hardly be said to deal with the lapse of time at all. He deals with the essential characteristics of the Divine government in time, whether it be long or short. Shall the revolving years be in our sense short, these characteristics will nevertheless come forth with a clearness that shall leave man without excuse. Shall they be in our sense long, the unfolding of God's eternal plan will only be again and again made manifest. He with whom we have to do is without beginning of days or end of years, the I am, unchangeable both in the attributes of His own nature, and in the execution of His purposes for the world's redemption. Let us cast our eyes along the centuries that have passed away since Jesus died and rose again. They are full of one great lesson. At every point at which we pause we see the Son of God going forth conquering and to conquer. We see the world struggling against His righteousness, refusing to submit to it, and dooming itself in consequence to every form of woe. We see the children of God following a crucified Redeemer, but preserved, sustained, animated, their cross, like His, their crown. Finally, as we realize more and more deeply what is going on around us, we feel that we are in the midst of a great earthquake, that the sun and the moon have become black, and that the stars of heaven are falling to the earth; yet by the eye of faith we pierce the darkness, and where are all our adversaries? Where are the kings and the potentates, the rich and the powerful of the earth, of an ungodly and persecuting world? They have hid themselves in the caves and in the rocks of the mountains; and we hear them say to the mountains and to the rocks, "Fall on us, and hide us from the face of Him that sitteth on the throne, and from the wrath of the Lamb: for the great day of their wrath is come; and who is able to stand?"

With the beginning of chap. vii. we might expect the seventh Seal to be opened; but it is the manner of the apocalyptic writer, before any final or particularly critical manifestation of the wrath of God, to present us with visions of consolation, so that we may enter into the thickest darkness, even into the valley of the shadow of death, without alarm. We have already met with this in chaps. iv. and v. We shall meet with it again. Meanwhile it is here illustrated:--

After this I saw four angels standing at the four corners of the earth, holding the four winds of the earth, that no wind should blow on the earth, or on the sea, or upon any tree. And I saw another angel ascend from the sun-rising, having the seal of the living God: and he cried with a great voice to the four angels, to whom it was given to hurt the earth and the sea, saying, Hurt not the earth, neither the sea, nor the trees, till we shall have sealed the servants of our God on their foreheads. And I heard the number of them which were sealed, a hundred and forty and four thousand, sealed out of every tribe of the children of Israel. Of the tribe of Judah were sealed twelve thousand; of the tribe of Reuben, twelve thousand; of the tribe of Gad, twelve thousand; of the tribe of Asher, twelve thousand; of the tribe of Naphtali, twelve thousand; of the tribe of Manasseh, twelve thousand; of the tribe of Simeon, twelve thousand; of the tribe of Levi, twelve thousand; of the tribe of Issachar, twelve thousand; of the tribe of Zebulun, twelve thousand; of the tribe of Joseph, twelve thousand; of the tribe of Benjamin were sealed twelve thousand (vii. 1-8).

Although various important questions, which we shall have to notice, arise in connexion with this vision, there never has been, as there scarcely can be, any doubt as to its general meaning. In its main features it is taken from the language of Ezekiel, when that prophet foretold the approaching destruction of Jerusalem: "He cried also with a loud voice in mine ears, saying, Cause them that have charge over the city to draw near, even every man with his destroying weapon in his hand. And, behold, six men came from the way of the higher gate, which lieth toward the north, and every man a slaughter weapon in his hand; and one man among them was clothed with fine linen, with a writer's inkhorn by his side.... And the Lord said unto him, Go through the midst of the city, through the midst of Jerusalem, and set a mark upon the foreheads of the men that sigh and that cry for all the abominations that be done in the midst thereof.... And, behold, the man clothed with linen, which had the inkhorn by his side, reported the matter, saying, I have done as Thou hast commanded me." [169] Preservation of the faithful in the midst of judgment on the wicked is the theme of the Old Testament vision, and in like manner it is the theme of this vision of St. John. The winds are the symbols of judgment; and, being in number four and held by four angels standing at the four corners of the earth, they indicate that the judgment when inflicted will be universal. There is no place to which the ungodly can escape, none where they shall not be overtaken by the wrath of God. "He that fleeth of them," says the Almighty by His prophet, "shall not flee away, and he that escapeth of them shall not be delivered. Though they dig into hell, thence shall Mine hand take them; though they climb up to heaven, thence will I bring them down: and though they hide themselves in the top of Carmel, I will search and take them out thence; and though they be hid from My sight in the bottom of the sea, thence will I command the serpent, and he shall bite them." [170]

In the midst of all this the safety of the righteous is secured, and that in a way, as compared with the way of the Old Testament, proportionate to the superior greatness of their privileges. They are marked as God's, not by a man out of the city, but by an angel ascending from the sun-rising, the quarter whence proceeds that light of day which gilds the loftiest mountain-tops and penetrates into the darkest recesses of the valleys. This angel, with his great voice, is probably the Lord Himself appearing by His angel. The mark impressed upon the righteous is more than a mere mark: it is a seal--a seal similar to that with which Christ was "sealed;" [171] the seal which in the Song of Songs the bride desires as the token of the Bridegroom's love to her alone: "Set me as a seal upon Thine heart, as a seal upon Thine arm;" [172] the seal which expresses the thought, "The Lord knoweth them that are His." [173] Finally, this seal is impressed on the forehead, on that part of the body on which the high-priest of Israel wore the golden plate, with its inscription, "Holiness to the Lord." Such a seal, manifest to the eyes of all, was a witness to all that they who bore it were acknowledged by the Redeemer before all, even before His Father and the holy angels. [174]

When we turn to the numbers sealed, every reader who reflects for a moment will allow that they must be symbolically, and not literally, understood. Twelve thousand out of each of twelve tribes, in all a hundred and forty and four thousand, bears upon its face the stamp of symbolism. It is more difficult to answer the question, Who are they? Are they Jewish Christians, or are they the whole multitude of God's faithful people belonging to the Church universal, but indicated by a figure taken from Judaism?

The question now asked is of greater than ordinary importance, for upon the answer given to it largely depends the solution of the problem whether the author of the fourth Gospel and the author of the Apocalypse are the same. If the first vision of the chapter relating to those sealed out of the tribes of Israel speak only of Jewish Christians, and the second vision, beginning at ver. 9, of "the great multitude which no man could number," speak of Gentile Christians, it will follow that the writer exhibits a particularistic tendency altogether at variance with the universalism of the author of the fourth Gospel. Gentile Christians will be, as they have been called, an "appendix" to the Jewish-Christian Church; and the followers of Jesus will fail to constitute one flock all the members of which are equal in the sight of God, occupy the same position, and enjoy the same privileges. The first impression produced by the vision of the sealed is undoubtedly that it refers to Jewish Christians, and to them alone. Many considerations, however, lead to the wider conclusion that, under a Jewish figure, they include all the followers of Christ, or the universal Church. Some of these at least ought to be noticed.

1. We have not yet found, and we shall not find in any later part of the Apocalypse, a distinction drawn between Jewish and Gentile Christians. To the eye of the Seer, the Church of the Lord Jesus Christ is one. There is in it neither Jew nor Greek, barbarian, Scythian, bond, nor free. He recognises in it in its collective capacity the Body of Christ, all the members of which occupy the same relation to their Lord, and stand equally in grace. He knows indeed of a distinction between the Jewish Church, which waited for the coming of the Lord, and the Christian Church, which rejoiced in Him as come; but he knows also that when Jesus did come the privileges of the latter were bestowed upon those in the

former who had looked onward to Christ's day, and that they were arrayed in the same "white robe." Under all the six Seals, accordingly, embracing the whole period of the Gospel dispensation, there is not a single word to suggest the thought that the Christian Church is divided into two parts. The struggle, the preservation, and the victory belong equally to all. A similar remark may be made on the epistles to the seven churches, which unquestionably contain a representation of that Church the fortunes of which are to be afterwards described. In these epistles Christ walks equally in the midst of every part of it; and promises are made, not in one form to one member and in another to another, but always in precisely the same terms to "him that overcometh." It would be out of keeping with this were we now, when a similar topic of preservation is on hand, to be introduced to a Jewish-Christian as distinguished from a Gentile-Christian Church.

2. It is the custom of the Seer to heighten and spiritualize all Jewish names. The Temple, the Tabernacle, the Altar, Mount Zion, and Jerusalem are to him the embodiments of ideas deeper than those literally conveyed by them. Analogy therefore might suggest that this also would be the case with the word "Israel." Nay, it would even be the more natural so to use that word, because it is so often used in the same spiritual sense in other parts of the New Testament: "But they are not all Israel which are of Israel;" "And as many as shall walk by this rule, peace be upon them, and mercy, and upon the Israel of God." [175] Nor need we be startled by that employment of the word tribes, which may seem to give more precision to the idea that Jewish Christians are designated by the term, for St. John, in his peculiar way of looking at men, beheld "tribes" not only among the Jews, but among all nations: "And all the tribes of the earth shall mourn over Him." [176] In chap. xxi. 12, too, the "twelve tribes" plainly include all believers.

3. The enumeration of the tribes of Israel given in these verses is different from any other enumeration of the kind contained in Scripture. Thus the tribe of Dan is omitted; and, contrary to the practice of at least the later books of the Old Testament, that of Levi is inserted; while Joseph also is substituted for Ephraim: and the order in which the twelve are given has elsewhere no parallel. Points such as these may appear trifling, but they are not without importance. No student of the Apocalypse will imagine that they are accidental or undesigned. He may not be able to satisfy either himself or others as to the grounds upon which St. John proceeded, but that there were grounds sufficient to the Apostle himself for what he did he will not for a moment doubt. One thing may, however, be said. If the changes can be explained at all, it must be by considerations springing out of the heart of the Christian community, and not out of any suggested by the relations of the tribes of Judaism to one another. Levi may thus be inserted, instead of standing apart as formerly, because in Christ Jesus there was no priestly tribe: all Christians were priests; Dan may be omitted because that tribe had chosen the serpent as its emblem, and St. John not only felt with peculiar power the direct antagonism to Christ of "the old serpent the devil," [177] but had been accustomed to see in the traitor Judas, who had been expelled from the apostolic band, and for whom another apostle had been substituted, the very impersonation or incarnation of Satan [178] ; Ephraim also may have been replaced by Joseph because of its enmity to Judah, the tribe out of which Jesus sprang; while Judah, the fourth son of Jacob, may head the list because it was the tribe in which Christ was born.

4. Some of the expressions of the passage are inconsistent with the limitation of the sealed to any special class of Christians. Why, for example, should the holding back of the winds be universal? Would it not have been enough to restrain the winds that blew on Jewish Christians, and not the winds of the whole earth? And again, why do we meet with language of so general a character as that of ver. 3: "till we shall have sealed the servants of our God"? This designation "servants" seems to include the whole number, and not some only, of God's children.

5. If God's servants from among the Gentiles are not now sealed, the Apocalypse mentions no other occasion when they were so. It is true that, according to the ordinary interpretation of the next vision, they are admitted to the happiness of heaven; but we may well ask whether, if the sealing be the emblem of preservation amidst worldly troubles, they ought not also, at one time or another, to have been sealed on earth.

6. The sealed are marked upon their foreheads, and in chap. xxii. 4 all believers are marked in a similar way.

7. We shall meet again this number of a hundred and forty-four thousand in chap. xiv.; and, while it can hardly be doubted that the same persons are on both occasions included in it, it will be seen that there at least the whole number of the redeemed is meant.

8. It is worthy of notice that the contrasts of the Apocalypse lead directly to a similar conclusion. St. John always sees light and darkness standing over against each other, and exhibiting themselves in a correspondence which, extending even to minute details, aids the task of the interpreter. Now in many passages of this book we find Satan not only marking his followers, but, precisely as here, marking them upon the "forehead;" [179] and it is impossible to resist the conclusion that the one marking is the antithesis of the other. But this mark is imprinted by Satan upon all his followers, and the inference is legitimate that the seal of the living God is in like manner imprinted upon all the followers of Jesus.

9. One more reason may be assigned for this conclusion. If ver. 4, with its "hundred and forty and four thousand out of every tribe of the children of Israel," is to be understood of Jewish Christians alone, the contrast between it and ver. 9, with its "great multitude, which no man can number, out of every nation, and of all tribes, and peoples, and tongues," makes it necessary to understand the latter of Gentile Christians alone. It will not do to say that the comprehensive enumeration of this verse may include Jewish as well as Gentile Christians. Placed over against the very definite statement of ver. 4, it can only, according to the style of the Apocalypse, be referred to persons who have come out of the heathen world in the fourfold conception of its parts. Now, whatever may be the precise interpretation of the second vision of the chapter, it is undeniable that it unfolds a higher stage of privilege and glory than the first. It will thus follow on the supposition now combated that at the very instant when the Apostle is said to be placing Gentile Christians in a position of inferiority to Jewish Christians, and when he is treating the one as simply an "appendix" to the other, he speaks of them as the inheritors of a far greater "weight of glory." St. John could not be thus inconsistent with himself.

The conclusion from all that has been said, is plain. The vision of the sealing does not apply to Jewish Christians only, but to the universal Church. When the judgments of God are abroad in the world, all the disciples of Christ are sealed for preservation against them.

Notwithstanding what has been said, the reader may still find it difficult to conceive that two pictures of the same multitude should be presented to us drawn on such entirely different lines. What is the meaning of it? he may exclaim. What is the Seer's motive in doing so? The explanation is not difficult. An attentive examination of the structural principles marking the writings of St. John will show that they are distinguished by a tendency to set forth the same object in two different lights, the latter of which is climactic to the former, as well as, for the most part at least, taken from a different sphere. The writer is not satisfied with a single utterance of what he desires to impress upon his readers. After he has uttered it for the first time, he brings it again before him, works upon it, enlarges it, deepens it, sets it forth with stronger and more vivid colouring. The fundamental idea is the same on both occasions; but on the second it is the centre of a circle of wider circumference, and it is uttered in a more impressive manner. Want of space will not permit the illustration of this by an appeal either to the nature of Hebrew thought in general, or to the other writings of the New Testament which owe their authorship to St. John. It must be enough to say that the fourth Gospel bears deep and important traces of this characteristic, and that difficult passages in it not otherwise explicable seem to be solved by its application. [180] The main point to be kept in view is that the principle in question may be traced on many different occasions both in the fourth Gospel and in the Apocalypse. One of these has indeed already come under our notice in the case of the "golden candlesticks" and of the "stars" in Chapter I. of this book. The two figures relate to the same object, but the second is climactic to the first, and it is taken from a larger field. The same principle meets us here. The second vision of chap. vii. is climactic to the first, and the field from which it is drawn is larger. The analogy, however, not of the golden candlesticks and of the stars only, but of many other passages of a similar kind, warrants the inference that both the visions relate to the same thing, although the aspect in which it is looked at is in each case different. Any difficulty therefore at first presented by the double picture disappears; while the peculiarity of structure exhibited not only helps to lead us to a Johannine authorship, but tends powerfully to establish the correctness of the interpretation now adopted.

We are thus entitled to conclude that the hundred and forty-four thousand of this first consolatory vision represent not Jewish Christians only, but the whole Church of God, and that the number used is intended to represent completeness: not one member of the true Church is lost. [181] Twelve, a sacred number, the number of the patriarchs, of the tribes of Israel, and of the Apostles of Jesus, is first multiplied by itself, and then by a thousand, the sign of the heavenly in contrast with the earthly. A hundred and forty and four thousand is the result.

It need only further be observed--and the observation will help to confirm what has been said--that St. John did not himself count the number of the sealed. He heard the number of them (ver. 4). Already they were "a multitude which no man could number" (ver. 9). But He who telleth the innumerable stars that sparkle in the midnight sky, and who "bringeth out their host by number," [182] could number them. He it was who communicated the number to the Seer.

The second vision of the chapter follows:--

After these things I saw, and, behold, a great multitude, which no man could number, out of every nation, and of all tribes, and peoples, and tongues, standing before the throne, and before the Lamb, arrayed in white robes, and palms in their hands; and they cry with a great voice, saying, Salvation unto our God which sitteth on the throne, and unto the Lamb. And all the angels were standing round about the throne, and about the elders and the four living creatures; and they fell before the throne on their faces, and worshipped God, saying, Amen: Blessing, and glory, and wisdom, and thanksgiving, and honour, and power, and might, be unto our God for ever and ever. Amen. And one of the elders answered, saying unto me, These which are arrayed in the white robes, who are they, and whence came they? And I said unto him, My lord, thou knowest. And he said to me, These are they which came out of the great tribulation, and they washed their robes, and made them white in the blood of the Lamb. Therefore are they before the throne of God, and they serve Him day and night in His temple: and He that sitteth on the throne shall spread His tabernacle over them. They shall hunger no more, neither thirst any more; neither shall the sun strike upon them, nor any heat: for the Lamb which is in the midst of the throne shall be their Shepherd, and shall guide them unto fountains of waters of life: and God shall wipe away every tear from their eyes (vii. 9-17).

Upon the magnificence and beauty of this description it is not only unnecessary, it would be a mistake, to dwell. Words of man would only mar the sublimity and pathos of the spectacle. Neither is it desirable to look at each expression of the passage in itself. These expressions are better considered as a whole. One point indeed ought to be carefully kept in view: that the palms spoken of in ver. 9 as in the hands of the happy multitude are not the palms of victory in any earthly contest, but the palms of the Feast of Tabernacles, and that upon the thought of that feast the scene is moulded.

The Feast of Tabernacles, it will be remembered, was at once the last, the highest, and the most joyful of the festivals of the Jewish year. It fell in the month of October, when the harvest not only of grain, but of wine and oil, had been gathered in, and when, therefore, all the labours of the year were past. It was preceded, too, by the great Day of Atonement, the ceremonial of which gathered together all the sacrificial acts of the previous months, beheld the sins of the people, from their highest to their lowest, carried away into the wilderness, and brought with it the blessing of God from that innermost recess of the sanctuary which was lightened by the special glory of His presence, and into which the high-priest even was permitted to enter upon that day alone. The feelings awakened in Israel at the time were of the most triumphant kind. They returned in thought to the independent life which their fathers, delivered from the bondage of Egypt, led in the wilderness; and, the better to realize this, they left their ordinary dwellings and took up their abode for the days of the feast in booths, which they erected in the streets or on the flat roofs of their houses. These booths were made of branches of their most prized, most fruit-bearing, and most umbrageous trees; and beneath them they raised their psalms of thanksgiving to Him who had delivered them as a bird out of the snare of the fowler. Even this was not all, for we know that in the later period of their history the Jews connected the Feast of Tabernacles with the brightest anticipations of the future as well as with the most joyful memories of the past. They beheld in it the promise of the Spirit, the great gift of the approaching Messianic age; and, that they might give full expression to this, they sent on the eighth, or great, day of the feast, a priest to the pool of Siloam with a golden urn, that he might fill it from the pool, and, bringing it up to the Temple, might pour it on the altar. This is the part of the ceremonial alluded to in John vii. 37-39, and during it the joy of the people reached its highest point. They surrounded the priest in crowds as he brought up the water from the pool, waved their lulabs--small branches of palm trees, the "palms" of ver. 9--and made the courts of the Temple re-echo with their song, "With joy shall ye draw water out of wells of salvation." [183] At night the great illumination of the Temple followed, that to which our Lord most probably alludes when, immediately after the Feast of Tabernacles spoken of in chap. viii. of the fourth Gospel, He exclaims, "I am the Light of the world: he that followeth Me shall not walk in the darkness, but shall have the light of life." [184]

Such was the scene the main particulars of which are here made use of by the apocalyptic Seer to set before us the triumphant and glorious condition of the Church when, after all her members have been sealed, they are admitted to the full enjoyment of the blessings of God's covenant, and when, washed in the blood of the Lamb and clothed with His righteousness, they keep their Feast of Tabernacles.

A most important and interesting question connected with this vision has still to be answered. It may be first asked in the words of Isaac Williams. "It is whether all this description is of the Church in heaven or on earth." The same writer has answered his question by saying, "The fact is that, like the expression 'the kingdom of heaven,' and many others of the same kind, it applies to both, and it is doubtless intended to do so--in fulness hereafter, but even here in part." [185] The answer thus given is no doubt correct when the question is asked in the particular form to which it is a reply. Yet we have still to ask whether, granting it to be so, the primary reference of the vision is to the Church of Christ during her present pilgrimage or after that pilgrimage has been completed, and she has entered on her eternal rest. To the question so put, the reply usually given is that the Seer has the latter aspect of the Church in view. The redeemed are sealed on earth; they bear their "palms," and rejoice with the joy afterwards spoken of, in heaven. Much in the passage may seem to justify this conclusion. But a recent writer on the subject has adduced such powerful considerations in favour of the former view, that it will be proper to examine them. [186]

Appeal is first made to Matt. xxiv. 13, a passage throwing no light upon the point. It is otherwise with many prophecies of the Old Testament next referred to, which describe the coming dispensation of the Gospel: "They shall not hunger nor thirst; neither shall the heat nor sun smite them: for He that hath mercy on them shall lead them, even by the springs of water shall He guide them;" "He will swallow up death in victory; and the Lord God will wipe away tears from off all faces;" "And it shall come to pass, that every one that is left of all the nations which came against Jerusalem shall even go up from year to year to worship the King, the Lord of hosts, and to keep the Feast of Tabernacles." [187] To passages such as these have to be added the promises of our Lord as to fountains of living waters even now opened to the believer, that he may drink and never thirst again: "Jesus answered and said unto her, Every one that drinketh of this water shall thirst again: but whosoever drinketh of the water that I shall give him shall never thirst; but the water that I shall give him shall become in him a springing fountain of water, unto eternal life;" "Now on the last day, the great day of the feast, Jesus stood and cried, saying, If any man thirst, let him come unto Me, and drink. He that believeth on Me, as the Scripture hath said, out of his belly shall flow rivers of living water." [188] St. John, too, it is urged, teaches us to look for a Tabernacle Feast on earth [189] ; while at the same time throughout all his writings eternal life is set before us as a present possession. Nor is this the case only in the writings of St. John. In the Epistle to the Hebrews we meet the same line of thought: "Ye are come" (not Ye shall come) "unto Mount Zion, and unto the city of the living God, the heavenly Jerusalem, and to innumerable hosts of angels, to the general assembly and Church of the first-born, who are enrolled in heaven." [190] Influenced by these considerations, the writer to whom we have referred is led, "though not without some hesitation," to conclude that the vision of the palm-bearing multitude is to be understood of the Church on earth, and not of the Church in heaven.

The conclusion may be accepted without the "hesitation." The colours on the canvas may indeed at first appear too bright for any condition of things on this side the grave. But they are not more bright than those employed in the description of the new Jerusalem in chap. xxi.; and, when we come to the exposition of that chapter, we shall find positive proof in the language of the Seer that he looks upon that city as one already come down from heaven and established among men. Not a few of its most glowing traits are even precisely the same as those that we meet in the corresponding vision of this chapter: "And I heard a great voice out of the throne saying, Behold, the tabernacle of God is with men, and He shall tabernacle with them, and they shall be His peoples, and God Himself shall be with them, and be their God; and He shall wipe away every tear from their eyes; and death shall be no more; neither shall there be mourning, nor crying, nor pain, any more: the first things are passed away." [191] If words like these may be justly applied, as we have yet to see that they may and must be, to one aspect of the Church on earth, there is certainly nothing to hinder their application to the same Church now. The truth is that in both cases the description is ideal, and that not less so than the description of the terrors of the worldly at the opening of the sixth Seal. Nor indeed shall we understand any part of the Apocalypse unless we recognise the fact that everything with which it is concerned is raised to an ideal standard. Reward and punishment, righteousness and sin, the martyrdoms of the Church and the fate of her oppressors, are all set before us in an ideal light. The Seer moves in the midst of conceptions which are fundamental, ultimate, and eternal. The "broken lights" which partially illuminate our progress in this world are to him absorbed in "the true Light." The clouds and darkness which obscure our path gather themselves together to his eyes in "the darkness" with which the light has to contend. Descriptions, accordingly, applicable in their fulness to the Church only after the glory of her Lord is manifested, apply also to her now, when she is thought of as living the life that is hid with Christ in God, the life of her exalted and glorified Redeemer. For this conception the colours of the picture before us are not too bright. [192]

The relation in which the two visions of this chapter stand to one another may now be obvious. Although the persons referred to are in both the same, they do not in both occupy the same position. In the first they are only sealed, and through that sealing they are safe. Their Lord has taken them under His protection; and, whatever troubles or perils may beset them, no one shall pluck them out of His hand. In the second they are more than safe. They have peace, and joy, and triumph, their every want supplied, their every sorrow healed. Death itself is swallowed up in victory, and every tear is wiped from every eye.

Thus also may we determine the period to which both the sealing of believers and their subsequent enjoyment of heavenly blessing belong. In neither vision are we introduced to any special era of Christian history. St. John has in view neither the Christians of his own day alone, nor those of any later time. As we found that each of the first six Seals embraced the whole Gospel age, so also is it with these consolatory visions. We are to dwell upon the thought rather than the time of preservation and of bliss. The Church of Christ never ceases to follow in the footsteps of her Lord. Like Him, when faithful to her high commission, she never ceases to bear the cross. The unredeemed world must always be her enemy; and in it she must always have tribulation. But not less continuous is her joy. We judge wrongly when we think that the Man of sorrows was never joyful. He spoke of "My peace," "My joy." [193] In one of His moments of deepest feeling we are told that He "rejoiced in spirit." [194] Outwardly the world troubled Him; and huge billows, raised by its tempestuous winds, swept across the surface of His soul. Beneath, the unfathomed depths were calm. In communion with His Father in heaven, in the thought of the great work which He was carrying to its completion, and in the prospect of the glory that awaited Him, He could rejoice in the midst of sorrow. So also with the members of His Body. They bear about with them a secret joy which, like their new name, no man knoweth saving he that receiveth it. As the friend of the bridegroom who standeth and heareth him rejoices greatly because of the bridegroom's voice, so their joy is fulfilled. [195] Nor does it ever cease to be theirs while their Lord is with them; and unless they grieve Him "lo, He is always with them, even unto the consummation of the age." [196] The two visions, therefore, of the sealing and of the palm-bearing multitude embrace the whole Christian dispensation within their scope, and express ideas which belong to the condition of the believer in all places and at all times.

Footnotes:

168. Ps. ii. 7; cx. 7.
169. Ezek. ix.
170. Amos ix. 1-3.
171. John vi. 27.
172. Cant. viii. 3.
173. 2 Tim. ii. 19.
174. Comp. Luke xii. 8.
175. Rom. ix. 6; Gal. vi. 16.
176. Chap. i. 7.
177. Comp. chap. xii. 9.
178. John xiii. 2.
179. Chaps. xiii. 16, 17; xiv. 9; xvi. 2; xix. 20; xx. 4.
180. The writer has treated this subject at considerable length in The Expositor (2nd series, vol. iv.).
181. Comp. John xvii. 12.
182. Isa. xl. 26.
183. Isa. xii. 3.
184. John viii. 12.
185. The Apocalypse, p. 126.
186. Professor Gibson, in The Monthly Interpreter, vol. ii., p. 9.
187. Isa. xlix. 10; xxv. 8; Zech. xiv. 16.
188. John iv. 13, 14; vii. 37, 38.
189. John i. 14.
190. Heb. xii. 22, 23.
191. Chap. xxi. 3, 4.
192. Comp. on the general thought Brown, The Second Advent, chap. vi.
193. John xiv. 27; xvii. 13.
194. Luke x. 21.
195. John iii. 29.
196. Matt. xxviii. 20.

CHAPTER VI - THE FIRST SIX TRUMPETS

Rev. viii., ix.

The two consolatory visions of chap. vii. have closed, and the Seer returns to that opening of the seven Seals which had been interrupted in order that these two visions might be interposed.

Six Seals had been opened in chap. vi.; the opening of the seventh follows:--

And when He opened the seventh seal, there followed silence in heaven about the space of half an hour. And I saw the seven angels which stand before God; and there were given unto them seven trumpets. And another angel came and stood over the altar, having a golden censer; and there was given unto him much incense, that he should give it unto the prayers of all the saints upon the golden altar which was before the throne. And the smoke of the incense, with the prayers of the saints, went up before God out of the angel's hand. And the angel taketh the censer; and he filled it with the fire of the altar, and cast it upon the earth: and there followed thunders, and voices, and lightnings, and an earthquake. And the seven angels which had the seven trumpets prepared themselves to sound (viii. 1-6).

Before looking at the particulars of this Seal, we have to determine the relation in which it stands to the Seals of chap. vi. as well as to the visions following it. Is it as isolated, as independent, as those that have come before it; and are its contents exhausted by the first six verses of the chapter? or does it occupy such a position of its own that we are to regard the following visions as developed out of it? And if the latter be the case, how far does the development extend?

In answering these questions, it can hardly be denied that if we are to look upon the seventh Seal as standing independent and alone, its contents have not the significance which we seem entitled to expect. It is the last Seal of its own series; and when we turn to the last member of the Trumpet series at chap. xi. 15, or of the Bowl series at chap. xvi. 17, we find them marked, not by less, but by much greater, force than had belonged in either case to the six preceding members. The seventh Trumpet and the seventh Bowl sum up and concentrate the contents of their predecessors. In the one the judgments of God represented by the Trumpets, in the other those represented by the Bowls, culminate in their sharpest expression and their most tremendous potency. There is nothing of that kind in the seventh Seal if it terminates with the preparation of the Trumpet angels to sound; and the analogy of the Apocalypse therefore, an analogy supplying in a book so symmetrically constructed an argument of greater than ordinary weight, is against that supposition.

Again, the larger portion of the first six verses of this chapter does not suggest the contents of the Seal. Rather would it seem as if these contents were confined to the "silence" spoken of in ver. 1, and as if what follows from ver. 2 to ver. 6 were to be regarded as no part of the Seal itself, but simply as introductory to the Trumpet visions. Everything said bears upon it the marks of preparation for what is to come, and we are not permitted to rest in what is passing as if it were a final and conclusive scene in the great spectacle presented to the Seer.

For these reasons the view often entertained that the visions to which we proceed are developed out of the seventh Seal may be regarded as correct.

If so, how far does the development extend? The answer invariably given to this question is, To the end of the Trumpets. But the answer is not satisfactory. The general symmetry of the Apocalypse militates against it. There is then no correspondence between the last Trumpet and the last Seal, nothing to suggest the thought of a development of the Bowls out of the seventh Trumpet in a manner corresponding to the development of the Trumpets out of the seventh Seal. In these circumstances the only probable conclusion is that both the Bowls and the Trumpets are developed out of the seventh Seal, and that that development does not close until we reach the end of chap. xvi.

If what has now been said be correct, it will throw important light upon the relation of the Seals to the two series of the Trumpets and the Bowls taken together; while, at the same time, it will lend us valuable aid in the interpretation of all the three series.

Returning to the words before us, it is said that, at the opening of the seventh Seal, there followed silence in heaven about the space of half an hour. This silence may perhaps include a cessation even of the songs which rise before the throne of God from that redeemed creation the voice of whose praise rests not either day or night. [197] Yet it is not necessary to think so. The probability rather is that it arises from a cessation only of the "lightnings and voices and thunders" which at chap. iv. 5 proceed out of the throne, and which are resumed at ver. 5 of the present chapter, when the fire of the altar is cast from the angel's censer upon the earth. A brief suspension of judgment is thereby indicated, a pause by and during which the Almighty would call attention to the manifestations of His wrath about to follow. The exact duration of this silence, "about the space of half an hour," has never been satisfactorily explained; and the general analogy of St. John's language condemns the idea of a literal interpretation. We shall perhaps be more in accordance with the spirit in which the Revelation is written if we consider--(1) that in that book the half of anything suggests, not so much an actual half, as a broken and interrupted whole,---five a broken ten, six a broken twelve, three and a half a broken seven; (2) that in the Gospel of St. John we find on more than one occasion mention made of an "hour" by which at one time the actions, at another the sufferings, of Jesus are determined: "Woman, what have I to do with thee? Mine hour is not yet come;" "Father, save Me from this hour: but for this cause came I unto this hour." [198] The "hour" of Jesus is thus to St. John the moment at which action, having been first resolved on by the Father, is taken by the Son; and a "half-hour" may simply denote that the course of events has been interrupted, and that the instant for renewed judgment has been delayed. Such an interpretation will also be in close correspondence with the verses following, as well as with what we have seen to be the probable meaning of the "silence" of ver. 1. Preparation for action, rather than action, marks as yet the opening of the seventh Seal.

That preparation is next described.

St. John saw seven trumpets given to the seven angels which stand before God. In whatever other respects these seven angels are to be distinguished from the hosts of angels which surround the throne, the commission now given shows that they are angels of a more exalted order and a more irresistible power. They are in fact the expression of the Divine Judge of men, or rather of the mode in which He chooses by judgment to express Himself. We are not even required to think of them as numerically seven, for seven in its sacred meaning is the number of unity, though of unity in the variety as well as the combination of its agencies. The "seven Spirits of God" are His one Spirit; the "seven churches," His one Church; the "seven horns" and "seven eyes" of the Lamb, His one powerful might and His one penetrating glance. In like manner the seven Seals, the seven Trumpets, and the seven Bowls embody the thought of many judgments which are yet in reality one. Thus also the angels here are seven, not because literally so, but because that number brings out the varied forms as well as the essential oneness of the action of Him to whom the Father has given "authority to execute judgment, because He is a Son of man." [199]

As yet the seven trumpets have only been given to the seven angels. More has to pass before they put them to their lips and sound. Another angel is seen who came and stood over the altar, having a golden censer in his hand. At the opening of the fifth Seal we read of an "altar" which it was impossible not to identify with the great brazen altar, the altar of burnt-offering, in the outer court of the sanctuary. Such identification is not so obvious here; and perhaps a majority of commentators agree in thinking that the altar now spoken of is rather the golden or incense altar which had its place within the Tabernacle, immediately in front of the second veil. To this altar the priest on ordinary occasions, and more particularly the high-priest on the great Day of Atonement, brought a censer with burning frankincense, that the smoke of the incense, as it rose into the air, might be a symbol to the congregation of Israel that its prayers, offered according to the Divine will, ascended as a sweet savour to God. It is possible that this may be the altar meant; yet the probabilities of the case rather lead to the supposition that allusion is made to the altar of sacrifice in the Tabernacle court; for (1) when the Seer speaks here and again in ver. 5 of "the altar," and in ver. 3 of "the golden altar," he seems to distinguish between the two. (2) The words fire of the altar are in favour of the same conclusion. According to the ritual of the Law, it was from the brazen altar that fire was taken in order to kindle the incense, [200] while at the same time fire continually burned upon that altar, but not upon the altar within the Tabernacle. (3) The thought represented by the symbolism seems to be that the sufferings of the saints gave efficacy to their prayers, and drew down the answer of Him who says, "Call upon Me in the day of trouble, and I will answer thee, and thou shalt glorify Me." [201] (4) The words of ver. 3, the prayers of all the saints, and the similar expression in ver. 4, remind us of the prayers of the fifth Seal, now swelled by the prayers of those New Testament saints who have been added to "the blessed fellowship" of the Old Testament martyrs. These prayers, it will be remembered, rose from beneath the altar of burnt-offering; and it is natural to think that the same altar is again alluded to in order to bring out the idea of a similar martyrdom. What we see, therefore, is an angel taking the prayers and adding to them much incense, so that we may behold them as they ascend up before God and receive His answer.

Further, it ought to be observed that the prayers referred to are for judgment upon sin. There is nothing to justify the supposition that they are partly for judgment upon, partly for mercy to, a sinful world. They are simply another form of the cry, "How long, O Master, the holy and true, dost Thou not judge and avenge our blood on them that dwell on the earth?" [202] They are a cry that God will vindicate the cause of righteousness. [203]

The cry is heard, for the angel takes of the fire of the altar on which the saints had been sacrificed as an offering to God, and casts it into the earth, that it may consume the sin by which it had been kindled. The lex talionis again starts to view; not merely punishment, but retribution, the heaviest of all retribution, because it is accompanied by a convicted conscience, retribution in kind.

Everything is now ready for judgment, and the seven angels which had the seven trumpets prepare themselves to sound:--

And the first sounded, and there followed hail and fire mingled with blood, and they were cast into the earth: and the third part of the earth was burnt up, and the third part of the trees was burnt up, and all green grass was burnt up (viii. 7).

To think, in interpreting these words, of a literal burning up of a third part of the "earth," of the "trees," and of the "green grass," would lead us astray. Comparing the first Trumpet with those that follow, we have simply a general description of judgment as it affects the land in contradistinction to the sea, the rivers and fountains of water, and the heavenly bodies by which the earth is lighted. The punishment is drawn down by a guilty world upon itself when it rises in opposition to Him who at first prepared the land for the abode of men, planted it with trees pleasant to the eye, cast over it its mantle of green, and pronounced it to be very good. Of every tree of the garden, except the tree of the knowledge of good and evil, might our first parents eat; while grass covered the earth for their cattle, and herb for their service. All nature was to minister to the wants of man, and in cultivating the garden and the field he was to find light and happy labour. But sin came in. Thorns and thistles sprang up on every side. Labour became a burden, and the fruitful field was changed into a wilderness which could only be subdued by constant, patient, and often-disappointed toil. This is the thought--a thought often dwelt upon by the prophets of the Old Testament--that is present to the Seer's mind.

One of the plagues of Egypt, however, may also be in his eye. When the Almighty would deliver His people from that land of their captivity, "He sent thunder and hail, and the fire ran along upon the ground; and the Lord rained hail upon the land of Egypt. So there was hail, and fire mingled with the hail, very grievous.... And the hail smote throughout all the land of Egypt all that was in the field, both man and beast; and the hail smote every herb of the field, and broke every tree of the field." [204] That plague the Seer has in his mind; but he is not content to use its traits alone, terrible as they were. The sin of a guilty world in refusing to listen to Him who speaks from heaven is greater than was the sin of those who refused Him that spake on earth, and their punishment must be in proportion to their sin. Hence the plague of Egypt is magnified. We read, not of hail and fire only, but of hail and fire mingled with (or rather in) blood, so that the blood is the outward and visible covering of the hail and of the fire. In addition to this, we have the herbs and trees of the field, not merely smitten and broken, but utterly consumed by fire. What is meant by the "third part" of the earth and its products being attacked it is difficult to say. The probability is that, as a whole consists of three parts, partial destruction only is intended, yet not destruction of a third part of the earth, leaving two-thirds untouched; but a third part of the earth and of its produce is everywhere consumed.

The second Trumpet is now blown:--

And the second angel sounded, and as it were a great mountain burning with fire was cast into the sea: and the third part of the sea became blood; and there died the third part of the creatures which were in the sea, even they that had life; and the third part of the ships was destroyed (viii. 8, 9).

As the first Trumpet affected the land, so the second affects the sea; and the remarks already made upon the one destruction are for the most part applicable to the other. The figure of removing a mountain from its place and casting it into the sea was used by our Lord to express what beyond all else it was impossible to accomplish by mere human power: "Verily I say unto you, If ye have faith, and doubt not, ye shall not only do what is done to the fig tree, but even if ye shall say unto this mountain, Be thou taken up and cast into the sea, it shall be done." [205] In so speaking, our Lord had followed the language of the prophets, who were accustomed to illustrate by the thought of the removal of mountains the greatest acts of Divine power: "What art thou, O great mountain? before Zerubbabel thou shalt become a plain;" "Therefore will we not fear, though the mountains be carried into the midst of the seas." [206]

Even the figure of a "burnt mountain" is not strange to the Old Testament, for the prophet Jeremiah thus denounces woe on Babylon: "Behold, I am against thee, O destroying mountain, saith the Lord, which destroyest all the earth: and I will stretch out Mine hand upon thee, and roll thee down from the rocks, and make thee a burnt mountain." [207]

The plagues of Egypt, too, are again taken advantage of by the Seer, for in the first of these Moses "lifted up the rod, and smote the waters that were in the river; ... and all the waters that were in the river were turned to blood. And the fish that was in the river died; and the river stank, and the Egyptians could not drink of the water of the river; and there was blood throughout all the land of Egypt." [208] Here, however, the plague is extended, embracing as it does not only the river of Egypt, but the sea, with all the ships that sail upon it, and all its fish. Again also, as before, the "third part" is not to be thought of as confined to one region of the ocean, while the remaining two-thirds are left untouched. It is to be sought everywhere over the whole compass of the deep.

The third Trumpet is now blown:--

And the third angel sounded, and there fell from heaven a great star, burning as a torch, and it fell upon the third part of the rivers, and upon the fountains of the waters; and the name of the star is called Wormwood: and the third part of the waters became wormwood; and many men died of the waters, because they were made bitter (viii. 10, 11).

The third Trumpet is to be understood upon the same principles and in the same general sense as the two preceding Trumpets. The figures are again such as meet us in the Old Testament, though they are used by the Seer in his own free and independent way. Thus the prophet Isaiah, addressing Babylon in his magnificent description of her fall, exclaims, "How art thou fallen from heaven, O Lucifer, son of the morning!" [209] and thus also the prophet Jeremiah denounces judgment upon rebellious Israel: "Therefore thus saith the Lord of hosts, the God of Israel; Behold, I will feed them, even this people, with wormwood, and give them water of gall to drink." [210] The bitter waters of Marah also lived in the recollections of Israel as the first, and not the least terrible, punishment of the murmuring of their fathers against Him who had brought them out into what seemed but a barren wilderness, instead of leaving them to quench their thirst by the sweet waters of the Nile. [211] Thus the waters which the world offers to its votaries are made bitter, so bitter that they become wormwood itself, the very essence of bitterness. Again the "third part" of them is thus visited, but this time with a feature not previously mentioned: the destruction of human life,--many men died of the waters. Under the first Trumpet only inanimate nature was affected; under the second we rose to creatures that had life; under the third we rise to "many men." The climax ought to be noticed, as illustrating the style of the Apostle's thought and aiding us in the interpretation of his words. A similar climax may perhaps also be intended by the agents successively employed under these Trumpets: hail and fire, a great mountain burning, and a falling star.

The fourth Trumpet is now blown:--

And the fourth angel sounded, and the third part of the sun was smitten, and the third part of the moon, and the third part of the stars; that the third part of them should be darkened, and the day should not shine for the third part of it, and the night in like manner (viii. 12).

This Trumpet offers no contradiction to what was previously said,--that the first four members of the three series of Seals, of Trumpets, and of Bowls deal with the material rather than the spiritual side of man, with man as a denizen of this world rather than of the next. [212] The heavenly bodies are here viewed solely in their relation to earth and its inhabitants. As to the judgment, it rests, like those of the first and second Trumpets, upon the thought of the Egyptian plague of darkness: "And the Lord said unto Moses, Stretch out thine hand toward heaven, that there may be darkness over the land of Egypt, even darkness that may be felt. And Moses stretched forth his hand toward heaven; and there was a thick darkness in all the land of Egypt three days: they saw not one another, neither rose any from his place for three days: but all the children of Israel had lights in their dwellings." [213] The trait of the Egyptian plague alluded to in this last sentence is not mentioned here; and we have probably, therefore, no right to say that it was in the Seer's thoughts. Yet it is in a high degree probable that it was; and at all events his obvious reference to that plague may help to illustrate an important particular to be afterwards noticed,--that all the Trumpet judgments fall directly upon the world, and not the Church. As under the first three Trumpets, the third part of the light of sun, and moon, and stars is alone darkened.

The first four Trumpets have now been blown, and we reach the line of demarcation by which each series of judgments is divided into its groups of four and three. That line is drawn in the present instance with peculiar solemnity and force:--

And I saw, and I heard an eagle flying in mid-heaven, saying with a great voice, Woe, woe, woe, for them that dwell on the earth by reason of the other voices of the three angels who are yet to sound (viii. 13).

Attention ought to be paid to the fact that the cry uttered in mid-heaven, and thus penetrating to the most distant corners of the earth, proceeds from an eagle, and not, as in the Authorised Version, from an "angel;" and the eagle is certainly referred to for the purpose of adding fresh terror to the scene. If we would enter into the Seer's mind, we must think of it as the symbol of rapine and plunder. To him the prominent characteristic of that bird is not its majesty, but its swiftness, its strength, and its hasting to the prey. [214]

Thus ominously announced, the fifth Trumpet is now blown:--

And the fifth angel sounded, and I saw a star out of heaven fallen unto the earth: and there was given to him the key of the well of the abyss. And he opened the well of the abyss; and there went up a smoke out of the well, as the smoke of a great furnace; and the sun and the air were darkened by reason of the smoke of the well. And out of the smoke came forth locusts upon the earth: and power was given them, as the scorpions of the earth have power. And it was said unto them that they should not hurt the grass of the earth, neither any green thing, neither any tree; but only such men as have not the seal of God on their foreheads. And it was given them that they should not kill them, but that they should be tormented five months: and their torment was as the torment of a scorpion, when it striketh a man. And in those days men shall seek death, and shall in no wise find it; and they shall desire to die, and death fleeth from them. And the shapes of the locusts were like unto horses prepared for war, and upon their heads as it were crowns like unto gold, and their faces were as faces of men. And they had hair as the hair of women, and their teeth were as the teeth of lions. And they had breastplates, as it were breastplates of iron; and the sound of their wings was as the sound of chariots of many horses rushing to war. And they have tails like unto scorpions, and stings: and in their tails is their power to hurt men five months. They have over them as king the angel of the abyss: his name in Hebrew is Abaddon, and in the Greek tongue he hath the name Apollyon (ix. 1-11).

Such is the strange but dire picture of the judgment of the fifth Trumpet; and we have, as usual, in the first place, to look at the particulars contained in it. As in several previous instances, these are founded upon the plagues of Egypt and the language of the prophets. In both these sources how terrible does a locust plague appear! In Egypt--"And the Lord said unto Moses, Stretch out thine hand over the land of Egypt for the locusts, that they may come up upon the land of Egypt, and eat every herb of the land, even all that the hail hath left. And Moses stretched forth his rod over the land of Egypt, and the Lord brought an east wind upon the land all that day, and all that night; and when it was morning, the east wind brought the locusts. And the locusts went up over all the land of Egypt, and rested in all the coasts of Egypt: very grievous were they; before them there were no such locusts as they, neither after them shall be such. For they covered the face of the whole earth, so that the land was darkened; and they did eat every herb of the land, and all the fruit of the trees which the hail had left: and there remained not any green thing in the trees, or in the herbs of the field, through all the land of Egypt." [215] Darker even than this is the language of the prophet Joel. When he sees locusts sweeping across a land, he exclaims, "The land was as the garden of Eden before them, and behind them a desolate wilderness;" [216] and from their irresistible and destructive ravages he draws not a few traits of the dread events by which the coming of the day of the Lord shall be accompanied: "The appearance of them is as the appearance of horses; and as horsemen, so shall they run. Like the noise of chariots on the tops of mountains shall they leap, like the noise of a flame of fire that devoureth the stubble, as a strong people set in battle array.... They shall run like mighty men; they shall climb the wall like men of war; and they shall march every one on his ways, and they shall not break their ranks.... They shall run to and fro in the city; they shall run upon the wall, they shall climb up upon the houses; they shall enter in at the windows like a thief. The earth shall quake before them; the heavens shall tremble: the sun and the moon shall be dark, and the stars shall withdraw their shining." [217]

It is no doubt true that in the description before us the qualities of its locusts are preternaturally magnified, but that is only what we might expect, and it is in keeping with the mode in which other figures taken from the Old Testament are treated in this book. There is a probability, too, that each trait of the description had a distinct meaning to St. John, and that it represents some particular phase of the calamities he intended to depict. But it is hardly possible now to discover such meanings; and that the Seer had in view general evil as much at least as evil in certain special forms is shown by the artificiality of structure marking the passage as a whole. For the description of the locusts is divided into three parts, the first general, the second special, the third the locust-king. The special characteristics of the insects, again, are seven in number: (1) upon their heads as it were crowns like unto gold; (2) and their faces were as faces of men; (3) and they had hair as the hair of women; (4) and their teeth were as the teeth of lions; (5) and they had breastplates, as it were breastplates of iron; (6) and the sound of their wings was as the sound of many chariots; (7) and they have tails like unto scorpions, and stings.

Whether the period of five months, during which these locusts are said to commit their ravages, is fixed on because the destruction caused by the natural insect lasts for that length of time, or for some other reason unknown to us, it is difficult to determine. There is a want of proof that a locust-plague generally continues for the number of months thus specified, and it is otherwise more in accordance with the style of the Apocalypse to regard that particular period of time as simply denoting that the judgment has definite limits.

One additional particular connected with the fifth Trumpet ought to be adverted to. It will be noticed that the well of the abyss whence the plague proceeds is opened by a star fallen (not "falling") out of heaven, to which the key of the well was given. We have here one of those contrasts of St. John a due attention to which is of such importance to the interpreter. This "fallen star" is the contrast and counterpart of Him who is "the bright, the morning star," and who "has the keys of death and of Hades." [218]

At this point the sixth angel ought to sound; but we are now in the midst of the three last woes, and each is of so terrible an import that it deserves to be specially marked. Hence the words of the next verse:--

The first Woe is past; behold, there come yet two Woes hereafter (ix. 12).
This warning given, the sixth Trumpet is now blown:--
And the sixth angel sounded, and I heard a voice from the horns of the golden altar which is before God, one saying to the sixth angel which had the trumpet, Loose the four angels which are bound at the great river Euphrates. And the four angels were loosed, which had been prepared for the hour, and day, and month, and year, that they should kill the third part of men. And the number of the armies of the horsemen was twice ten thousand times ten thousand; I heard the number of them. And thus I saw the horses in the vision, and them that sat on them, having breastplates as of fire, and of hyacinth, and of brimstone. By these three plagues was the third part of men killed, by the fire, and the smoke, and the brimstone, which proceeded out of their mouths. For the power of the horses is in their mouth, and in their tails: for their tails are like unto serpents, and with them they do hurt. And the rest of mankind which were not killed with these plagues repented not of the works of their hands, that they should not worship demons, and the idols of gold, and of silver, and of brass, and of stone, and of wood: which can neither see, nor hear nor walk: and they repented not of their murders, nor of their sorceries, nor of their fornication, nor of their thefts (ix. 13-21).

There is much in this Trumpet that is remarkable even while we confine ourselves to the more outward particulars contained in it. Thus we are brought back by it to the thought of those prayers of the saints to which all the Trumpets are a reply, but which have not been mentioned since the blowing of the Trumpets began. [219] Once more we read of the golden altar which was before God, in His immediate presence. On that altar the prayers of all the saints had been laid, that they might rise to heaven with the much incense added by the angel, and might be answered in God's own time and way. The voice heard from the four horns of this altar--that is, from the four projecting points at its four corners, representing the altar in its greatest potency--shows us, what we might have been in danger of forgetting, that the judgment before us continues to be an answer of the Almighty to His people's prayers. Again it may be noticed that in the judgment here spoken of we deal once more with a third part of the class upon which it falls. Nothing of the kind had been said under the fifth Trumpet. The inference to be drawn from these particulars is important. We learn that, however distinct the successive members of any of the three series of the Seals, the Trumpets, or the Bowls may seem to be, they are yet closely connected with one another. Though seven in number, there is a sense in which they are also one; and any characteristic thought which appears in a single member of the series ought to be carried through all its members. [220]

The judgment itself is founded, as in the others already considered, upon thoughts and incidents connected with Old Testament history.

The first of these is the river Euphrates. That great river was the boundary of Palestine upon the northeast. "In the same day the Lord made a covenant with Abram, saying, Unto thy seed have I given this land, from the river of Egypt unto the great river, the river Euphrates;" [221] and in the days of Solomon this part of the covenant appears to have been fulfilled, for we are told that "Solomon reigned over all kingdoms from the river" (that is, the Euphrates) "unto the land of the Philistines, and unto the border of Egypt." [222] The Euphrates, however, was not only the boundary between Israel and the Assyrians. It was also Israel's line of defence against its powerful and ambitious neighbour, who had to cross its broad stream before he could seize any part of the Promised Land. By a natural transition of thought, the Euphrates next became a symbol of the Assyrians themselves, for its waters, when they rose in flood, overflowed Israel's territory and swept all before them. Then the prophets saw in the rush of the swollen river a figure of the scourge of God upon those who would not acknowledge Him: "The Lord spake also unto me again, saying, Forasmuch as this people refuseth the waters of Shiloah that go softly, and rejoice in Rezin and Remaliah's son; now therefore behold, the Lord bringeth up upon them the waters of the river, strong and many, even the king of Assyria, and all his glory: and he shall come up over all his channels, and go over all his banks: and he shall pass through Judah; he shall overflow and go over, he shall reach even to the neck; and the stretching out of his wings shall fill the breadth of Thy land, O Immanuel." [223] When accordingly the Euphrates is here spoken of, it is clear that with the river as such we have nothing to do. It is simply a symbol of judgment; and the four angels which had been bound at it, but were now loosed, are a token--four being the number of the world--that the judgment referred to, though it affects but a third part of men, reaches men over the whole surface of the globe. When the hour, and the day, and the month, and the year--that is, when the moment fixed in the counsels of the Almighty--come, the chains by which destruction has been kept back shall be broken, and the world shall be overwhelmed by the raging stream.

The second Old Testament thought to be noted in this vision is that of horses. To the Israelite the horse presented an object of terror rather than admiration, and an army of horsemen awakened in him the deepest feelings of alarm. Thus it is that the prophet Habakkuk, describing the coming judgments of God, is commissioned to exclaim, "Behold ye among the heathen, and regard, and wonder marvellously: for I will work a work in your days, which ye will not believe, though it be told you. For, lo, I raise up the Chaldeans, that bitter and hasty nation, which shall march through the breadth of the land, to possess the dwelling-places that are not theirs. They are terrible and dreadful: their judgment and their dignity shall proceed of themselves. Their horses also are swifter than the leopards, and are more fierce than the evening wolves: and their horsemen shall spread themselves, and their horsemen shall come from far; they shall fly as the eagle that hasteth to eat. They shall come all for violence: their faces shall sup up as the east wind, and they shall gather the captivity as the sand. And they shall scoff at the kings, and the princes shall be a scorn unto them: they shall deride every stronghold; for they shall heap dust, and take it." [224] Like the locusts of the previous vision, the "horses" now spoken of are indeed clothed with preternatural attributes; but the explanation is the same. Ordinary horses could not convey images of sufficient terror.

The last two verses of chap. ix., which follow the sixth Trumpet, deserve our particular attention. They describe the effect produced upon the men who did not perish by the previous plagues, and they help to throw light upon a question most intimately connected with a just interpretation of the Apocalypse. The question is, Does the Seer, in any of his visions, anticipate the conversion of the ungodly? or does he deal, from the beginning to the end of his descriptions, with righteousness and sin in themselves rather than with righteous persons who may decline from the truth or sinful persons who may own and welcome it? The question will meet us again in the following chapters of this book, and will demand a fuller discussion than it can receive at present. In the meantime it is enough to say that, in the two verses now under consideration, no hint as to the conversion of any ungodly persons by the Trumpet plagues is given. On the contrary, the "men"--that is, the two-thirds of the inhabitants of the earth or of the ungodly world--who were not killed by these plagues repented neither of their irreligious principles nor of their immoral lives. They went on as they had done in the grossness of their idolatries and in the licentiousness of their conduct. They were neither awakened nor softened by the fate of others. They had deliberately chosen their own course; and, although they knew that they were rushing against the thick bosses of the Almighty's buckler, they had resolved to persevere in it to the end.

Two brief remarks on these six Trumpet visions, looked at as a whole, appear still to be required.

1. No attempt has been made to interpret either the individual objects of the judgments or the instruments by which judgment is inflicted. To the one class belong the "earth," the "trees," the "green grass," the "sea," the "ships," the "rivers and fountains of the waters," the "sun," the "moon," and the "stars;" to the other belong the details given in the description first of the "locusts" of the fifth Trumpet and then of the "horses" of the sixth. Each of these particulars may have a definite meaning, and interpreters may yet be successful in discovering it. The object kept in view throughout this commentary makes any effort to ascertain that meaning, when it is doubtful if it even exists, comparatively unimportant. We are endeavouring to catch the broader interpretation and spirit of the book; and it may be a question whether our impressions would in that respect be deepened though we saw reason to believe that all the objects above mentioned had individual force. One line of demarcation certainly seems to exist, traced by the Seer himself, between the first four and the two following judgments, the former referring to physical disasters flowing from moral evil, the latter to the more dreadful intensification of intellectual darkness and moral corruption visited upon men when they deliberately choose evil rather than good. Further than this it is for our present purpose unnecessary to go.

2. The judgments of these Trumpets are judgments on the world rather than the Church. Occasion has been already taken to observe that the structure of this part of the Apocalypse leads to the belief that both the Trumpets and the Bowls are developed out of the Seals. Yet there is a difference between the two, and various indications in the Trumpet visions appear to confine them to judgments on the world.

There is the manner in which they are introduced, as an answer to the prayers of "all the saints." [225] It is true, as we shall yet see, that the degenerate Church is the chief persecutor of the people of God. But against her the saints cannot pray. To them she is still the Church. They remember the principle laid down by their Lord when He spoke of His kingdom in the parable of the tares: "Let both grow together until the harvest." [226] God alone can separate the false from the true within her pale. There is a sense in which the Church can never be overthrown, and there is not less a sense in which the world shall be subdued. Only for the subjugation of the world, therefore, can "all the saints" pray; and the Trumpets are an answer to their prayers.

Again, the three Woe-Trumpets are directed against "them that dwell on the earth." [227] But, as has been already said, it is a principle of interpretation applicable to all the three series of the Seals, the Trumpets, and the Bowls, that traits filling up the picture in one member belong also to the other members of the group, and that the judgments, while under one aspect seven, are under another one. The three Woes therefore fall upon the same field of judgment as that visited by the plagues preceding them. In other words, all the six plagues of this series of visions are inflicted upon "them that dwell on the earth;" and that is simply another form of expression for the ungodly world.

Again, under the fifth Trumpet the children of God are separated from the ungodly, so that the particulars of that judgment do not touch them. The locusts are instructed that they should not hurt the grass of the earth, neither any green thing, neither any tree; but only such men as have not the seal of God in their foreheads. [228]

Again, the seventh Trumpet, in which the series culminates, and which embodies its character as a whole, will be found to deal with judgment on the world alone: "The nations were roused to wrath, and Thy wrath came, and the time of the dead to be judged," ... and "the time to destroy them that destroy the earth." [229]

Finally, the description given at the end of the sixth Trumpet of those who were hardened rather than softened by the preceding judgments leads directly to the same conclusion: And the rest of mankind which were not killed by these plagues repented not of the works of their hands, that they should not worship devils, and the idols of gold, and of silver, and of brass, and of stone, and of wood. [230]

These considerations leave no doubt that the judgments of the Trumpets are judgments on the world. The Church, it is true, may also suffer from them, but not in judgment. They may be part of her trial as she mixes with the world during her earthly pilgrimage. Trial, however, is not judgment. To the children of God it is the discipline of a Father's hand. In the midst of it the Church is safe, and it helps to ripen her for the fulness of the glory of her heavenly inheritance.

Footnotes:

197. Chap. iv. 8.
198. John ii. 4; xii. 27.
199. John v. 27.
200. Smith's Dictionary of the Bible, Incense.
201. Ps. l. 15.
202. Chap. vi. 10.
203. Comp. p. 103.
204. Exod. ix. 23-25.
205. Matt. xxi. 21.
206. Zech. iv. 7; Ps. xlvi. 2.
207. Jer. li. 25.
208. Exod. vii. 20, 21.
209. Isa. xiv. 12.
210. Jer. ix. 15.
211. Exod. xv. 23.
212. Comp. p. 97.
213. Exod. x. 21-23.
214. Comp. Job ix. 26.
215. Exod. x. 12-15.
216. Joel ii. 3.
217. Joel ii. 4-10.
218. Chaps. xxii. 16; i. 18.
219. Vers. 3-5.
220. Comp. p. 268.
221. Gen. xv. 18.
222. 1 Kings iv. 21.
223. Isa. viii. 5-8.
224. Hab. i. 5-10.
225. Chap. viii. 3.
226. Matt. xiii. 30.
227. Chap. viii. 13.
228. Chap. ix. 4.
229. Chap. xi. 18.
230. Chap. ix. 20.

CHAPTER VII - FIRST CONSOLATORY VISION

Rev. x.

At the point now reached by us the regular progress of the Trumpet judgments is interrupted, in precisely the same manner as between the sixth and seventh Seals, by two consolatory visions. The first is contained in chap. x., the second in chap. xi. 1-13. At chap. xi. 14 the series of the Trumpets is resumed, reaching from that point to the end of the chapter.

And I saw another strong angel coming down out of heaven, arrayed with a cloud: and the rainbow was upon his head, and his face was as the sun, and his feet as pillars of fire: and he had in his hand a little book-roll open: and he set his right foot upon the sea, and his left upon the earth: and he cried with a great voice, as a lion roareth: and when he cried, the seven thunders uttered their voices. And when the seven thunders uttered their voices, I was about to write: and I heard a voice from heaven saying, Seal up the things which the seven thunders uttered, and write them not. And the angel which I saw standing upon the sea and upon the earth lifted up his right hand to heaven, and sware by Him that liveth for ever and ever, who created the heaven, and the things that are therein, and the earth, and the things that are therein, and the sea, and the things that are therein, that there shall be time no longer: but in the days of the voice of the seventh angel, when he is about to sound, then is finished the mystery of God, according to the good tidings which He declared to His servants the prophets. And the voice which I heard from heaven, I heard it again speaking with me, and saying, Go, take the book-roll which is open in the hand of the angel that standeth upon the sea and upon the earth. And I went unto the angel, saying unto him that he should give me the little book-roll. And he saith unto me, Take it, and eat it up; and it shall make thy belly bitter, but in thy mouth it shall be sweet as honey. And I took the little book-roll out of the angel's hand, and ate it up; and it was in my mouth sweet as honey: and when I had eaten it, my belly was made bitter. And they say unto me, Thou must prophesy again over many peoples, and nations, and tongues, and kings (x. 1-11).

Many questions of deep interest, and upon which the most divergent opinions have been entertained, meet us in connexion with this passage. To attempt to discuss these various opinions would only confuse the reader. It will be enough to allude to them when it seems necessary to do so. In the meantime, before endeavouring to discover the meaning of the vision, three observations may be made; one of a general kind, the other two bearing upon the interpretation of particular clauses.

1. Like almost all else in the Revelation of St. John, the vision is founded upon a passage of the Old Testament. "And when I looked," says the prophet Ezekiel, "behold, an hand was sent unto me; and, lo, a roll of a book was therein.... Moreover He said unto me, Son of man, eat what thou findest; eat this roll, and go speak unto the house of Israel. So I opened my mouth, and He caused me to eat that roll. And He said unto me, Son of man, cause thy belly to eat, and fill thy bowels with this roll that I give thee. Then did I eat it; and it was in my mouth as honey for sweetness. And He said unto me, Son of man, go, get thee unto the house of Israel, and speak with My words unto them." [231]

2. In one expression of ver. 6 it is doubtful whether the translation of the Authorised and Revised Versions, or the marginal translation of the latter, ought to be adopted, whether we ought to read, "There shall be time" or "There shall be delay" no longer. But the former is not only the natural meaning of the original; it would almost seem, from the use of the same word in other passages of the Apocalypse, [232] that it is employed by St. John to designate the whole Christian age. That age is now at its very close. The last hour is about to strike. The drama of the world's history is about to be wound up. "For the Lord will execute His word upon the earth, finishing it and cutting it short." [233]

3. The last verse of the chapter deserves our attention for a moment: And they say unto me, Thou must prophesy again over many peoples, and nations, and tongues, and kings. Although prophecy itself is spoken of in several passages of this book, [234] we read only once again of prophesying: when it is said in chap. xi. 3 of the two witnesses that they shall prophesy. A comparison of these passages will show that both words are to be understood in the sense of proclaiming the righteous acts and judgments of the Almighty. The prophet of the Apocalypse is not the messenger of mercy only, but of the just government of God.

From these subordinate points we hasten to questions more immediately concerning us in our effort to understand the chapter. Several such questions have to be asked.

1. Who is the angel introduced to us in the first verse of the vision? He is described as another strong angel; and, as the epithet "strong" has been so used only once before--in chap. v. 2, in connexion with the opening of the book-roll sealed with seven seals--we are entitled to conclude that this angel is said to be "another" in comparison with the angel there spoken of rather than with the many angels that surround the throne of God. But the "strong angel" in chap. v. is distinguished both from God Himself, and from the Lamb. In some sense, therefore, a similar distinction must be drawn here. On the other hand, the particulars mentioned of this angel lead directly to the conclusion not only that he has Divine attributes, but that he represents no other than that Son of man beheld by St. John in the first vision of his book. He is arrayed with a cloud; and in every passage of the Apocalypse where mention is made of such investiture, or in which a cloud or clouds are associated with a person, it is with the Saviour of the world as He comes to judgment. [235] Similar language marks also the other books of the New Testament. [236] The rainbow was upon his head; and the definite article employed takes us back, not to the rainbow spoken of in the book of Genesis, or to the rainbow which from time to time appears, a well-known object, in the sky, but to that of chap. iv. 3, where we have been told, in the description of the Divine throne, that "there was a rainbow round about the throne, like an emerald to look upon." The words his face was as the sun do not of themselves prove that the reference is to chap. i. 16, where it is said of the One like unto a son of man that "His countenance was as the sun shineth in his strength;" but the propriety of this reference is made almost indubitable by the mention of his feet as pillars of fire, for this last circumstance can only be an allusion to the trait spoken of in chap. i. 15, "And His feet like unto fine brass, as if it had been refined in a furnace." The combination of these particulars shows how close is the connexion between the "strong angel" of this vision and the Divine Redeemer; and the explanation of both the difference and the correspondence between the two is to be found in the remark previously made that in the Apocalypse the "angel" of any person or thing expresses that person or thing in action. [237] Here, therefore, we have the action of Him who is the Head, and King, and Lord of His Church.

2. In what character does the Lord appear? As to the answer to this question there can be no dubiety. He appears in judgment. The rainbow upon His head is indeed the symbol of mercy, but it is sufficiently accounted for by the fact that He is Saviour as well as Judge. So far is the Apocalypse from representing the ideas of judgment and mercy as incompatible with each other that throughout the whole book the most terrible characteristic of the former is its proceeding from One distinguished by the latter. If even in itself the Divine wrath is to be dreaded by the sinner, the dread which it ought to inspire reaches its highest point when we think of it as "the wrath of the Lamb." The other features of the description speak directly of judgment: the "cloud," the "sun," the "pillars of fire."

3. What notion are we to form of the contents of the little book-roll? They are certainly not the same as those of the book-roll of chap. v., although the word here used for the roll, a diminutive from the other, may suggest the idea that there is an intimate connexion between the two books, and that the second, like the first, is full of judgment. Other circumstances mentioned lead to the same conclusion. Thus the great voice, as a lion roareth, cannot fail to remind us of the voice of "the Lion that is of the tribe of Judah" in chap. v. The thought of the seven thunders which uttered their voices deepens the impression, for in that number we have the general conception of thunder in all the varied terrors that belong to it; and, whatever the particulars uttered by the thunders were--a point into which it is vain to inquire, as the writing of them was forbidden--their general tone must have been that of judgment. But these thunders are a response to the strong angel as he was about to take action with the little book,-- "when he cried, the seven thunders uttered their voices,"--and the response must have been related to the action. It is clear, therefore, that the contents of the little book cannot have been tidings of mercy to a sinful world; and that that book cannot have been intended to tell the Seer that, notwithstanding the opposition of the powers of darkness, the Church of Christ was to make her way among the nations, growing up from the small seed into the stately tree, and at last covering the earth with the shadow of her branches. Even on the supposition that a conception of this kind could be traced in other parts of the Apocalypse, it would be out of keeping with the particulars accompanying it here. We may without hesitation conclude that the little book-roll has thus the general character of judgment, although, like the larger roll of chap. v., it may also include in it the preservation of the saints.

We are thus in a position to inquire what the special contents of the little book-roll were. Before doing so one consideration may be kept in view.

Calling to mind the symmetrical structure of the Apocalypse, it seems natural to expect that the relation to one another of the two consolatory visions falling between the Trumpets and the Bowls will correspond to that of the two between the Seals and the Trumpets. The two companies, however, spoken of in these two latter visions, are the same, the hundred and forty and four thousand "out of every tribe of the children of Israel" being identical with the great multitude "out of every nation;" while the contents of the second vision are substantially the same as those of the first, though repeated on a fuller and more perfect scale. Now we shall shortly see that the second of our present consolatory visions--that in chap. xi.--brings out the victory and triumph of a faithful remnant of believers within a degenerate, though professing, Church. How probable does it become that the first consolatory vision--that in chap. x.--will relate to the same remnant, though on a lower plane alike of battle and of conquest!

Thus looked at, we have good ground for the supposition that the little book-roll contained indications of judgment about to descend on a Church which had fallen from her high position and practically disowned her Divine Master; while at the same time it assured the faithful remnant within her that they would be preserved, and in due season glorified. The little book thus spoke of the hardest of all the struggles through which believers have to pass: that with foes of their own household; but, so speaking, it told also of judgment upon these foes, and of a glorious issue for the true members of Christ's Body out of toil and suffering.

With this view of the contents of the little book-roll everything that is said of it appears to be in harmony.

1. We thus at once understand why it is named by a diminutive form of the word used for the book-roll in chap. v. The latter contained the whole counsel of God for the execution of His plans both in the world and in the Church. The former has reference to the Church alone. A smaller roll therefore would naturally be sufficient for its tidings.

2. The action which the Seer is commanded to take with the roll receives adequate explanation. He was to take it out of the hand of the strong angel and to eat it up. The meaning is obvious, and is admitted by all interpreters. The Seer is in his own actual experience to assimilate the contents of the roll in order that he may know their value. The injunction is in beautiful accord with what we otherwise know of the character and feelings of St. John. The power of Christian experience to throw light upon Christian truth and upon the fortunes of Christ's people is one of the most remarkable characteristics of the fourth Gospel. It penetrates and pervades the whole. We listen to the expression of the Evangelist's own feelings as he is about to present to the world the image of his beloved Master, and he cries, "We beheld His glory, glory as of the only-begotten from the Father;" "Of His fulness we all received, and grace for grace." [238] We notice his comment upon words of Jesus dark to his fellow-Apostles and himself at the time when they were spoken, and he says, "When therefore He was raised from the dead, His disciples remembered that He spake this; and they believed the word which Jesus had said." [239] Finally, we hear him as he remembers the promise of the Spirit of truth, who was to instruct the disciples, not by new revelations of the Divine will, but by unfolding more largely the fulness that was to be found in Christ: "Howbeit when He, the Spirit of truth, is come, He shall guide you into all the truth: for He shall not speak from Himself; but what things soever He shall hear, these shall He speak: and He shall declare unto you the things that are to come. He shall glorify Me: for He shall take of Mine, and shall declare it unto you." [240] Everywhere and always Christian experience is the key that unlocks what would otherwise be closed, and sheds light upon what would otherwise be dark. To such experience, accordingly, the contents of the little roll, if they were such as we have understood them to be, must have appealed with peculiar power. In beholding judgment executed on the world, the believer might need only to stand by and wonder, as Moses and Israel stood upon the shore of the Red Sea when the sea, returning to its bed, overwhelmed their enemies. They were safe. They had neither part nor lot with those who were sinking as lead in the mighty waters. It would be otherwise when judgment came upon the Church. Of that Church believers were a part. How could they explain the change that had come over her, the purification that she needed, the separation that must take place within what had hitherto been to all appearance the one Zion which God loved? In the former case all was outward; in the latter all is inward, personal, experimental, leading to inquiry and earnest searchings of heart and prayer. A book containing these things was thus an appeal to Christian experience, and St. John might well be told to "eat it up."

3. The effect produced upon the Seer by eating the little roll is also in accord with what has been said. It shall make thy belly bitter, it was said to him, but in thy mouth it shall be sweet as honey; and the effect followed. It was in my mouth, he says, sweet as honey; and when I had eaten it, my belly was made bitter. Such an effect could hardly follow the mere proclamation of judgment on the world. When we look at that judgment in the light in which it ought to be regarded, and in which we have hitherto regarded it--as the vindication of righteousness and of a Divine and righteous order--the thought of it can impart nothing but joy. But to think that the Church of the living God, the bride of Christ, shall be visited with judgment, and to be compelled to acknowledge that the judgment is deserved; to think that those to whom so much has been given should have given so little in return; to think of the selfishness which has prevailed where love ought to have reigned, of worldliness where there ought to have been heavenliness of mind, and of discord where there ought to have been unity--these are the things that make the Christian's reflections "bitter;" they, and they most of all, are his perplexity, his burden, his sorrow, and his cross. The world may disappoint him, but from it he expected little. When the Church disappoints him, the "foundations are overturned," and the honey of life is changed into gall and wormwood.

Combining the particulars which have now been noticed, we seem entitled to conclude that the little book-roll of this chapter is a roll of judgment, but of judgment relating less to the world than to the Church. It tells us that that sad experience of hers which is to meet us in the following chapters ought neither to perplex nor overwhelm us. The experience may be strange, very different from what we might have expected and hoped for; but the thread by which the Church is guided has not passed out of the hands of Him who leads His people by ways that they know not into the hands of an unsympathizing and hostile power. As His counsels in reference to the world, and to the Church in her general relation to it, contained in the great book-roll of chap. v., shall stand, so the internal relations of the two parts of His Church to each other, together with the issues depending upon them, are equally under His control. If judgment falls upon the Church, it is not because God has forgotten to be gracious, or has in anger shut up His tender mercies, but because the Church has sinned, because she is in need of chastisement, and because she must be taught that only in direct dependence upon the voice of the Good Shepherd, and not in the closest "fold" that can be built for her, is she safe. Let her "know" Him, and she shall be known of Him even as He is known of the Father. [241]

Footnotes:

231. Ezek. ii. 9; iii. 4.
232. Comp. chaps. vi. 11; xx. 3.
233. Rom. ix. 28.
234. Comp. chaps. i. 3; xxii. 7, 10, 18, 19.
235. Chaps. i. 7; xiv. 14-16. In chap. xi. 12 "the cloud" is the well-known cloud in which Christ ascended, and in which He comes to judgment.
236. Matt. xxiv. 30; Mark xiii. 26; Luke xxi. 27; 1 Thess. iv. 17.
237. Comp. p. 25.
238. John i. 14, 16.
239. John ii. 22.
240. John xvi. 13, 14.
241. Comp. John x. 1-15.

CHAPTER VIII - SECOND CONSOLATORY VISION AND THE SEVENTH TRUMPET

Rev. xi.

From the first consolatory vision we proceed to the second:--

And there was given unto me a reed like unto a rod: and one said, Rise, and measure the temple of God, and the altar, and them that worship therein. And the court which is without the temple cast without, and measure it not; for it hath been given unto the nations: and the holy city shall they tread under foot forty and two months (xi. 1, 2).

Various points connected with these verses demand examination before any attempt can be made to gather the meaning of the vision as a whole.

1. What is meant by the measuring of the Temple? As in so many other instances, the figure is taken from the Old Testament. In the prophet Zechariah we read, "I lifted up mine eyes again, and looked, and behold a man with a measuring line in his hand. Then said I, Whither goest thou? And he said unto me, To measure Jerusalem, to see what is the breadth thereof, and what is the length thereof." [242] To the same effect, but still more particularly, the prophet Ezekiel speaks: "In the visions of God brought He me into the land of Israel, and set me upon a very high mountain, by which was as the frame of a city on the south. And He brought me thither, and, behold, there was a man, whose appearance was like the appearance of brass, with a line of flax in his hand, and a measuring reed; and he stood in the gate.... And behold a wall on the outside of the house round about, and in the man's hand a measuring reed of six cubits long by the cubit and an handbreadth, so he measured," [243] whereupon follows a minute and lengthened description of the measuring of all the parts of that Temple which was to be the glory of God's people in the latter days. From these passages we not only learn whence the idea of the "measuring" was taken, but what the meaning of it was. The account given by Ezekiel distinctly shows that thus to measure expresses the thought of preservation, not of destruction. That the same thought is intended by Zechariah is clear from the words immediately following the instruction given him to measure: "For I, saith the Lord, will be unto her a wall of fire round about, and will be the glory in the midst of her;" [244] while, if further proof upon this point were needed, it is found in the fact that the measuring of this passage does not stand alone in the Apocalypse. The new Jerusalem is also measured: "And he that spake with me had for a measure a golden reed to measure the city, and the gates thereof, and the wall thereof. And he measured the wall thereof, an hundred and forty and four cubits, according to the measure of a man, that is, of an angel." [245] When God therefore measures, He measures, not in indignation, but that the object measured may be in a deeper than ordinary sense the habitation of His glory.

2. What is meant by the temple, the altar, and the casting without of the court which is without the temple? In other words, are we to interpret these objects and the action taken with the latter literally or figuratively? Are we to think of the things themselves, or of certain spiritual ideas which they are used to represent? The first view is not only that of many eminent commentators; it even forms one of the chief grounds upon which they urge that the Herodian temple upon Mount Moriah was still in existence when the Apocalyptist wrote. He could not, it is alleged, have been instructed to "measure" the Temple if that building had been already thrown down, and not one stone left upon another. Yet, when we attend to the words, it would seem as if this view must be set aside in favour of a figurative interpretation. For-

(1) The word "temple" misleads. The term employed in the original does not mean the Temple-buildings as a whole, but only their innermost shrine or sanctuary, that part known as the "Holy of holies," which was separated from every other part of the sacred structure by the second veil. No doubt, so far as the simple act of measuring was concerned, a part might have been as easily measured as the whole. But closer attention to what was in the Seer's mind will show that when he thus speaks of the naos or shrine he is not thinking of the Temple at Jerusalem at all, but of the Tabernacle in the wilderness upon which the Temple was moulded. The nineteenth verse of the chapter makes this clear. In that verse we find him saying, "And there was opened the temple" (the naos) "of God that is in heaven, and there was seen in His temple" (His naos) "the ark of His covenant." We know, however,

that the ark of the covenant never had a place in the Temple which existed in the days of Christ. It had disappeared at the destruction of the first Temple, long before that date. The Temple spoken of in the nineteenth verse is indeed said to be "in heaven;" and it may be thought that the ark, though not on earth, might have been seen there. But no reader of the Revelation of St. John can doubt that to him the sanctuary of God on earth was an exact representation of the heavenly sanctuary, that what God had given in material form to men was a faithful copy of the ideas of His spiritual and eternal kingdom. He could not therefore have placed in the original what, if he had before his mind the Temple at Jerusalem, he knew had no existence within its precincts; and the conclusion is irresistible that when he speaks of a naos that was to be measured he had turned his thoughts, not to the stone building upon Mount Moriah, but to its ancient prototype. On this ground alone then, even could no other be adduced, we seem entitled to maintain that a literal interpretation of the word "temple" is here impossible.

(2) Even should it be allowed that the sanctuary and the altar might be measured, the injunction is altogether inapplicable to the next following clause: them that worship therein. And it is peculiarly so if we adopt the natural construction, by which the word "therein" is connected with the word "altar." We cannot literally speak of persons worshipping "in" an altar. Nay, even though we connect "therein" with "the temple," the idea of measuring persons with a rod is at variance with the realities of life and the ordinary use of human language. A figurative element is thus introduced into the very heart of the clause the meaning of which is in dispute.

(3) A similar observation may be made with regard to the words cast without in ver. 2. The injunction has reference to the outer court of the Temple, and the thought of "casting out" such an extensive space is clearly inadmissible. So much have translators felt this that both in the Authorised and Revised Versions they have replaced the words "cast without" by the words "leave without." The outer court of the Temple could not be "cast out;" therefore it must be "left out." The interpretation thus given, however, fails to do justice to the original, for, though the word employed does not always include actual violence, it certainly implies action of a more positive kind than mere letting alone or passing by. More than this. We are under a special obligation in the present instance not to strip the word used by the Apostle of its proper force, for we shall immediately see that, rightly interpreted, it is one of the most interesting expressions of his book, and of the greatest value in helping us to determine the precise nature of his thought. In the meanwhile it is enough to say that the employment of the term in the connexion in which it here occurs is at variance with a simply literal interpretation.

(4) It cannot be denied that almost every other expression in the subsequent verses of the vision is figurative or metaphorical. If we are to interpret this part literally, it will be impossible to apply the same rule to other parts; and we shall have such a mixture of the literal and metaphorical as will completely baffle our efforts to comprehend the meaning of the Seer.

(5) We have the statement from the writer's own lips that, at least in speaking of Jerusalem, he is not to be literally understood. In ver. 8 he refers to "the great city, which spiritually is called Sodom and Egypt." The hint thus given as to one point of his description may be accepted as applicable to it all.

We conclude, therefore, that the "measuring," the "temple" or naos, the "altar," the "court which is without," and the "casting without" of the latter are to be regarded as figurative.

3. Our third point of inquiry is, What is the meaning of the figure? There need be no hesitation as to the things first spoken of: "the temple, the altar, and them that worship therein." These, the most sacred parts of the Temple-buildings, can only denote the most sacred portion of the true Israel of God. They are those disciples of Christ who constitute His shrine, His golden altar of incense whence their prayers rise up continually before Him, His worshippers in spirit and in truth. These, as we have already often had occasion to see, shall be preserved safe amidst the troubles of the Church and of the world. In one passage we have been told that they are numbered [246] ; now we are further informed that they are measured.

It is more difficult to explain who are meant by "the court which is without the temple." But three things are clear. First, they are a part of the Temple-buildings, although not of its inner shrine. Secondly, they belong to Jerusalem; and Jerusalem, notwithstanding its degenerate condition, was still the city of God, standing to Him in a relation different from that of the "nations," even when it had sunk beneath them and had done more to merit His displeasure. Thirdly, they cannot be the Gentiles, for from them they are manifestly distinguished when it is said that the outer court "hath been given unto the nations: and the holy city shall they tread under foot forty and two months." [247] One conclusion alone remains. The "court that is without" must symbolize the faithless portion of the Christian Church, such as tread the courts of the house of God, but to whom He speaks as He spoke to Jerusalem of old: "Bring no more vain oblations; incense is an abomination unto Me; the new moons and sabbaths, the calling of assemblies, I cannot away with; it is iniquity, even the solemn meeting. Your new moons and your appointed feasts My soul hateth: they are a trouble unto Me; I am weary to bear them." [248]

The correctness of the sense thus assigned to this part of the vision is powerfully confirmed by what appears to be the true foundation of the singular expression already so far spoken of, "cast without." Something must lie at the bottom of the figure; and nothing seems so probable as this: that it is the "casting out" which took place in the case of the man blind from his birth, and the opening of whose eyes by Jesus is related in the fourth Gospel. Of that man we are told that when the Jews could no longer answer him "they cast him out." [249] The word is the same as that now employed, and the thought is most probably the same also. Excommunication from the synagogue is in the Seer's mind, not a temporal punishment, not a mere worldly doom, but a spiritual sentence depriving of spiritual privileges misunderstood and abused. Such a casting out, however, can apply only to those who had been once within the courts of the Lord's house or to the faithless members of the Christian Church. They, like the Jews of old, would "cast out" the humble disciples whom Jesus "found"; [250] and He cast them out.

If the explanation now given of the opening verses of this chapter be correct, we have reached a very remarkable stage in these apocalyptic visions. For the first time, except in the letters to the churches, [251] we have a clear line of distinction drawn between the professing and the true portions of the Church of Christ, or, as it may be otherwise expressed, between the "called" and the "chosen." [252] How far the same distinction will meet us in later visions of this book we have yet to see. For the present it may be enough to say that the drawing of such a distinction corresponds exactly with what we might have been prepared to expect. Nothing can be more certain than that in the things actually around him St. John beheld the mould and type of the things that were to come. Now Jerusalem, the Church of God in Israel, contained two classes within its walls: those who were accomplishing their high destiny and those by whom that destiny was misunderstood, despised, and cast away. Has it not always been the same in the Christian Church? If the world entered into the one, has it not entered as disastrously into the other? That field which is "the kingdom of heaven" upon earth has never wanted tares as well as wheat. They grow together, and no man may separate them. When the appropriate moment comes, God Himself will give the word; angels will carry off the tares, and the great Husbandman will gather the wheat into His garner.

4. One question still remains: What is the meaning of the forty and two months during which the holy city is to be trodden under foot of the nations? The same expression meets us in chap. xiii. 5, where it is said that "there was given to the beast authority to continue forty and two months." But forty and two months is also three and a half years, the Jewish year having consisted of twelve months, except when an intercalary month was inserted among the twelve in order to preserve harmony between the seasons and the rotation of time. The same period is therefore again alluded to in chap. xii. 14, when it is said of the woman who fled into the wilderness that she is there nourished for "a time, and times, and half a time." Once more, we read in chap. xi. 3 and in chap. xii. 6 of a period denoted by "a thousand two hundred and threescore days;" and a comparison of this last passage with ver. 14 of the same chapter distinctly shows that it is equivalent to the three and a half times or years. Three and a half multiplied by three hundred and sixty, the number of days in the Jewish year, gives us exactly the twelve hundred and sixty days. These three periods, therefore, are the same. Why the different designations should be adopted is another question, to which, so far as we are aware, no satisfactory reply has yet been given, although it may be that, for some occult reason, the Seer beholds in "months" a suitable expression for the dominion of evil, in "days" one appropriate to the sufferings of the good.

The ground of this method of looking at the Church's history is found in the book of Daniel, where we read of the fourth beast, or the fourth kingdom, "And he shall speak great words against the Most High, and shall wear out the saints of the Most High, and think to change times and laws: and they shall be given into his hand until a time and times and the dividing of time." [253] The same book helps us also to answer the question as to the particular period of the Church's history denoted by the days, or months, or years referred to, for in another passage the prophet says, "And He shall confirm the covenant with many for one week: and in the midst of the week He shall cause the sacrifice and the oblation to cease." [254] The three and a half years therefore, or the half of seven years, denote the whole period extending from the cessation of the sacrifice and oblation. In other words, they denote the Christian era from its beginning to its close, and that more especially on the side of its disturbed and broken character, of the power exercised in it by what is evil, of the troubles and sufferings of the good. During it the disciples of the Saviour do not reach the completeness of their rest; their victory is not won. Ideally it is so; it always has been so since Jesus overcame: but it is not yet won in the actual realities of the case; and, though in one sense every heavenly privilege is theirs, their difficulties are so great, and their opponents so numerous and powerful, that the true expression for their state is a broken seven years, or three years and a half. During this time, accordingly, the holy city is represented as trodden under foot by the nations. They who are at ease in Zion may not feel it; but to the true disciples of Jesus their Master's prophecy is fulfilled, "In the world ye shall have tribulation." [255]

The vision now proceeds:--

And I will give power unto My two witnesses, and they shall prophesy a thousand two hundred and threescore days, clothed in sackcloth. These are the two olive trees, and the two candlesticks standing before the Lord of the earth. And if any man desireth to hurt them, fire proceedeth out of their mouth, and devoureth their enemies: and if any man shall desire to hurt them, in this manner must he be killed. These have the power to shut the heaven, that it rain not during the days of their prophecy: and they have power over the waters to turn them into blood, and to smite the earth with every plague, as often as they shall desire. And when they shall have finished their testimony, the beast that cometh up out of the abyss shall make war with them, and overcome them, and kill them. And their dead body lies in the street of the great city, which spiritually is called Sodom and Egypt, where also their Lord was crucified. And from among the peoples and tribes and tongues and nations do men look upon their dead body three days and an half, and suffer not their dead bodies to be laid in a tomb. And they that dwell on the earth rejoice over them, and make merry: and they shall send gifts one to another; because these two prophets tormented them that dwell on the earth. And after the three days and an half the breath of life from God entered into them, and they stood upon their feet; and great fear fell upon them which beheld them. And they heard a great voice from heaven saying unto them, Come up hither. And they went up into heaven in the cloud; and their enemies beheld them. And in that hour there was a great earthquake, and the tenth part of the city fell; and there were killed in the earthquake seven thousand persons: and the rest were affrighted, and gave glory to the God of heaven (xi. 3-13).

The figures of this part of the vision, like those of the first part, are drawn from the Old Testament. That the language is not to be literally understood hardly admits of dispute, for, whatever might have been thought of the "two witnesses" had we read only of them, the description given of their persons, or of their person (for in ver. 8, where mention is made of their dead body--not "bodies"--they are treated as one), of their work, of their death, and of their resurrection and ascension, is so obviously figurative as to render it necessary to view the whole passage in that light. The main elements of the figure are supplied by the prophet Zechariah. "And the angel that talked with me," says the prophet, "came again, and waked me, as a man that is wakened out of sleep, and said unto me, What seest thou? And I said, I have looked, and behold a candlestick all of gold, with a bowl upon the top of it, and his seven lamps thereon, and seven pipes to the seven lamps, which are upon the top thereof: and two olive trees by it, one upon the right side of the bowl, and the other upon the left side thereof. So I answered and spake to the angel that talked with me, saying, What are these, my lord?... Then he answered and spake unto me, saying, This is the word of the Lord unto Zerubbabel, saying, Not by might, nor by power, but by My Spirit, saith the Lord of hosts Who art thou, O great mountain? before Zerubbabel thou shalt become a plain: and he shall bring forth the headstone thereof with shoutings, crying, Grace, grace unto it.... Then answered I, and said unto him, What are these two olive trees upon the right side of the candlestick and upon the left side thereof? And I answered again, and said unto him, What be these two olive branches which through the two golden pipes empty the golden oil out of themselves? And he answered and said unto me, Knowest thou not what these be? And I said, No, my lord. Then said he, These are the two anointed ones, that stand by the Lord of the whole earth." [256] In these words indeed we read only of one golden candlestick, while now we read of two. But we have already found that the Seer of the Apocalypse, in using the figures to which he had been accustomed, does not bind himself to all their details; and the only inference to be drawn from this difference, as well as from the circumstance already noted in ver. 8, is that the number "two" is to be regarded less in itself than as a strengthening of the idea of the number one. This circumstance further shows that the two witnesses cannot be divided between the two olive trees and the two candlesticks, as if the one witness were the former and the other the latter. Both taken together express the idea of witnessing, and to the full elucidation of that idea belong also the olive tree and the candlestick. The witnessing is fed by perpetual streams of that heavenly oil, of that unction of the Spirit, which is represented by the olive tree; and it sheds light around like the candlestick. The two witnesses, therefore, are not two individuals to be raised up during the course of the Church's history, that they may bear testimony to the facts and principles of the Christian faith. The Seer indeed may have remembered that it had been God's plan in the past to commission His servants, not singly, but in pairs. He may have called to mind Moses and Aaron, Joshua and Caleb, Elijah and Elisha, Zerubbabel and Joshua, or he may have thought of the fact that our Lord sent forth His disciples two by two. The probability, however, is that, as he speaks of "witnessing," he thought mainly of that precept of the law which required the testimony of two witnesses to confirm a statement. Yet he does not confine himself to the thought of two individual witnesses, however eminent, who shall in faithful work fill up their own short span of human life and die. The witness he has in view is that to be borne by all Christ's people, everywhere, and throughout the whole Christian age. From the first to the last moment of the Church's history in this world there shall be those raised up who shall never fail to prophesy, or, in other words, to testify to the truth of God as it is in Jesus. The task will be hard, but they will not shrink from it. They shall be clothed in sackcloth, but they shall count their robes of shame to be robes of honour. They shall occupy the position of Him who, in the days of His humiliation, was the "faithful and true Witness." Nourished by the Spirit that was in Him, they shall, like Him, be the light of the world, [257] so that God shall never be left without some at least to witness for Him.

Having spoken of the persons of the two witnesses, St. John next proceeds to describe the power with which, amidst their seeming weakness, their testimony is borne; and once more he finds in the most striking histories of the Old Testament the materials with which his glowing imagination builds.

In the first place, fire proceedeth out of their mouth, and devoureth their enemies, so that these enemies are killed by the manifest judgment of God, and even, in His righteous retribution, by the very instrument of destruction they would have themselves employed. Elijah and the three companions of Daniel are before us, when at the word of Elijah fire descended out of heaven, and consumed the two captains and their fifties, [258] and when the companions of Daniel were not only left unharmed amidst the flames, but when the fire leaped out upon and slew the men by whom they had been cast into the furnace. [259] This fire proceeding out of the mouth of the two witnesses is like the sharp two-edged sword proceeding out of the mouth of the Son of man in the first vision of the book. [260] In the second place, the witnesses have the power to shut the heaven, that it rain not during the days of their prophecy. Elijah is again before us when he exclaimed in the presence of Ahab, "As the Lord God of Israel liveth, before whom I stand, there shall not be dew nor rain these years, but according to my word," and when "it rained not on the earth for three years and six months." [261] Finally, when we are told that the witnesses have power over the waters to turn them into blood, and to smite the earth with every plague, as often as they shall desire, we are reminded of Moses and of the plagues inflicted through him upon the oppressors of Israel in Egypt.

The three figures teach the same lesson. No deliverance has been effected by the Almighty for His people in the past which He is not ready to repeat. The God of Moses, and Elijah, and Daniel is the unchangeable Jehovah. He has made with His Church an everlasting covenant; and the most striking manifestations of His power in bygone times "happened by way of example, and were written for our admonition, upon whom the ends of the ages are come." [262]

Hence, accordingly, the Church finishes her testimony. [263] So was it with our Lord in His high-priestly prayer and on the Cross: "I glorified Thee on the earth, having accomplished the work which Thou hast given Me to do;" "It is finished." [264] But this "finishing" of their testimony on the part of the two witnesses points to more than the end of the three and a half years viewed simply as a period of time. Not the thought of time alone, but of the completion of testimony, is present to the Seer's mind. At every moment in the history of Christ's true disciples that completion is reached by some or others of their number. Through all the three and a half years their testimony is borne with power, and is finished with triumph, so that the world is always without excuse.

Having spoken of the power of the witnesses, St. John next turns to the thought of their evil fate. The beast that cometh up out of the abyss shall make war with them, and overcome them, and kill them. This "beast" has not yet been described; but it is a characteristic of the Apostle, both in the fourth Gospel and in the Apocalypse, to anticipate at times what is to come, and to introduce persons to our notice whom we shall only learn to know fully at a later point in his narrative. That is the case here. This beast will again meet us in chap. xiii. and chap. xvii., where we shall see that it is the concentrated power of a world material and visible in its opposition to a world spiritual and invisible. It may be well to remark, too, that the representation given of the beast presents us with one of the most striking contrasts of St. John, and one that must be carefully remembered if we would understand his visions. Why speak of its "coming up out of the abyss"? Because the beast is the contrast of the risen Saviour. Only after His resurrection did our Lord enter upon His dominion as King, Head, and Guardian of His people. In like manner only after a resurrection mockingly attributed to it does this beast attain its full range of influence. Then, in the height of its rage and at the summit of its power, it sets itself in opposition to Christ's witnesses. It cannot indeed prevent them from accomplishing their work; they shall finish their testimony in spite of it: but, when that is done, it shall gain an apparent triumph. As the Son of God was nailed to the Cross, and in that hour of His weakness seemed to be conquered by the world, so shall it be with them. They shall be overcome and killed.

Nor is that all, for their dead body (not dead bodies [265]) is treated with the utmost contumely. It lies in the broad open street of the great city, which the words where also their Lord was crucified show plainly to be Jerusalem. But Jerusalem! In what aspect is she here beheld? Not as "the holy city," "the beloved city," the Zion which God had desired for His habitation, and of which He had said, "This is My rest for ever: here will I dwell; for I have desired it," [266] but degenerate Jerusalem, Jerusalem become as Sodom for its wickedness, and as Egypt for its oppression of the Israel of God. The language is strong, so strong that many interpreters have deemed it impossible to apply it to Jerusalem in any sense, and have imagined that they had no alternative but to think of Rome. Yet it is not stronger than the language used many a time by the prophets of old: "Hear the word of the Lord, ye rulers of Sodom; give ear unto the law of our God, ye people of Gomorrah. How is the faithful city become an harlot! ... righteousness lodged in it; but now murderers." [267]

If, however, this city be Jerusalem, what does it represent? Surely, for reasons already stated, neither the true disciples of Jesus, nor the heathen nations of the world. We have the degenerate Church before us, the Church that has conformed to the world. That Church beholds the faithful witnesses for Christ the Crucified lie in the open way. Their wounds make no impression upon her heart, and draw no tear from her eyes. She even invites the world to the spectacle; and the world, always eager to hear the voice of a degenerate Church, responds to the invitation. It "looks," and obviously without commiseration, upon the prostrate, mangled form that has fallen in the strife. This it does for three days and a half, the half of seven, a broken period of trouble; and it will not suffer the dead body to be laid in a tomb. Nay, the world is not content even with its victory. After victory it must have its triumph; and that triumph is presented to us in one of the most wonderful pictures of the Apocalypse, when they that dwell on the earth--that is, the men of the world--from among the peoples and tribes and tongues and nations, having listened to the degenerate Church's call, make high holiday at the thought of what they have done. They rejoice over the dead bodies, and make merry: and they send gifts one to another; because these two prophets tormented them that dwell on the earth. We are reminded of Herod and Pilate, who, when the Jewish governor sent Jesus to his heathen brother, "became friends that very day." [268] But we are reminded of more. In the book of Nehemiah we find mention of that great feast of Tabernacles which was observed by the people when they heard again, after long silence, the book of the law, and when "there was very great gladness." In immediate connexion with this feast, Nehemiah said to the people, "Go your way, eat the fat, and drink the sweet, and send portions unto them for whom nothing is prepared: for this day is holy unto the Lord: neither be ye sorry; for the joy of the Lord is your strength" [269] ; while it constituted a part also of the joyful ceremonial of the feast of the dedication of the Temple that the Jews made the days of the feast "days of feasting and joy, and of sending portions one to another, and gifts to the poor." [270] Taking these passages into account, and remembering the general style and manner of St. John, we can have no hesitation in recognising in the festival of these verses the world's Feast of Tabernacles, the contrast and the counterpart of the Church's feast already spoken of in the second consolatory vision of chap. vii.

If so, what a picture does it present!--the degenerate Church inviting the world to celebrate a feast over the dead bodies of the witnesses for Christ, and the world accepting the invitation; the former accommodating herself to the ways of the latter, and the latter welcoming the accommodation; the one proclaiming no unpleasant doctrines and demanding no painful sacrifices, the other hailing with satisfaction the prospect of an easy yoke and of a cheap purchase of eternity as well as time. The picture may seem too terrible to be true. But let us first remember that, like all the pictures of the Apocalypse, it is ideal, showing us the operation of principles in their last, not their first, effect; and then let us ask whether we have never read of, or ourselves seen, such a state of things actually realized. Has the Church never become the world, on the plea that she would gain the world? Has she never uttered smooth things or prophesied deceits in order that she might attract those who will not endure the thought of hardness in religious service, and would rather embrace what in their inward hearts they know to be a lie than bitter truth? Such a spectacle has been often witnessed, and is yet witnessed every day, when those who ought to be witnesses for a living and present Lord gloze over the peculiar doctrines of the Christian faith, draw as close as possible the bonds of their fellowship with unchristian men, and treat with scorn the thought of a heavenly life to be led even amidst the things of time. One can understand the world's own ways, and, even when lamenting that its motives are not higher, can love its citizens and respect their virtues. But a far lower step in declension is reached when the Church's silver becomes dross, when her wine is mixed with water, and when her voice no longer convicts, no longer "torments them that dwell on the earth."

In the midst of all their tribulation, however, the faithful portion of the Church have a glorious reward. They have suffered with Christ, but they shall also reign with Him. After all their trials in life, after their death, and after the limited time during which even when dead they have been dishonoured, they live again. The breath of life from God entered into them. Following Him who is the first-fruits of them that sleep, they stood upon their feet. [271] They heard a great voice from heaven saying unto them, Come up hither. They went up into heaven in the cloud; and there they sit down with the conquering Redeemer in His throne, even as He overcame and sat down with His Father in His throne. [272] All this, too, takes place in the very presence of their enemies, upon whom great fear fell. Even nature sympathizes with them. Having waited for the revealing of the sons of God, and in hope that she also shall be delivered from the bondage of corruption into the liberty of the glory of the children of God, [273] she hails their final triumph. There was a great earthquake, the tenth part of the city (that is, of Jerusalem) fell; and there were killed in the earthquake seven thousand persons. It is unnecessary to say that the words are figurative and symbolical, denoting in all probability simply judgment, but judgment restrained.

The last words of the vision alone demand more particular attention: The rest were affrighted, and gave glory to the God of heaven. The thought is the same as that which met us when we were told at the close of the sixth Trumpet that "the rest of mankind which were not killed with these plagues repented not." [274] There is no repentance, no conversion. There is terror; there is alarm; there is a tribute of awe to the God of heaven who has so signally vindicated His own cause; but there is nothing more. Nor are we told what may or may not follow in some future scene. For the Seer the final triumph of good and the final overthrow of evil are enough. He can be patient, and, so far as persons are concerned, can leave the issue in the hands of God.

The two consolatory visions interposed between the sixth and seventh Trumpets are now over, and we cannot fail to see how great an advance they are upon the two visions of a similar kind interposed between the sixth and seventh Seals. The whole action has made progress. At the earlier stage the Church may be said to have been hidden in the hollow of the Almighty's hand. In the thought of the "great tribulation" awaiting her she has been sealed, while the peace and joy of her new condition have been set before us, as she neither hungers nor thirsts, but is guided by her Divine Shepherd to green pastures and to fountains of the waters of life. At this later stage she is in the midst of her conflict and her sufferings. She is in the heat of her warfare, in the extremity of her persecuted state. From the height on which we stand we do not look over a quiet and peaceful plain, with flocks of sheep resting in its meadows; we look over a field where armed men have met in the shock of battle. There is the stir, the excitement, the tumult of deadly strife for higher than earthly freedom, for dearer than earthly homes. There may be temporary repulse and momentary yielding even on the side of the good, but they still press on. The Captain of their salvation is at their head; and foot by foot fresh ground is won, until at last the victory is sounded, and we are ready for the seventh Trumpet.

Before it sounds there is a warning similar to that which preceded the sounding of the fifth and sixth [275] :--

The second Woe is past; behold, the third Woe cometh quickly (xi. 14).

These words are to be connected with the close of chap. ix., all that is contained in chaps. x. and xi. 1-13 being, as we have seen, episodical.

The seventh Trumpet is now sounded:--

And the seventh angel sounded; and there followed great voices in heaven, and they said, The kingdom of the world is become the kingdom of our Lord, and of His Christ; and He shall reign for ever and ever. And the four-and-twenty elders, which sit before God on their thrones, fell upon their faces, and worshipped God, saying, We give Thee thanks, O Lord, God, the Almighty, which art and which wast; because Thou hast taken Thy great power, and didst reign. And the nations were roused to wrath, and Thy wrath came, and the time of the dead to be judged, and the time to give their reward to Thy servants the prophets, both the saints and them that fear Thy name, the small and the great, and to destroy them that destroy the earth. And there was opened the temple of God that is in heaven, and there was seen in His temple the ark of His covenant: and there followed lightnings, and voices, and thunders, and an earthquake, and great hail (xi. 15-19).

1. By the kingdom of the world here spoken of is meant, that dominion over the world as a whole has become the possession of our Lord and of His Christ; and it is to be His for ever and ever. There is no contradiction between this statement of St. John and that of St. Paul when, speaking of the Son, the latter Apostle says, "And when all things have been subjected unto Him, then shall the Son also Himself be subjected to Him that did subject all things unto Him, that God may be all in all." [276] The "kingdom" thus spoken of by St. Paul is that exercised by our Lord in subduing His enemies, and it must necessarily come to an end when there are no more enemies to subdue. The kingdom here referred to is Christ's dominion as Head and King of His Church, and of that dominion there is no end. Of more consequence perhaps is it to observe that when it is said in the words before us, The kingdom of the world is become the kingdom of our Lord, and of His Christ, there is nothing to lead to the supposition that this "kingdom" becomes Christ's by the conversion of the world. The meaning simply is that evil has been finally and for ever put down, that good is finally and for ever triumphant. No inference can be drawn as to the fate of wicked persons further than this: that they shall not be found in "the new heavens and the new earth wherein dwelleth righteousness." [277] Were additional proof needed upon this point, it would be supplied by the fact that in almost the next following words we read of the nations being roused to wrath. These are the wicked upon whom judgment falls; and, instead of being converted, they are roused to the last and highest outburst of the wickedness which springs from despair.

2. The song of the four-and-twenty elders. We have already had occasion to notice that song of the representatives of redeemed creation in which the four living creatures celebrated "the Lord, God, the Almighty, which was and which is and which is to come." [278] The song now before us, sung by the representatives of the glorified Church, is cast in precisely the same mould of three ascriptions of praise to the Lord. But in the third member there is an important difference, the words "and which is to come" being omitted. The explanation is that the Lord is come. The present dispensation is at its close.

3. The events of the close are next described. It is the time of the dead to be judged, and the time to give reward to God's faithful servants, to whatever part of mankind they have belonged, and whatever the position they have filled in life. The whole family of man is divided into two great classes, and for the one there is judgment, for the other reward.

4. Before passing on it may be well to call attention to one or two particulars in these verses which, though not specially connected with that general meaning of the passage which it is the main object of this commentary to elicit, may help to throw light upon the style of the Apostle and the structure of his work.

(1) Thus it is important to observe his use of the word prophets. The persons spoken of are obviously in contrast with "the nations" and "the dead to be judged," and they must include all who are faithful unto death. Already we have seen that every true follower of Christ is in St. John's eyes a martyr, and that when he thinks of the martyrs of the Church he has a far wider circle in view than that of those who meet death by the sword or at the stake. [279] To his ideal conceptions of things the martyr spirit makes the martyr, and the martyr spirit must rule in every disciple of the Crucified. In like manner the prophetic spirit makes the prophet, and of that spirit no true follower of Him in whom prophecy culminated can be devoid. In this very chapter we have read of "prophesying" as the work of the two witnesses who are a symbol of the whole Christian Church, and who prophesy through the thousand two hundred and threescore days of her pilgrimage. We are not therefore to suppose that those here called "prophets" are either prophets in the stricter sense of the word, or commissioned ministers of Christ. All Christ's people are His "servants the prophets," and the idealism of St. John distinctly appears in the designation given them.

(2) The next following clause, which we have translated in a manner slightly different from that of both the Authorised and the Revised Versions, is not less important: both the saints and them that fear Thy name, instead of "and to the saints, and to them that fear Thy name." It is the manner of St. John to dwell in the first instance upon one characteristic of the object of which he speaks, and then to add other characteristics belonging to it, equally important, it may be, in themselves, but not occupying so prominent a place in the line of thought which he happens to be pursuing at the moment. An illustration of this is afforded in John xiv. 6, where the words of Jesus are given in the form, "I am the Way, and the Truth, and the Life." The context shows that the emphasis rests wholly on Jesus as "the Way," and that the addition of the words "the Truth, and the Life," is only made to enhance and complete the thought. Here in like manner the contents of what is involved in the term "the prophets" are completed by a further statement of what the prophets are. They are "the saints and they that fear God's name." The twofold structure of this statement, however, again illustrates the manner of St. John. "The saints" is, properly speaking, a Jewish epithet, while every reader of the Acts of the Apostles is familiar with the fact that "they that fear God" was a term applied to Gentile proselytes to Judaism. We have thus an instance of St. John's method of regarding the topic with which he deals from a double point of view, the first Jewish, the second Gentile. He is not thinking of two divisions of the Church. The Church is one; all her members constitute one Body in Christ. But looked at from the Jewish standpoint, they are "the saints;" from the Gentile, they are those that "fear Thy name."

(3) The verses under consideration afford a marked illustration of St. John's love of presenting judgment under the form of the lex talionis. The nations were "roused to wrath," and upon them God's "wrath came." They had "destroyed the earth," and God would "destroy" them. In studying the Apocalypse, all peculiarities of style or structure ought to be present to the mind. They are not unfrequently valuable guides to interpretation.

The seventh Trumpet has sounded, and the end has come. A glorious moment has been reached in the development of the Almighty's plan; and the mind of the Seer is exalted and ravished by the prospect. Yet he beholds no passing away of the present earth and heavens, no translation of the reign of good to an unseen spiritual and hitherto unvisited region of the universe. It would be out of keeping with the usual phraseology of his book to understand by heaven, in which he sees the ark of God's covenant, a locality, a place "beyond the clouds and beyond the tomb." His employment of the contrasted words "earth" and "heaven" throughout his whole series of visions rather leads to the supposition that by the latter we are to understand that region, wherever it may be, in which spiritual principles alone bear sway. It may be here; it may be elsewhere; it seems hardly possible to say: but the more the reader enters into the spirit of this book, the more difficult will he find it to resist the impression that St. John thinks of this present world as not only the scene of the great struggle between good and evil, but also, when it has been cleansed and purified, as the seat of everlasting righteousness. These in the present instance are striking words: "to destroy them that destroy the earth." Why not destroy the earth itself if it is only to be burned up? Why speak of it in such terms as lead almost directly to the supposition that it shall be preserved though its destroyers perish? While, on the other hand, if God at first pronounced it to be "very good;" if it may be a home of truth, and purity, and holiness; and if it shall be the scene of Christ's future and glorious reign,--then may we justly say, Woe to them that destroy the habitation, the palace, now preparing for the Prince of peace.

However this may be, it was a fitting close to the judgments of the seven Trumpets that the "temple" of God--that is, the innermost shrine or sanctuary of His temple--should be opened. There was no need now that God should be "a God that hideth Himself." [280] When earth had in it none but the pure in heart, why should they not see Him? [281] He would dwell in them and walk in them. [282] The Tabernacle of the Lord would be again with men. [283]

When too the shrine was opened, what more appropriate spectacle could be seen than "the ark of His covenant," the symbol of His faithfulness, the pledge of that love of His which remains unchanged when the mountains depart and the hills are removed? The covenant-keeping God! No promise of the past had failed, and the past was the earnest of the future.

Nor need we wonder at the lightnings, and voices, and thunders, and the earthquake, and the great hail that followed. For God had "promised, saying, Yet once more will I make to tremble not the earth only, but also the heaven. And this word, Yet once more, signifieth the removing of those things that are shaken, as of things that are made, that those things which are not shaken may remain." [284]

Footnotes:

242. Zech. ii. 1, 2.
243. Ezek. xl. 2-5.
244. Zech. ii. 5.
245. Chap. xxi. 15, 17.
246. John vii. 4.
247. Ver. 2.
248. Isa. i. 13, 14.
249. John ix. 34.
250. John ix. 35.
251. Chaps. ii. 24; iii. 1, 4.
252. Comp. Matt. xxii. 14.
253. Dan. vii. 25.
254. Dan. ix. 27.
255. John xvi. 33.
256. Zech. iv.
257. John viii. 12. Comp. Matt. v. 14.
258. 2 Kings i. 10, 12.
259. Dan. iii. 22.
260. Chap. i. 16.
261. 1 Kings xvii. 1; James v. 17.
262. 1 Cor. x. 11.
263. Ver. 7.
264. John xvii. 4; xix. 30.
265. See margin of R.V.
266. Ps. cxxxii. 13, 14.
267. Isa. i. 10, 21.
268. Luke xxiii. 12.
269. Neh. viii. 10.
270. Esther ix. 22.
271. Comp. chap. v. 6.
272. Chap. iii. 21.
273. Rom. viii. 19, 21.
274. Chap. ix. 20.
275. Chaps. viii. 13; ix. 12.
276. 1 Cor. xv. 28.
277. 2 Pet. iii. 13.
278. Chap. iv. 8.
279. Comp. p. 102.
280. Isa. xlv. 15.
281. Matt. v. 8.
282. 2 Cor. vi. 16.
283. Chap. xxi. 3.
284. Heb. xii. 26, 27.

CHAPTER IX – THE FIRST GREAT ENEMY OF THE CHURCH

Rev. xii.

The twelfth chapter of the Revelation of St. John has been felt by every commentator to be one more than usually difficult to interpret, and that whether we look at it in relation to its special purpose, or to its position in the structure of the book. If we can satisfy ourselves as to the first of these two points, we shall be better able to form correct notions as to the second.

Turning then for a moment to chap. xiii., we find it occupied with a description of two of the great enemies with which the Church has to contend. These are spoken of as "a beast" (ver. 1) and "another beast" (ver. 11), the latter being obviously the same as that described in chap. xix. 20 as "the false prophet that wrought the signs" in the sight of the former. At the same time, it is evident that these two beasts are regarded as enemies of the Church in a sense peculiar to themselves, for the victorious Conqueror of chap. xix. makes war with them, and "they twain are cast into the lake of fire that burneth with brimstone." [285] This fate next overtakes, in chap. xx. 10, "the dragon, the old serpent, which is the devil, and Satan," so that no doubt can rest upon the fact that to St. John's view the great enemies of the Church are three in number. When, accordingly, we find two of them described in chap. xiii., and chap. xii. occupied with the description of another, we are warranted in concluding that the main purpose of the chapter is to set before us a picture of this last.

Thus also we are led to understand the place of the chapter in the structure of the book. We have already seen that the seven Trumpets are occupied with judgments on the world. The seven Bowls, forming the next and highest series of judgments, are to be occupied with judgments on the degenerate members of the Church. It is a fitting thing, therefore, that we should be able to form a clear idea of the enemies by which these faithless disciples are subdued, and in resisting whom the steadfastness of the faithful remnant shall be proved. To describe them sooner was unnecessary. They are the friends, not the enemies, of the world. They are the enemies only of the Church. Hence the sudden transition made at the beginning of chap. xii. There is no chronological relation between it and the chapters which precede. The thoughts embodied in it refer only to what follows. The chapter is obviously divided into three parts, and the bearing of these parts upon one another will appear as we proceed.

And a great sign was seen in heaven; a woman arrayed with the sun, and the moon under her feet, and upon her head a crown of twelve stars: and she was with child; and she crieth out, travailing in birth, and in pain to be delivered. And there was seen another sign in heaven; and behold a great red dragon, having seven heads and ten horns, and upon his heads seven diadems. And his tail draweth the third part of the stars of heaven, and did cast them into the earth: and the dragon stood before the woman that was about to be delivered, that when she was delivered he might devour her child. And she was delivered of a son, a man-child, who as a shepherd shall tend all the nations with a sceptre of iron: and her child was caught up unto God, and unto His throne. And the woman fled into the wilderness, where she hath a place prepared of God, that there they may nourish her a thousand two hundred and threescore days (xii. 1-6).

In the first chapter of the book of Genesis we read, "And God made two great lights; the greater light to rule the day, and the lesser light to rule the night: He made the stars also." [286] Sun, and moon, and stars exhaust the Biblical notion of the heavenly bodies which give light upon the earth. They therefore, taken together, clothe this woman; and there is no need to search for any recondite meaning in the place which they severally occupy in her investiture. She is simply arrayed in light from head to foot. In other words, she is the perfect emblem of light in its brightness and purity. The use of the number twelve indeed suggests the thought of a bond of connexion between this light and the Christian Church. The tribes of Israel, the type of God's spiritual Israel, were in number twelve; our Lord chose to Himself twelve Apostles; the new Jerusalem has "twelve gates, and at the gates twelve angels, and names written thereon, which are the names of the twelve tribes of the children of Israel." [287]

But though the light is thus early connected with the thought of the Christian Church, and though the subsequent portion of the chapter confirms the connexion, the woman is not yet to be regarded as, in the strictest sense, representative of that community or Body historically viewed. By-and-by she will be so. In the meantime a comparison of ver. 6 with ver. 14, where her fleeing into the wilderness and her nourishment in it for precisely the same period of time as in ver. 6 are again mentioned, together with what we have already seen to be a peculiarity of St. John's mode of thought, forbids the supposition. The Apostle would not thus repeat himself. We are entitled therefore to infer that at the opening of the chapter he deals less with actual history than with the "pattern" of that history which had existed from all eternity in the mount. Hence also it would seem that the birth of the child, though undoubtedly referring to the birth of Jesus, is not the actual birth. It, too, is rather the eternal "pattern" of that event. Similar remarks apply to the dragon, who is not yet the historical Satan, and will only be so in the second paragraph, at ver. 9. The whole picture, in short, of these verses is one of the ideal which precedes the actual, and of which the actual is the counterpart and realization.

The resemblance, accordingly, borne by the first paragraph of this chapter (vers. 1-6) to the first paragraph of the fourth Gospel (vers. 1-5), is of the most striking kind. In neither is there any account of the actual birth of our Lord. In both (and we shall immediately see this still more fully brought out in the apocalyptic vision) we are introduced to Him at once, not as growing up to be the Light of the world, but as already grown up and as perfect light. In both we have the same light and the same darkness, and in both the same contrariety and struggle between the two. Nor does the comparison end here. We have also the same singular method of expressing the deliverance of the light from the enmity of the darkness. In John i. 5, correctly translated, we read "The light shineth in the darkness, and the darkness overcame it not," the thought being rather negative than positive, rather that of preservation than of victory. In the Apocalypse we read, And her child was caught up unto God, and unto His throne, the idea being again that of preservation rather than of victory.

Such is the general conception of the first paragraph of this chapter. The individual expressions need not detain us long. The woman's raiment of light has been already spoken of. Passing therefore from that, it need occasion no surprise that He who is Himself the Giver of light should be represented as the Son of light. God "is light, and in Him is no darkness at all." [288] Jesus, as the Son of God, is thus also the Son of light. No doubt the conception is continued even after we behold the woman in her actual, not her ideal, state. Jesus is still her Son. [289] Yet there is a true sense in which we may describe our Lord not only as the Foundation, but also as the Son, of the Church. He is "the First-born among many brethren," [290] the elder Brother in a common Father's house. He is begotten by the power of the Holy Spirit [291] ; and they that believe in His name are "born, not of blood, nor of the will of the flesh, nor of the will of man, but of God." [292] So close linked in the teaching of St. John is the identification of Christ and His people, that whatever is said of Him may be said of them, and what is said of them may be said of Him. Human thought and language fail to do justice to a relation so profound and mysterious. But it is everywhere the teaching of the beloved disciple--in his Gospel, in his Epistles, in his Revelation--although the Church may not fully understand it until she has lived herself more into it than she has done. Her "life" will then bring her "light." [293]

The dragon of the passage is great and red: "great" because of the power which he possesses; "red," the colour of blood, because of the ferocity with which he destroys men: "He was a murderer from the beginning;" "Cain was of the evil one, and slew his brother;" "And I saw the woman" (that is, the woman who rode upon the scarlet-coloured beast) "drunk with the blood of the saints, and with the blood of the martyrs of Jesus." [294] The dragon has further seven heads,--seven, the number of completeness, so that he possesses everything to enable him to execute his plans; and ten horns, the emblem at once of his strength and of his rule over all the kingdoms of the world. Upon the heads, too, are seven diadems, a word different from that which had been employed for the woman's "crown" in the first verse of the chapter. Hers is a crown of victory; the diadems of the dragon are only marks of royalty, and may be worn, as they will be worn, in defeat. The dragon's tail, again, like the tails of the locusts of the fifth Trumpet and of the horses of the sixth, is the instrument with which he destroys [295] ; and the third part of the stars of heaven corresponds to "the third part" mentioned in each of the first four Trumpets. The figure of casting the stars into the earth is taken from the prophecy of Daniel, in which it is said of the "little horn" that "it waxed great, even to the host of heaven; and it cast down some of the host and of the stars to the ground, and stamped upon them." [296]

The dragon next takes up his position before the woman which was about to be delivered, that when she was delivered he might devour her child; and the first historical circumstances to which the idea corresponds, and in which it is realized, may be found in the effort of Pharaoh to destroy the infant Moses. Pharaoh is indeed often compared in the Old Testament to a dragon: "Thou didst divide the sea by Thy strength: Thou brakest the heads of the dragons in the waters;" "Speak, and say, Thus saith the Lord God; Behold, I am against thee, Pharaoh king of Egypt, the great dragon that lieth in the midst of his rivers, which hath said, My river is mine own, and I have made it for myself." [297] The power, and craft, and cruelty of the Egyptian king could hardly have been absent from the Seer's mind when he employed the figure of the text. But he was certainly not thinking of Pharaoh alone. He remembered also the plot of Herod to destroy the Child Jesus. [298] Pharaoh and Herod--men quailed before them;

yet both were no more than instruments in the hands of God. Both worked out His "determinate counsel and foreknowledge." [299]

The child is born, and is described in language worthy of our notice. He is a son, a man-child; and the at first sight tautological information appears to hint at more than the mere sex of the child. He is already more than a child: he is a man. There is a similar emphasis in the words of our Lord when He said to His disciples in His last consolatory discourse, "A woman when she is in travail hath sorrow, because her hour is come: but when she is delivered of the child, she remembereth no more the anguish, for the joy that a man is born into the world." [300] From the first the child is less a child than a man, strong, muscular, and vigorous, who as a shepherd shall tend all the nations with a sceptre of iron. Strange that we should be invited to dwell on this ideal aspect of the Son's work rather than any other! No doubt the words are quoted from the second Psalm. This, however, only removes the difficulty a step further back. Why either there or here should the shepherd work of the Messiah be connected with an iron sceptre rather than a peaceful crook? The explanation is not difficult. Both the Psalm and the Apocalypse are occupied mainly with the victory of Christ over His adversaries. His friends have already been secured in the possession of a complete salvation. It remains only that His foes shall be finally put down. Hence the "sceptre of iron." Strange also, it may be thought, that in this ideal picture we should find no "pattern" of the life of our Lord on earth, of His labours, or sufferings, or death; and that we should only be invited to behold Him in His incarnation and ascension into heaven! But again the explanation is not difficult. Over against Satan stands, not a humbled merely, but a risen and glorified, Redeemer. The process by which He conquered it is unnecessary to dwell upon. Enough that we know the fact.

The woman's child being thus safe, the woman herself fled into the wilderness, where she hath a place prepared of God, and where she shall be nourished by heavenly sustenance. Thus Israel wandered forty years, fed with the manna that fell from heaven and the water that flowed from the smitten rock. [301] Thus Elijah fled to the brook Cherith, and afterwards to the wilderness, where his wants were supplied in the one case by the ravens, in the other by an angel. [302] And thus was our Lord upheld for forty days by the words that proceeded out of the mouth of God. [303] This wilderness life of the Church, too, continues during the whole Christian era, during the whole period of witnessing. [304] Always in the wilderness so long as her Lord is personally absent, she eats heavenly food and drinks living water.

Such is the first scene of this chapter; and, glancing once more over it, it would seem as if its chief purpose were to present to us the two great opposing forces of light and darkness, of the Son and the dragon, considered in themselves.

The second scene follows:--

And there was war in heaven, Michael and his angels going forth to war with the dragon; and the dragon warred and his angels: and they prevailed not, neither was their place found any more in heaven. And the great dragon was cast down, the old serpent, he that is called the devil, and Satan, the deceiver of the whole inhabited earth: he was cast down into the earth, and his angels were cast down with him. And I heard a great voice in heaven, saying, Now is come the salvation, and the power, and the kingdom of our God, and the authority of His Christ: for the accuser of our brethren is cast down, which accuseth them before our God day and night. And they overcame him because of the blood of the Lamb, and because of the word of their testimony; and they loved not their life even unto death. Therefore rejoice, O heavens, and ye that tabernacle in them. Woe for the earth and for the sea! because the devil is gone down unto you, having great wrath, knowing that he hath but a short season (xii. 7-12).*

If our conception of the first six verses of the chapter be correct, it will be evident that the idea often entertained, that the verses following them form a break in the narrative which is only resumed at ver. 13, is wrong. There is no break. The progress of the thought is continuous. The combatants have been set before us, and we have now the contest in which they are engaged. This consideration also helps us to understand the personality of Michael and the particular conflict in the Seer's view.

For, as to the first of these two points, it is even in itself probable that the Leader of the hosts of light will be no other than the Captain of our salvation, the Lord Jesus Christ Himself. The dragon leads the hosts of darkness. The Son has been described as the opponent against whom the enmity of the dragon is especially directed. When the war begins, we have every reason to expect that as the one leader takes the command, so also will the other. There is much to confirm this conclusion. The name Michael leads to it, for that word signifies, "Who is like God?" and such a name is at least more appropriate to a Divine than to a created being. In the New Testament, too, we read of "Michael the archangel" [305] --there seems to be only one, for we never read of archangels [306] --and an archangel is again spoken of in circumstances that can hardly be associated with the thought of any one but God: "The Lord Himself shall descend from heaven with a shout, with the voice of the archangel, and with the trump of God." [307] Above all, the prophecies of Daniel, in which the name Michael first occurs, may be said to decide the point. A person named Michael there appears on different occasions as the defender of the Church against her enemies, [308] and once at least in a connexion leading directly to the thought of our Lord Himself: "And at that time shall Michael stand up, the great prince which standeth for the children of Thy people: and there shall be a time of trouble, such as never was since there was a nation even to that same time: and at that time Thy people shall be delivered, every one that shall be found written in the book. And many of them that sleep in the dust of the earth shall awake, some to everlasting life, and some to shame and everlasting contempt. And they that be wise shall shine as the brightness of the firmament; and they that turn many to righteousness as the stars for ever and ever." [309] These considerations justify the conclusion that the Michael now spoken of is the representative of Christ; and we have already seen, in examining the vision of the "strong angel" in chap. x., that such a mode of speaking is in perfect harmony with the general method of St. John.

Light is thus thrown also upon the second point above mentioned: the particular conflict referred to in these verses. The statement that there was war in heaven, and that when the dragon was defeated he was cast down into the earth, might lead us to think of an earlier conflict between good and evil than any in which man has part: of that mentioned by St. Peter and St. Jude, when the former consoles the righteous by the thought that "God spared not angels when they sinned, but cast them down to hell, and committed them to pits of darkness, to be reserved unto judgment," [310] and when the latter warns sinners to remember that "angels which kept not their own principality, but left their proper habitation, He hath kept in everlasting bonds under darkness unto the judgment of the great day." [311] The circumstances, however, of the war, lead rather to the thought of a conflict in which the Son, incarnate and glorified, takes His part. For this "Son" is the opponent of the dragon introduced to us in the first paragraph of the chapter. "Heaven" is not so much a premundane or supramundane locality as the spiritual sphere within which believers dwell even during their earthly pilgrimage, when that pilgrimage is viewed upon its higher side. And the means by which the victory is gained--for the victors overcame by the blood of the Lamb, and by the word of their testimony--distinctly indicate that the struggle referred to took place after the work of redemption had been completed, not before it was begun.

Several other passages of the New Testament are in harmony with this supposition. Thus it was that when the seventy returned to our Lord with joy after their mission, saying, "Lord, even the demons are subject unto us in Thy name," He, beholding in this the pledge of His completed victory, exclaimed, "I beheld Satan fallen as lightning from heaven." [312] Thus it was that when charged with casting out demons by Beelzebub, the prince of the demons, our Lord pointed out to His accusers that His actions proved Him to be the Conqueror, and that the kingdom of God was come unto them: "When the strong man fully armed guardeth his own court, his goods are in peace: but when a stronger than he shall come upon him, and overcome him, he taketh from him his whole armour wherein he trusted, and divideth his spoils." [313] To the same effect are all those passages where our Lord or His Apostles speak, not of a partial, but of a complete, victory over Satan, so that for His people the great enemy of man is already judged, and overthrown, and bruised beneath their feet: "Now is a judgment of this world: now shall the prince of this world be cast out;" "And when He" (the Advocate) "is come, He will convince the world of judgment, because the prince of this world hath been judged;" "Since then the children are sharers in flesh and blood, He also Himself in like manner partook of the same; that through death He might bring to nought him that had the power of death, that is, the devil; and might deliver all them who through fear of death were all their lifetime subject to bondage;" "Whatsoever is begotten of God overcometh the world: and this is the victory that overcometh the world, even our faith;" "We know that whosoever is begotten of God sinneth not; but He that was begotten of God keepeth him, and the evil one toucheth him not." [314]

In passages such as these we have the same thought as that before us in this vision. Satan has been cast out of heaven; that is, in his warfare against the children of God he has been completely overthrown. Over their higher life, their life in a risen and glorified Redeemer, he has no power. They are for ever escaped from his bondage, and are free. But he has been cast down into the earth, and his angels with him; that is, over the men of the world he still exerts his power, and they are led captive by him at his will. Hence, accordingly, the words of the great voice heard in heaven which occupy all the latter part of the vision, words which distinctly bring out the difference between the two aspects of Satan now adverted to,--(1) his impotence as regards the disciples of Jesus who are faithful unto death: Rejoice, O heavens, and ye that dwell in them; (2) his mastery over the ungodly: Woe for the earth and for the sea! for the devil is gone down unto you in great wrath, knowing that he hath but a short season. Although, therefore, the fall of the angels from their first estate may be remotely hinted at, the vision refers to the spiritual contest begun after the resurrection of Jesus; and we ask our readers only to pay particular regard to the double relation of Satan to mankind which is referred to in it: his subjection to the righteous and the subjection of the wicked to him. One phrase only may seem inconsistent with this view. In ver. 9 Satan is described as the deceiver of the whole inhabited earth, for that, and not "the whole world," is the true rendering of the original. [315] "The whole inhabited earth" cannot be the same as "the earth." The latter is simply the wicked; the former includes all men. But the words describe a characteristic of Satan in himself, and not what he actually effects. He is the deceiver of the whole inhabited earth. He lays his snares for all. He tempted Jesus Himself in the wilderness, and many a time thereafter during His labours and His sufferings. The vision gives no ground for the supposition that God's children are not attacked by him. It assures us only that when the attack is made it is at the same instant foiled. There is a battle, but Christians advance to it as conquerors; before it begins victory is theirs. [316]

One other expression of these verses may be noted: the short season spoken of in ver. 12. This period of time is not to be looked at as if it were a brief special season at the close of the Christian age, when the wrath of Satan is aroused to a greater than ordinary degree because the last hour is about to strike. The great wrath with which he goes forth is that stirred in him by his defeat through the death, resurrection, and ascension of our Lord. It was roused in him when he was "cast into the earth," and from that moment of defeat therefore the "short season" begins.

The third paragraph of the chapter follows:--

And when the dragon saw that he was cast down into the earth, he persecuted the woman which brought forth the man-child. And there were given to the woman the two wings of the great eagle, that she might fly into the wilderness, unto her place, where she is nourished for a time, and times, and half a time, from the face of the serpent. And the serpent cast out of his mouth after the woman water as a river, that he might cause her to be carried away by the stream. And the earth helped the woman, and the earth opened her mouth, and swallowed up the river which the dragon cast out of his mouth. And the dragon waxed wroth with the woman, and went away to make war with the rest of her seed, which keep the commandments of God, and hold the testimony of Jesus; and he stood upon the sand of the sea (xii. 13-xiii. 1a).

We have already seen that the woman introduced to us in the first paragraph of this chapter is the embodiment and the bearer of light. She is there indeed set before us in her ideal aspect, in what she is in herself, rather than in her historical position. Now we meet her in actual history, or, in other words, she is the historical Church of God in the New Testament phase of her development. As such she has a mission to the world. She is "the sent" of Christ, as Christ was "the sent" of the Father. [317] In witnessing for Christ, she has to reveal to the children of men what Divine love is. But she has to do this in the midst of trouble. This world is not her rest; and she must bear the Saviour's cross if she would afterwards wear His crown.

Persecuted, however, she is not forsaken. She had given her the two wings of the great eagle, that she might fly into the wilderness, unto her place--the place prepared of God for her protection. There can be little doubt as to the allusion. The "great eagle" is that of which God Himself spoke to Moses in the mount: "Ye have seen what I did unto the Egyptians, and how I bare you on eagles' wings, and brought you unto Myself;" [318] and that alluded to by Moses in the last song taught by him to the people: "As an eagle stirreth up her nest, fluttereth over her young, spreadeth abroad her wings, taketh them, beareth them on her wings: so the Lord alone did lead him, and there was no strange god with him." [319] The same eagle was probably in view of David when he sang, "How excellent is Thy lovingkindness, O God! therefore the children of men put their trust under the shadow of Thy wings;" [320] while it was also that on the wings of which the members of the Church draw continually nearer God: "They mount up with wings as eagles." [321] To the woman then there was given a "refuge from the storm," a "covert from the heat," of trial, that she might abide in it, nourished with her heavenly food, for a time, and times, and half a time. Of this period we have already spoken. It is the same as that of the three and a half years, the "forty-two months," the "thousand two hundred and threescore days." It is thus the whole period of the Church's militant history upon earth. During all of it she is persecuted by Satan; during all of it she is preserved and nourished by the care of God. At first sight indeed it may seem as if this shelter in the wilderness were incompatible with the task of witnessing assigned to her. But it is one of the paradoxes of the position of the children of God in this present world that while they are above it they are yet in it; that while they are seated "in the heavenly places" they are exposed to the storms of earth; that while their life is hid with Christ in God they witness and war before the eyes of men. The persecution and the nourishment, the suffering and the glory, run parallel with each other. One other remark may be made. There is obviously an emphasis upon the word "two" prefixed to "wings." Though founded upon the fact that the wings of the bird are two in number, a deeper meaning would seem to be intended; and that meaning is suggested by the fact that the witnesses of chap. xi. were also two. The protection extended corresponds exactly to the need for it. The "grace" of God is in all circumstances "sufficient" for His people. [322] No temptation can assail them which He will not enable them to endure, or out of which He will not provide for them a way of escape. [323] Therefore may they always take up the language of the Apostle and say, "Most gladly will I rather glory in my weaknesses, that the strength of Christ may spread a tabernacle over me. Wherefore I take pleasure in weaknesses, in injuries, in necessities, in persecutions, in distresses for Christ's sake: for when I am weak, then am I strong." [324]

The woman fled into the wilderness, but she was not permitted to flee thither without a final effort of Satan to overwhelm her; and in the manner in which this effort is made we again recognise the language of the Old Testament. There the assaults of the ungodly upon Israel are frequently compared to those floods of waters which, owing to the sudden risings of the streams, are in the East so common and so disastrous. Isaiah describes the enemy as coming in "like a flood." [325] Of the floods of the Euphrates and the destruction which they symbolized we have already spoken [326] ; and in hours of deliverance from trouble the Church has found the song of triumph most suitable to her condition in the words of the Psalmist, "If it had not been the Lord who was on our side, when men rose up against us: then they had swallowed us up quick, when their wrath was kindled against us: then the waters had overwhelmed us, the stream had gone over our soul: then the proud waters had gone over our soul. Blessed be the Lord, who hath not given us as a prey to their teeth." [327] The main reference is, however, in all probability to the passage of Israel across the Red Sea, for then, says David, calling to mind that great deliverance in the history of his people, and finding in it the type of deliverances so often experienced by himself, "the sorrows of death compassed me, and the floods of ungodly men made me afraid.... In my distress I called upon the Lord, and cried unto my God.... He sent from above, He took me. He drew me out of many waters." [328]

The most remarkable point to be noticed here is, however, not the deliverance itself, but the method by which it is accomplished. To understand this, as well as the wrath of Satan immediately afterwards described, it is necessary to bear in mind that twofold element in the Church the existence of which is the key to so many of the most intricate problems of the Apocalypse. The Church embraces both true and false members within her pale. She is the "vine" of our Lord's last discourse to His disciples, some of the branches of which bear much fruit, while others are only fit to be cast into the fire and burned. [329] The thought of these latter members is in the mind of St. John when he tells us, in a manner so totally unexpected, that the earth helped the woman, and the earth opened her mouth, and swallowed up the river which the dragon cast out of his mouth. He is thinking of the nominal members of the Church, of the merely nominal Christianity which she has so often exhibited to the world. That Christianity the world loves. When the Church's tone and life are lowered by her yielding to the influence of the things of time, then the world, "the earth," is ready to hasten to her side. It offers her its friendship, courts alliance with her, praises her for the good order which she introduces, by arguments drawn from eternity, into the things of time, and swallows up the river which the dragon casts out of his mouth against her. When Christ's disciples are of the world, the world loves its own. [330] They are helping "the earth" to do its work. Why should the earth not recognise and welcome the assistance given it by foolish foes as well as friends? Therefore it helps the woman.

But side by side with this aspect of the Church which met the approbation of "the earth," the dragon saw that she had another aspect of determined hostility to his claims; and he waxed wroth with her. She had within her not only degenerate but true members, not only worldly professors, but those who were one with her Divine and glorified Lord. These were the rest of her seed, which keep the commandments of God and the testimony of Jesus. They were the "few names in Sardis which did not defile their garments," [331] "the remnant according to the election of grace," [332] "the seed which the Lord hath blessed." [333] Such disciples of Jesus the dragon could not tolerate, and he went away to make war with them. Thus is the painful distinction still kept up which marks all the later part of the Apocalypse. The spectacle was one over which St. John had mourned as he beheld it in the Church of his own day: "They went out from us, but they were not of us; for if they had been of us, they would have continued with us: but they went out, that they might be made manifest that not all are of us. Little children, it is the last hour." [334] It was a spectacle which he knew would be repeated so long as the Church of Christ was in contact with the world; and he notes it now.

One other point ought to be noticed in connexion with these verses. The helping of the woman by the earth seems to be the Scripture parallel to the difficult words of St. Paul when he says in writing to the Thessalonians, "And now ye know that which restraineth to the end that he may be revealed in his own season. For the mystery of lawlessness doth already work: only there is one that restraineth now, until he be taken out of the way." [335] This "restraining" power, generally, and in all probability correctly, understood of the Roman State, is "the earth" of St. John helping the woman because it is helped by her.

We have been introduced to the first great enemy of the Church of Christ. It remains only that he shall take up his position on the field. The next clause therefore which meets us, and which ought to be read, not as the first clause of chap. xiii., but as the last of chap. xii., and in which the third person ought to be substituted for the first, describes him as doing so: And he stood upon the sand of the sea, upon the shore between the earth and the sea, where he could so command them both as to justify the "Woe" already uttered over both in the twelfth verse of the chapter. There we leave him for a time, only remarking that we are not to think of ocean lying before us in a calm, but of the restless and troubled sea, raised into huge waves by the storm-winds contending upon it for the mastery and dashing its waves upon the beach.

Footnotes:

285. Chap. xix. 20.
286. Gen. i. 16.
287. Chap. xxi. 12.
288. 1 John i. 5.
289. Comp. ver. 17.
290. Rom. viii. 29.
291. Matt. i. 20.
292. John i. 13.
293. Comp. John i. 4.
294. John viii. 44; 1 John iii. 12; Rev. xvii. 6.
295. Chap. ix. 10, 19.
296. Dan. viii. 10.
297. Ps. lxxiv. 13; Ezek. xxix. 3.
298. Matt. ii. 16.
299. Acts ii. 23.
300. John xvi. 21.
301. 1 Cor. x. 3, 4.
302. 1 Kings xvii. 6; xix. 5.
303. Matt. iv. 4.
304. Chap. xi. 3.
305. Jude 9.
306. Brown, The Book of Revelation, p. 69.
307. 1 Thess. iv. 16.
308. Dan. x. 13, 21.
309. Dan. xii. 1-3.
310. 2 Pet. ii. 4.
311. Jude 6.
312. Luke x. 17, 18.
313. Luke xi. 21, 22.
314. John xii. 31; xvi. 11; Heb. ii. 14, 15; 1 John v. 4, 18.
315. Comp. R.V. (margin).
316. Comp. 1 John v. 4.
317. John xx. 21.
318. Exod. xix. 3, 4.
319. Deut. xxxii. 11, 12.
320. Ps. xxxvi. 7.
321. Isa. xl. 31.
322. 2 Cor. xii. 9.
323. 1 Cor. x. 13.
324. 2 Cor. xii. 9, 10.
325. Isa. lix. 19.
326. Comp. p. 150.
327. Ps. cxxiv. 2-6.
328. Ps. xviii. 4-16.
329. John xv. 5, 6.
330. John xv. 19.
331. Chap. iii. 4.
332. Isa. lxi. 9.
333. Rom. xi. 5.
334. 1 John ii. 18, 19.
335. 2 Thess. ii. 6, 7.

CHAPTER X – THE SECOND AND THIRD GREAT ENEMIES OF THE CHURCH

Rev. xiii.

We have seen that the main purpose of chap. xii. was to introduce to our notice the dragon, or Satan, the first great enemy of the Church. The object of chap. xiii. is to make us acquainted with her second and third great enemies, and thus to enable us to form a distinct conception of the powerful foes with which the followers of Christ have to contend. The two enemies referred to are respectively styled "a beast" (ver. 1) and "another beast" (ver. 11), or, as they are generally termed, the first beast and the second beast. To the word "beast" must be assigned in both cases its fullest and most pregnant sense. The two "beasts" are not only beasts, but wild beasts, strong, fierce, rapacious, and cruel, even the apparent softness and tenderness of the second being associated with those dragon words which can proceed only from a dragon heart. [336]

The first is thus described:--

And I saw a beast coming up out of the sea, having ten horns and seven heads, and on his horns ten diadems, and upon his heads names of blasphemy. And the beast which I saw was like unto a leopard, and his feet were as the feet of a bear, and his mouth as the mouth of a lion: and the dragon gave him his power, and his throne, and great authority. And I saw one of his heads as though it had been slaughtered unto death; and the stroke of his death was healed: and the whole earth marvelled after the beast. And they worshipped the dragon because he gave his authority unto the beast: and they worshipped the beast, saying, Who is like unto the beast, and who is able to war with him? And there was given to him a mouth speaking great things and blasphemies; and there was given to him authority to continue forty and two months. And he opened his mouth for blasphemies against God, to blaspheme His name, and His tabernacle, even them that tabernacle in the heaven. And it was given unto him to make war with the saints, and to overcome them: and there was given to him authority over every tribe, and people, and tongue, and nation. And all that dwell on the earth shall worship him, every one whose name hath not been written from the foundation of the world in the book of life of the Lamb that hath been slaughtered. If any one hath an ear, let him hear. If any one leadeth into captivity, into captivity he goeth: if any one shall kill with the sword, with the sword must he be killed. Here is the patience and the faith of the saints (xiii. 1b-10).

The description carries us back to the prophecies of Daniel, and the language of the prophet helps us to understand that of the Seer. It is thus that the former speaks: "Daniel spake and said, I saw in my vision by night, and, behold, the four winds of the heaven brake forth upon the great sea. And four great beasts came up from the sea, diverse one from another. The first was like a lion, and had eagle's wings: I beheld till the wings thereof were plucked, and it was lifted up from the earth, and made to stand upon two feet as a man, and a man's heart was given to it. And behold another beast, a second, like to a bear, and it was raised up on one side, and three ribs were in his mouth between its teeth: and they said thus unto it, Arise, devour much flesh. After this I beheld, and lo another, like a leopard, which had upon the back of it four wings of a fowl; the beast had also four heads; and dominion was given to it. After this I saw in the night visions, and behold a fourth beast, terrible and powerful, and strong exceedingly; and it had great iron teeth: it devoured and brake in pieces, and stamped the residue with his feet: and it was diverse from all the beasts that were before it; and it had ten horns. I considered the horns, and, behold, there came up among them another horn, a little one, before which three of the first horns were plucked up by the roots: and, behold, in this horn were eyes like the eyes of a man, and a mouth speaking great things." [337] These particulars embody the prophet's picture of the world-power in four successive phases of its manifestation, until it culminates in the "little horn;" and it is not possible to doubt that the Seer, while modifying them with characteristic freedom, finds in them the foundation of his figure.

In both cases there is the same origin,--the sea swept by strong winds from every point of the compass, until the opposing forces rush upon one another, mingle in wild confusion, send up their spray into the air, and then, dark with the reflection of the clouds above and turbid with sand, exhaust themselves with one long, sullen roar upon the beach. In both cases the same animals are referred to, though in the vision of Daniel they are separated, in that of St. John combined: the leopard, with his sudden, cruel spring; the bear, with his slow, relentless brutishness; and the lion, with his all-conquering power. Finally, in the case of both mention is made also of "ten horns," which are distinct from the lineal succession of the heads. So far, therefore, we can have little hesitation in affirming the conclusion arrived at by most commentators that in this beast coming up out of the sea we have an emblem of that power of the world which, under the guidance of "the prince of the world," opposes and persecutes the Church of Christ. Several particulars regarding it, however, still demand our notice.

1. The horns are not to be thought of as distributed among the heads, but rather as a group by themselves, constituting along with the seventh head a manifestation of the beast distinct from that expressed by each of the separate heads. In a certain sense the seventh head, with its ten horns, is thus one of the seven, for in them the beast expresses himself. In another sense it is like the "fourth beast" of the prophet Daniel: "diverse from all the beasts that were before it" and even more terrible than they.

2. The seven heads seem most fittingly to represent seven powers of the world by which the children of God had been persecuted in the past or were to be persecuted in the future. The supposition has indeed been often made that they represent seven forms of Roman government or seven emperors who successively occupied the imperial throne. But neither of these sevens can be definitely fixed by the advocates of the general thought; while the whole strain of the passage suggests that the beast which, in the form now dealt with, unquestionably represents a world-power conterminous with the whole earth, grows up into this form only in his seventh head and ten horns manifestation. The other heads are rather preparatory to the last than to be ranked equally along with it. Making a natural beginning, therefore, with the oldest persecuting power mentioned in that Bible history of which the Apocalyptist makes such extensive use, and following the line down to the Seer's time, the seven heads appear to represent the Egyptian, Assyrian, Babylonian, Medo-Persian, Greek, and Roman powers, together with that power, wider even than the Roman, which St. John saw was about to rage in the hurried days of "the last time" against the simplicity, purity, holiness, and unworldliness of Christ's little flock. Each of these powers is a "head." The last is the concentrated essence, the most universal, the most penetrating, influence of them all. Taken together, they supply, as no other interpretation does, what is absolutely essential to a correct understanding of the figure,--the idea of completeness.

3. By such a rendering also we gain a natural interpretation of the head beheld as though it had been slaughtered unto death; and the stroke of his death was healed. Other renderings fail to afford this, for no successive forms of government at Rome and no successive emperors furnish a member of their series of which it may be said that it is first slain and then brought back to a life of greater energy and more quickened action. Yet without the thought of death and resurrection it is impossible to fulfil the conditions of the problem. The head spoken of in ver. 3 had not been merely wounded or smitten: it had been "slaughtered unto death;" and it was not merely his "deadly wound," [338] or even "his death-stroke:" [339] it was the "stroke of his death" that had been healed. There had been actual death and resurrection from death, the contrast and travesty of that death and resurrection which had befallen the Lamb slaughtered and raised again. [340] Such a death and resurrection can only be fittingly applied to that system of worldly influence, or, in other words, to that "prince of the world," whose power over His people Jesus was not simply to modify, but to extinguish. The Redeemer of the world came, not to wound or weaken only, but to "bring to nought," him that had the power of death--that is, the devil--and to give perfect and eternal freedom to all who would allow the chains in which Satan had bound them to be broken. [341] But the death, if we may so speak, of Satan in relation to them was accompanied by his resurrection in relation to the world, over which the great enemy of souls was thenceforward to exercise a more irresistible sway than ever. The time is that already spoken of in the previous chapter, when the devil went down into the earth, "having great wrath, knowing that he hath but a short season." [342] Nor is there any difficulty in determining to which of the seven heads of the beast the death and resurrection spoken of apply, for a comparison of chap. xvii. 8-11 with the present passage shows that it is to the sixth, or Roman, head that St. John intends his language to refer.

4. Particular attention must be paid to the fact that it is upon the beast in his resurrection state that we are to dwell, for the whole earth marvels after the beast not previously, but subsequently, to the point of time at which the stroke of his death is healed. [343] In that condition, too, he is not thought of as raging only in the Roman empire. His influence is universal. Wherever men are he is: And there was given to him authority over every tribe, and people, and tongue, and nation. [344] The fourfold division indicates absolute universality; and the whole earth--that is, all ungodly ones--worships the beast, even every one whose name has not been written in the Lamb's book of life. [345] Thus raging with an extent of power never possessed by any form of Roman government or any emperor of Rome, he rages also throughout all time, from the first to the second coming of the Lord, for he has authority given to him to continue forty and two months, [346] the period so denoted embracing the whole Christian era from its beginning to its close. [347]

5. Three points more may be noticed before drawing the general conclusion to which all this leads. In the first place, the beast is the vicegerent of another power which acts through him and by means of

him. The dragon gave him his power, and his throne, and great authority. The dragon himself does not directly act. He has his representative, or vicar, or substitute, in the beast. In the second place, the worship paid by "the whole earth" to the beast, when it cries, Who is like unto the beast? and who is able to make war with him? is an obvious imitation of the ascriptions of praise to God contained in not a few passages of the Old Testament: "Who is like unto the Lord our God, that hath His seat on high?"; "To whom then will ye liken Me, that I should be equal to him? saith the Holy One;" "Hearken unto Me, O house of Jacob, and all the remnant of the house of Israel.... To whom will ye liken Me, and make Me equal, and compare Me, that we may be like?" [348] In the third place, the beast opens his mouth, not only to blaspheme against God, but against His tabernacle, even them that tabernacle in the heaven,[349] expressions in which the use of the word "tabernacle" leads directly to the thought of opposition to Him who became flesh and tabernacled among us, and who now spreads His tabernacle over His saints. [350]

The whole description of the beast is thus, in multiplied particulars, a travesty of the Lord Jesus Christ Himself, the Head and King, the Guardian and Protector, of His people. Like the latter, the former is the representative, the "sent," of an unseen power, by whom all authority is "given" him; he has his death and his resurrection from the dead; he has his throngs of marvelling and enthusiastic worshippers; his authority over those who own his sway is limited by no national boundaries, but is conterminous with the whole world; he gathers up and unites in himself all the scattered elements of darkness and enmity to the truth which had previously existed among men, and from which the Church of God had suffered.

What then can this first beast be? Not Rome, either pagan or papal; not any single form of earthly government, however strong; not any Roman emperor, however vicious or cruel; but the general influence of the world, in so far as it is opposed to God, substituting the human for the Divine, the seen for the unseen, the temporal for the eternal. He is the impersonation of that world of which St. Paul writes, "We received, not the spirit of the world, but the spirit which is of God," [351] of which St. James speaks when he says, "Whosoever therefore would be a friend of the world maketh himself an enemy of God," [352] and in regard to which St. John exhorts, "Love not the world, neither the things that are in the world. If any man love the world, the love of the Father is not in him. For all that is in the world, the lust of the flesh, and the lust of the eyes, and the vain-glory of life, is not of the Father, but is of the world." [353] This beast, in short, is the world viewed in that aspect in which our Lord Himself could say of it that the devil was its prince, which He told His disciples He had overcome, and in regard to which He prayed in His high-priestly prayer, "I pray not that Thou shouldest take them out of the world, but that Thou shouldest keep them out of the evil one. They are not of the world, even as I am not of the world." [354]

The influence of the beast here spoken of is therefore confined to no party, or sect, or age. It may be found in the Church and in the State, in every society, in every family, or even in every heart, for wherever man is ruled by the seen instead of the unseen or by the material instead of the spiritual, there "the world" is. "Our wrestling is not against flesh and blood, but against the principalities, against the powers, against the world-rulers of this darkness, against the spiritual hosts of wickedness in the heavenly places." [355]

Against this foe the true life of the saints will be preserved. Nothing can harm the life that is hid with Christ in God. But the saints may nevertheless be troubled, and persecuted, and killed, as were the witnesses of chap. xi., by the beast that had given unto him to make war with them, and to overcome them. Such is the thought that leads to the last words of the paragraph with which we are now dealing: If any one leadeth into captivity, into captivity he goeth; if any one shall kill with the sword, with the sword must he be killed. In the great law of God, the lex talionis, consolation is given to the persecuted. Their enemies would lead them into captivity, but a worse captivity awaits themselves. They would kill with the sword, but with a sharper sword than that of human power they shall themselves be killed. Is there not enough in that to inspire the saints with patience and faith? Well may they endure with unfainting hearts when they remember who is upon their side, for "it is a righteous thing with God to recompense affliction to them that afflict them," and to them that are afflicted "rest" [356] --rest with Apostles, prophets, martyrs, the whole Church of God, rest never again to be disturbed either by sin or sorrow. Here is the patience and the faith of the saints.

The second enemy of the Church, or the first beast, has been described. St. John now proceeds to the third enemy, or the second beast:--

And I saw another beast coming up out of the earth; and he had two horns like unto a lamb, and he spoke as a dragon. And he exerciseth all the authority of the first beast in his sight; and he maketh the earth and them that dwell therein to worship the first beast, the stroke of whose death was healed. And he doeth great signs, that he should even make fire to come down out of heaven upon the earth in the sight of men. And he deceiveth them that dwell on the earth by reason of the signs which it was given him to do in the sight of the beast; saying to them that dwell on the earth, that they should make an image to the beast, who hath the stroke of the sword, and lived. And it was given unto him to give breath to it, even to the image of the beast, that the image of the beast should both speak, and cause that as many as should not worship the image of the beast should be killed. And he causeth all, the small and the great, and the rich and the poor, and the free and the bond, that there be given them a mark on their right hand, or upon their forehead: and that no man should be able to buy or to sell, save he that hath the mark, even the name of the beast or the number of his name (xiii. 11-17).

The first beast came up out of "the sea" (ver. 1); the second beast comes up out of the earth: and the contrast, so strongly marked, between these two sources, makes it necessary to draw a clear and definite line of distinction between the origin of the one beast and that of the other. The "sea," however, both in the Old Testament and in the New, is the symbol of the mass of the Gentile nations, of the heathen world in its condition of alienation from God and true religious life. In contrast with this, the "earth," as here used, must be the symbol of the Jews, among whom, to whatever extent they had abused their privileges, the Almighty had revealed Himself in a special manner, showing "His word unto Jacob, His statutes and His judgments unto Israel." [357] The Jews were an agricultural, not a commercial, people; and upon that great highway along which the commerce of the nations poured they looked with suspicion and dislike. Hence the sea, in its restlessness and barrenness, became to them the emblem of an irreligious world; the land, in its quiet and fruitfulness, the emblem of religion with all its blessings. In this sense the contrast here must be understood; and the statement as to the different origin of the first and second beasts is of itself sufficient to determine that, while the former belongs to a secular, the latter belongs to a religious, sphere. Many other particulars mentioned in connexion with the second beast confirm this conclusion.

1. The two horns like unto a lamb are unquestionably a travesty of the "seven horns" of the Lamb, so often spoken of in these visions; and the description carries us to the thought of Antichrist, of one who sets himself up as the true Christ, of one who, professing to imitate the Redeemer, is yet His opposite.

2. The words And he spoke as a dragon remind us of the description given by our Lord of those false teachers who "come in sheep's clothing, but inwardly are ravening wolves," [358] as well as of the language of St. Paul when he warns the Ephesian elders that after his departing "grievous wolves shall enter in among them, not sparing the flock." [359]

3. The function to which this beast devotes himself is religious, not secular. He maketh the earth and them that dwell therein to worship the first beast; and, having persuaded them to make an image to that beast, it was given unto him to give breath to it, even to the image of the beast, that the image of the beast should both speak, and cause that as many as should not worship the image of the beast should be killed. [360]

4. The great signs and wonders done by this beast, such as making fire to come down out of heaven upon the earth in the sight of men, are a reminiscence of the prophet Elijah at Carmel; while the signs by which he successfully deceives the world take us again to the words of Jesus: "There shall arise false Christs, and false prophets, and shall show great signs and wonders, so as to lead astray, if possible, even the elect." [361] St. Paul's words also, when he speaks of the man of sin, make similar mention of his "signs:" "Whose coming is according to the working of Satan with all power and signs and lying wonders, and with all deceit of unrighteousness for them that are perishing; because they received not the love of the truth, that they might be saved." [362]

5. Finally, the fact that this beast bears the name of "the false prophet," [363] the very term used by St. John when speaking of the false teachers who had arisen in his day, [364] may surely be accepted as conclusive that we have here a symbol of the antichrists of the first Epistle of that Apostle. Of the antichrists, let it be observed, not of Antichrist as a single individual manifestation. For there is a characteristic of this beast which leads to the impression that more than one agent is included under the terms of the symbol. The beast has two horns. Why two? We may be sure that the circumstance is not without a meaning, and that it is not determined only by the fact that the animal referred to has in its natural condition the rudiments of no more than two. In other visions of the Apocalypse we read of a lamb with "seven horns," and of a head of the beast with "ten horns," the numbers in both cases being symbolical. The "two horns" now spoken of must also be symbolical; and thus viewed, the expression leads us to the thought of the two witnesses, of the two prophets of truth, spoken of in chap. xi. But these two witnesses represent all faithful witnesses for Christ; and, in like manner, the two horns represent the many perverters of the Christian faith beheld by the Seer springing up around him, who, professing to be Apostles of the Lamb, endeavoured to overthrow His Gospel.

These considerations lead to a natural and simple interpretation of what is meant by the second beast. The plausible interpretation suggested by many of the ablest commentators on this book, that by the second beast is meant "worldly wisdom, comprehending everything in learning, science and art which human nature of itself, in its civilized state, can attain to, the worldly power in its more refined and spiritual elements, its prophetical or priestly class," [365] must be unhesitatingly dismissed. It fails to apprehend the very essence of the symbol. It speaks of a secular and mundane influence, when the whole point of St. John's words lies in this,--that the influence of which he speaks is religious. Not in anything springing out of the world in its ordinary sense, but in something springing out of the Church and the Church's faith, is the meaning of the Apostle to be sought.

Was there anything then in St. John's own day that might have suggested the figure thus employed? Had he ever witnessed any spectacle that might have burned such thoughts into his soul? Let us turn to his Gospel and learn from it to look upon the world as it was when it met his eyes. What had he seen, and seen with an indignation that penetrates to the core his narrative of his Master's life? He had seen the Divine institution of Judaism, designed by the God of Israel to prepare the way for the Light and the Life of men, perverted by its appointed guardians, and made an instrument for blinding instead of enlightening the soul. He had seen the Eternal Son, in all the glory of His "grace" and "truth," coming to the things that were His own, and yet the men that were His own rejecting Him, under the influence of their selfish religious guides. He had seen the Temple, which ought to have been filled with the prayers of a spiritual worship, profaned by worldly traffic and the love of gain. Nay more, he remembered one scene so terrible that it could never be forgotten by him, when in the judgment-hall of Pilate even that unscrupulous representative of Roman power had again and again endeavoured to set Jesus free, and when the Jews had only succeeded in accomplishing their plan by the argument, "If thou release this man, thou art not Cæsar's friend." [366] They Cæsar's friends! They attach value to honours bestowed by Cæsar! O vile hypocrisy! O dark extremity of hate! Judaism at the feet of Cæsar! So powerfully had the thought of these things taken possession of the mind of the beloved disciple, so deeply was he moved by the narrowness and bigotry and fanaticism which had usurped the place of generosity and tenderness and love, that, in order to find utterance for his feelings, he had been compelled to put a new meaning into an old word, and to concentrate into the term "the Jews" everything most opposed to Christ and Christianity.

Nor was it only in Judaism that St. John had seen the spirit of religion so overmastered by the spirit of the world that it became the world's slave. He had witnessed the same thing in Heathenism. It is by no means improbable that when he speaks of the image of the beast he may also think of those images of Cæsar the worshipping of which was everywhere made the test of devotion to the Roman State and of abjuration of the Christian faith. There again the forms and sanctions of religion had been used to strengthen the dominion of secular power and worldly force. Both Judaism and Heathenism, in short, supplied the thoughts which, translated into the language of symbolism, are expressed in the conception of the second beast and its relation to the first.

Yet we are not to imagine that, though St. John started from these things, his vision was confined to them. He thinks not of Jew or heathen only at a particular era, but of man; not of human nature only as it appears amidst the special circumstances of his own day, but as it appears everywhere and throughout all time. He is not satisfied with dwelling upon existing phenomena alone. He penetrates to the principles from which they spring. And wherever he sees a spirit professing to uphold religion, but objecting to all the unpalatable truths with which it is connected in the Christian faith, wherever he sees the gate to future glory made wide instead of narrow and the way broad instead of straitened, there he beholds the dire combination of the first and second beasts presented in this chapter. The light has become darkness, and how great is the darkness! [367] The salt has lost its savour, and is fit neither for the land nor for the dunghill. [368]

In speaking of the subserviency of the second to the first beast, the Seer had spoken of a mark given to all the followers of the latter on their right hand, or upon their forehead, and without which no one was to be admitted to the privileges of their association or of buying or selling in their city. He had further described this mark as being either the name of the beast or the number of his name. To explain more fully the nature of this "mark" appears to be the aim of the last verse of the chapter:--

Here is wisdom. He that hath understanding, let him count the number of the beast: for it is the number of a man; and his number is six hundred and sixty and six (xiii. 18).

To discuss with anything like fulness the difficult questions connected with these words would require a volume rather than the few sentences at the close of a chapter that can be here devoted to it. Referring, therefore, his readers to what he has elsewhere written on this subject, [369] the writer can only make one or two brief remarks, in order to point out the path in which the solution of the problems suggested by the words must be sought.

It is indeed remarkable that the Seer should speak at all of "the number" of the name of the beast; that is, of the number which would be gained by adding together the numbers represented by the several letters of the name. Why not be content with the name itself? Throughout this book the followers of Christ are never spoken of as stamped with a number, but either with the name of the Father or the Son, or with a new name which no one "knoweth" saving he that receiveth it. [370] Now the principle of Antithesis or Contrast, which so largely rules the structure of the Apocalypse, might lead us to expect a similar procedure in the case of the followers of the beast. Why then is it not resorted to?

1. St. John may not himself have known the name. He may have been acquainted only with the character of the beast, and with the fact, too often overlooked by inquirers, that to that character its name, when made known, must correspond. It is not any name, any designation, by which the beast may be individualized, that will fulfil the conditions of his thought. No reader of St. John's writings can have failed to notice that to him the word "name" is far more than a mere appellative. It expresses the inner nature of the person to whom it is applied. The "name" of the Father expresses the character of the Father, that of the Son the character of the Son. The Seer, therefore, might be satisfied in the present instance with his conviction that the name of the beast, whatever it be, must be a name which will express the inner nature of the beast; and he may have asked no more. Not only so. When we enter into the style of the Apostle's thought, we may even inquire whether it was possible for a Christian to know the name of the beast in the sense which the word "name" demands. No man could know the new name written upon the white stone given to him that overcometh "but he that receiveth it." [371] In other words, no one but a Christian indeed could have that Christian experience which would enable him to understand the "new name." In like manner now, St. John may have felt that it was not possible for the followers of Christ to know the name of Antichrist. Antichristian experience alone could teach the name of Antichrist, service of the beast the name of the beast; and such experience no Christian could have. But this need not hinder him from giving the number. The "number" spoke only of general character and fate; and knowledge of it did not imply, like knowledge of the "name," communion of spirit with him to whom the name belonged.

2. From this it follows that not the "name," but the "number" of the name, is of importance in the Apostle's view. The name no doubt must have a meaning which, taken even by itself, would be portentous; but, according to the artificial system of thought here followed, the "number" is the real portent, the real bearer of the Divine message of wrath and doom.

3. This is precisely the lesson borne by the number 666. The number six itself awakened a feeling of dread in the breast of the Jew who felt the significance of numbers. It fell below the sacred number seven just as much as eight went beyond it. This last number denoted more than the simple possession of the Divine. As in the case of circumcision on the eighth day, of the "great day" of the feast on the eighth day, or of the resurrection of our Lord on the first day of the week, following the previous seven days, it expressed a new beginning in active power. By a similar process the number six was held to signify inability to reach the sacred point and hopeless falling short of it. To the Jew there was thus a doom upon the number six even when it stood alone. Triple it; let there be a multiple of it by ten and then a second time by ten until you obtain three mysterious sixes following one another, 666; and we have represented a potency of evil than which there can be none greater, a direfulness of fate than which there can be none worse. The number then is important, not the name. Putting ourselves into the position of the time, we listen to the words, His number is six hundred sixty and six; and we have enough to make us tremble. Nay, there is in them a depth of sin and a weight of punishment which no one can "know" but he who has committed the sin and shared the punishment.

From all that has been said it would seem that there is no possibility of finding the name of the beast in the name of any single individual who has yet appeared upon the stage of history. It may well be that in Nero, or Domitian, or any other persecutor of the Church, the Seer beheld a type of the beast; but the whole strain of the chapter forbids the supposition that the meaning of the name is exhausted in any single individual. No merely human ruler, no ruler over merely a portion of the world however large, no ruler who had not died and risen from the grave, and who after his resurrection had not been hailed with enthusiasm by "every tribe, and tongue, and people, and nation," can be the beast referred to. Whether St. John expected such a ruler in the future; whether this beast, like the "little horn" of Daniel, which had "eyes like the eyes of a man, and a mouth speaking great things," [372] was not only bestial, but human; or whether in its individuality it was no more than a personification of antichristian sin and cruelty, is another and a more difficult question. Yet his tendency to represent abstract ideas by concrete images would lead to the latter rather than the former supposition. One thing is clear: that the bestial principle was already working, although it might not have reached its full development. The "many antichrists" [373] might be the precursors of a still more terrible Antichrist, but they worked in the same spirit and towards the same end. Nor are they to be less the object of alienation and abhorrence to the Christian now than when they may be concentrated in "the lawless one, whom the Lord Jesus shall slay with the breath of His mouth, and bring to nought by the manifestation of His coming." [374]

Footnotes:

336. Ver. 11.

337. Dan. vii. 2-8.

338. Chap. xiii. 3, A.V.

339. Chap. xiii. 3, R.V.

340. Chap. v. 6.

341. Heb. ii. 14.

342. Chap. xii. 12.

343. Vers. 3, 4.

344. Ver. 7.

345. Ver. 8.

346. Ver. 5.

347. Comp. p. 175.

348. Ps. cxiii. 5; Isa. xl. 25, xlvi. 3, 5.

349. Ver. 6.

350. John i. 14; Rev. vii. 15.

351. 1 Cor. ii. 12. Comp. Gal. vi. 14.

352. James iv. 4.

353. 1 John ii. 15, 16.

354. John xiv. 30; xvi. 33; xvii. 15, 16.

355. Eph. vi. 12.

356. 2 Thess. i. 6, 7.

357. Ps. cxlvii. 19.

358. Matt. vii. 15.

359. Acts xx. 29.

360. Vers. 12, 15.

361. Matt. xxiv. 24.

362. 2 Thess. ii. 9, 10.

363. Comp. chaps. xvi. 13; xix. 20; xx. 10.

364. 1 John iv. 1.

365. Fairbairn, On Prophecy, p. 328.

366. John xix. 12.

367. Matt. vi. 23.

368. Luke xiv. 34, 35.

369. The Revelation of St. John: Baird Lectures published by Macmillan and Co., second edition, p. 142, etc., 319, etc.

370. Comp. chaps. iii. 12; xiv. 1; ii. 17.

371. Chap. ii. 17. Comp. John i. 31; iv. 32.

372. Dan. vii. 8.

373. Comp. 1 John ii. 18.

374. 2 Thess. ii. 8.

CHAPTER XI – THE LAMB ON THE MOUNT ZION AND THE HARVEST AND VINTAGE OF THE WORLD.

Rev. xiv.

The twelfth and thirteenth chapters of this book were designed to set before us a picture of the three great enemies of the Church of Christ. We have been told of the dragon, the principle and root of all the evil, whether inward or outward, from which that Church suffers. He is the first enemy. We have been further told of the first beast, of that power or prince of the world to whom the dragon has committed his authority. He is the second enemy. Lastly, we have been told of that false spirit of religion which unites itself to the world, and which, even more opposed than the world itself to the unworldly spirit of Christianity, makes the relation of God's children to the world worse than it might otherwise have been. The picture thus presented is in the highest degree fitted to depress and to discourage. The thought more especially of faithlessness in the Church fills the heart with sorrow. The saddest feature in the sufferings of Jesus was that He was "wounded in the house of His friends;" and there is a greater than ordinary depth of pathos in the words with which the beloved disciple draws to a close his record of his Master's struggle with the Jews: "These things spake Jesus; and He departed, and was hidden from them. But though He had done so many signs before them, yet they believed not on Him: that the word of Isaiah the prophet might be fulfilled, which he spake, Lord, who hath believed our report? and to whom hath the arm of the Lord been revealed?" [375]

Even then, however, it was not wholly darkness and defeat, for the Evangelist immediately adds, "Nevertheless even of the rulers many believed on Him;" and he closes the struggle with the words of calm self-confidence on the part of Jesus, "The things therefore which I speak, even as the Father hath said unto Me, so I speak." [376] Thus also is it here, and we pass from the dark spectacle on which our eyes have rested to a scene of heavenly light, and beauty, and repose. The reader may indeed at first imagine that the symmetry of structure which has been pointed out as a characteristic of the Apocalypse is not preserved by the arrangement of its parts in the present instance. We are about to meet in the following chapter the third and last series of plagues; and we might perhaps expect that the consolatory visions contained in this chapter ought to have found a place between the sixth and seventh Bowls, just as the consolatory visions of chap. vii. and of chaps. x. and xi. found their place between the sixth and seventh Seals and the sixth and seventh Trumpets. Instead of this the seventh Bowl, at chap. xv. 17, immediately follows the sixth, at ver. 12 of the same chapter; and the visions of encouragement contained in the chapter before us precede all the Bowls. The explanation may be that the Bowls are the last and highest series of judgments, and that when they begin there can be no more pause. One plague must rush upon another till the end is reached. The final judgments brook neither interruption nor delay.

In this spirit we turn to the first vision of chap. xiv.:--

And I saw, and, behold, the Lamb standing on the mount Zion, and with Him a hundred and forty and four thousand, having His name and the name of His Father written on their foreheads. And I heard a voice from heaven, as the voice of many waters, and as the voice of a great thunder: and the voice which I heard was as the voice of harpers harping with their harps: and they sang as it were a new song before the throne, and before the four living creatures, and the elders: and no man could learn the song save the hundred and forty and four thousand, even they that had been purchased out of the earth. These are they which were not defiled with women; for they are virgins. These are they which follow the Lamb whithersoever He goeth. These were purchased from among men, a first-fruits unto God and unto the Lamb. And in their mouth was found no lie; they are without blemish (xiv. 1-5).

The scene of the vision is "the mount Zion," that Zion so often spoken of both in the Old and in the New Testament as God's peculiar seat, and in the eyes of Israel famous for the beauty of its morning dews. [377] It is the Zion in which God "dwells," [378] the mount Zion which He "loved," [379] and "out of which salvation comes." [380] It is that "holy hill of Zion" upon which God set the Son as King when He said to Him, "Thou art My Son; this day have I begotten Thee." [381] It is that Zion, too, to which "the ransomed of the Lord shall return, and come with singing; and everlasting joy shall be upon their heads." [382] Finally, it is that home of which the sacred writer, writing to the Hebrews, says, "Ye are come unto Mount Zion, and unto the city of the living God, the heavenly Jerusalem, and to innumerable hosts of angels, to the general assembly and Church of the first-born, who are enrolled in heaven, and to God the Judge of all, and to the spirits of just men made perfect, and to Jesus the Mediator of a new covenant, and to the blood of sprinkling, that speaketh better than that of Abel." [383] Upon this mount Zion the Lamb--that is, the crucified and risen Lamb of chap. v.--stands, firm, self-possessed, and calm.

There is more, however, than outward beauty or sacred memories to mark the scene to which we are introduced. Mount Zion may be "beautiful in elevation, the joy of the whole earth, on the sides of the north, the city of the great King." [384] But there is music for the ear as well as beauty for the eye. The mount resounds with song, rich and full of meaning to those who can understand it. A voice is heard from heaven which seems to be distinguished from the voice of the hundred and forty and four thousand to be immediately spoken of. We are not told from whom it comes; but it is there, as the voice of many waters, and as the voice of a great thunder, and as the voice of harpers harping with their harps. Majesty and sweetness mark it. It is the music that is ever in God's presence, not the music of angels only, or glorified saints, or a redeemed creation. More probably it is that of all of them together. And the song which they sing is new, like that of chap. v. 9, which is sung by "the four living creatures and the four-and-twenty elders, who have each one a harp, and golden bowls of incense, which are the prayers of the saints." That song the Church on earth understands, and she alone can understand. It spoke of truths which the redeemed alone could appreciate, and of joys which they alone could value. There is a communion of saints, of all saints on earth and of all who fill the courts of the Lord's house on high. Even now the Church can listen with ravished ear to songs which she shall hereafter join in singing.

Standing beside the Lamb upon Mount Zion, there are a hundred and forty and four thousand, having the Lamb's name and the name of His Father written on their foreheads, in token of their priestly state. We cannot avoid asking, Are these the same hundred and forty and four thousand of whom we have read in chap. vii. as sealed upon their foreheads, or are they different? The natural inference is that they are the same. To use such a peculiar number of two different portions of the Church of God would lead to a confusion inconsistent with the usually plain and direct, even though mystical, statements of this book. Besides which they have the mark or seal of God in both cases on the same part of their bodies,--the forehead. It is true that the definite article is not prefixed to the number; but neither is that article prefixed to the "glassy sea" of chap. xv. 1, and yet no one doubts that this is the same "glassy sea" as that of chap. iv. Besides which the absence of the article may be accounted for by the fact that the reference is not directly to the hundred and forty and four thousand of chap. vii. 4, but to the innumerable multitude of chap. vii. 9. [385] We have already seen, however, that these two companies are the same, although the persons composing them are viewed in different lights; and the hundred and forty and four thousand here correspond, not to the first, but to the second, company. They are in full possession of their Christian privileges and joys. They are not "in heaven," in the ordinary meaning of that term. They are on earth. But the two companies formerly mentioned meet in them. They are both sealed, and in the presence of the Lamb.

The character of the hundred and forty and four thousand next claims our thoughts.

1. They were not defiled with women, for they are virgins. The words cannot be literally understood, but must be taken in the sense of similar words of the Apostle Paul, when, writing to the Corinthians, he says, "For I am jealous over you with a godly jealousy: for I espoused you to one Husband, that I might present you as a pure virgin to Christ." [386] Such "a pure virgin" were the hundred and forty and four thousand now standing upon the mount Zion. They had renounced all that unfaithfulness to God and to Divine truth which is so often spoken of in the Old Testament as spiritual fornication or adultery. They had renounced all sin. In the language of St. John in his first Epistle, they had "the true God, and eternal life." They had "guarded themselves from idols." [387]

2. They follow the Lamb whithersoever He goeth. They shrink from no part of the Redeemer's life whether on earth or in heaven. They follow Him in His humiliation, labours, sufferings, death, resurrection, and ascension. They obey the command "Follow thou Me" [388] in prosperity or adversity, in joy or sorrow, in persecution or triumph. Wherever their Lord is they also are, one with Him, members of His Body and partakers of His Spirit.

3. They are purchased from among men, a first-fruits unto God and unto the Lamb. And in their mouth was found no lie; they are without blemish. Upon the fact that they are "purchased" it is unnecessary to dwell. We have already met with the expression in chap. v. 9, in one of the triumphant songs of the redeemed. Nor does it seem needful to speak of the moral qualifications here enumerated, further than to observe that in other parts of this book the "lie" is expressly said to exclude from the new Jerusalem, and to be a mark of those upon whom the door is shut, [389] while the epithet "without blemish" is elsewhere, on more than one occasion, applied to our Lord. [390]

The appellation "a first-fruits" demands more notice. The figure is drawn from the well-known offering of "first-fruits" under the Jewish law, in which the first portion of any harvest was dedicated to God, in token that the whole belonged to Him, and was recognised as His. Hence it always implies that something of the same kind will follow it, and in this sense it is often used in the New Testament: "If the first-fruit is holy, so is the lump;" "Epænetus, who is the first-fruits of Asia unto Christ;" "Now hath Christ been raised from the dead, the first-fruits of them that are asleep;" "Ye know the house of Stephanas, that it is the first-fruits of Achaia." [391] In like manner the mention of the hundred and forty and four thousand as "first-fruits" suggests the thought of something to follow. What that is it is more difficult to say. It can hardly be other Christians belonging to a later age of the Church's history upon earth, for the end is come. It can hardly be Christians who have done or suffered more than other members of the Christian family, for in St. John's eyes all Christians are united to Christ, alike in work and martyrdom. Only one supposition remains. The hundred and forty and four thousand, as the whole Church of God, are spoken of in the sense in which the same expression is used by the Apostle James: "Of His own will He brought us forth by the word of truth, that we should be a kind of first-fruits of His creatures." [392] Not as the first portion of the Church on earth, to be followed by another portion, but as the first portion of a kingdom of God wider and larger than the Church, are the words to be understood. The whole Church is God's first-fruits; and when she is laid upon His altar, we have the promise that a time is coming when creation shall follow in her train, when "it shall be delivered from the bondage of corruption into the liberty of the glory of the children of God," [393] when "the mountains and the hills shall break forth before the Redeemer into singing, and all the trees of the field shall clap their hands." [394]

Why shall nature thus rejoice before the Lord? Let the Psalmist answer: "For He cometh, for He cometh to judge the earth: He shall judge the world with righteousness, and the people with His truth." [395] This thought may introduce us to the next portion of the chapter:--

And I saw another angel flying in mid-heaven, having an eternal gospel to proclaim over them that sit on the earth, and over every nation, and tribe, and tongue, and people; and he saith with a great voice, Fear God, and give Him glory; for the hour of His judgment is come: and worship Him that made the heaven, and the earth, and sea, and fountains of waters.

And another, a second angel, followed, saying, Fallen, fallen, is Babylon the great, which hath made all the nations to drink of the wine of the wrath of her fornication.

And another angel, a third, followed them, saying with a great voice, If any man worshippeth the beast and his image, and receiveth a mark on his forehead, or upon his hand, he also shall drink of the wine of the wrath of God, which is mingled unmixed in the cup of His anger; and he shall be tormented with fire and brimstone in the presence of the holy angels, and in the presence of the Lamb: and the smoke of their torment goeth up unto ages of ages: and they have no rest day and night, they that worship the beast and his image, and whoso receiveth the mark of his name. Here is the patience of the saints, they that keep the commandments of God, and the faith of Jesus. And I heard a voice from heaven saying, Write, Blessed are the dead which die in the Lord from henceforth: Yea, saith the Spirit, that they may rest from their toils; for their works follow with them.

And I saw, and behold a white cloud, and on the cloud I saw One sitting like unto a Son of man, having on His head a golden crown, and in His hand a sharp sickle.

And another angel came out from the temple, crying with a great voice to Him that sat on the cloud, Send forth Thy sickle, and reap: for the hour to reap is come; for the harvest of the earth is fully ripe. And He that sat on the cloud cast His sickle upon the earth; and the earth was reaped.

And another angel came out from the temple which is in heaven, he also having a sharp sickle.

And another angel came out from the altar, he that hath power over fire; and he called with a great voice to him that had the sharp sickle, saying, Send forth thy sharp sickle, and gather the clusters of the vine of the earth; for her bunches of grapes are ripe. And the angel cast his sickle into the earth, and gathered the vine of the earth, and cast it into the winepress, the great winepress, of the wrath of God. And the winepress was trodden without the city, and there came out blood from the winepress, even unto the bridles of the horses, as far as a thousand and six hundred furlongs (xiv. 6-20).

The first point to be noticed in connexion with these verses is their structure, for the structure is of importance to the interpretation. The passage as a whole, it will be easily observed, consists of seven parts, the first three and the last three being introduced by an "angel," while the central or chief part is occupied with One who, from the description, can be no other than our Lord Himself. In this part it is also obvious that the Lord comes to wind up the history of the world, and to gather in that harvest of His people which is already fully or even overripe. There can be no doubt, therefore, that we are here at the very close of the present dispensation; and, as five out of the six parts which are grouped around the central figure are occupied with judgment on the wicked, the presumption is that the only remaining part, the first of the six, will be occupied with the same topic.

In this first part indeed we read of an eternal gospel proclaimed over them that sit on the earth, and over every nation, and tribe, and tongue, and people; and the first impression made upon us is that we have here a universal and final proclamation of the glad tidings of great joy, in order that the world may yet, at the last moment, repent, believe, and be saved. But such an interpretation, however plausible and generally accepted, must be set aside. The light thrown upon the words by their position in the series of seven parts already spoken of is a powerful argument against it. Everything in the passage itself leads to the same conclusion. We do not read, as we ought, were this the meaning, to have read, of "the," but of "an," eternal gospel. This gospel is proclaimed, not "unto," but "over," those to whom it is addressed. Its hearers do not "dwell," as in both the Authorised and Revised Versions, but, as in the margin of the latter, "sit," on the earth, in the sinful world, in the carelessness of pride and self-confident security. Thus the great harlot "sitteth upon many waters;" and thus Babylon says in her heart, "I sit a queen, and am no widow, and shall in no wise see mourning." [396] There is no humiliation, no spirit of repentance, no preparation for the Gospel, here; while the mention of the "earth" and the fourfold division of its inhabitants lead us to think of men continuing in their sins, over whom a doom is to be pronounced. [397] Still further, the words put into the mouth of him who speaks "with a great voice," and which appear to contain the substance of the gospel thus proclaimed, have in them no sound of mercy, no story of love, no mention of the name of Jesus. They speak of fearing God and giving glory to Him, as even the lost may do, [398] of the hour, not even the "day," of His judgment; and they describe the rule of the great Creator by bringing together the four things--the heaven, and the earth, and sea, and fountains of waters--upon which judgment has already fallen in the series of the Trumpets, and is yet to fall in that of the Bowls. [399] Lastly, the description given of the angel reminds us so much of the description given of the "eagle" in chap. viii. 13 as to make it at least probable that his mission is a similar one of woe.

In the light of all these circumstances, we seem compelled to come to the conclusion that the "gospel" referred to is a proclamation of judgment, that it is that side of the Saviour's mission in which He appears as the winnowing fan by which His enemies are scattered as the chaff, while His disciples are gathered as the wheat. There is no intimation here, then, of a conversion of the world. The world stands self-convicted before the bar of judgment, to hear its doom.

The cry of the second angel corresponds to that of the first. It proclaims the fall of Babylon and its cause. The deeply interesting questions relating to this city will meet us at a later point. In the meantime it is enough to observe that Babylon is described as fallen. The Judge is not only standing at the door: He has begun His work.

The words of the third angel continue the strain thus begun, and constitute the most terrible picture of the fate of the ungodly to be found in Scripture. The eye shrinks from the spectacle. The heart fails with fear when the words are read. That wine of the wrath of God which is mingled unmixed in the cup of His anger, that wine into which, contrary to the usage of the time, no water, no mitigating element, has been allowed to enter; that torment with fire and brimstone in the presence of the holy angels, and in the presence of the Lamb; that smoke of their torment going up unto ages of ages; that no-rest day and night, of so different a kind from the no-rest of which we have read in chap. iv. 8--all present a picture from which we can hardly do aught else than turn away with trembling. Can this be the Gospel of Jesus, the Lamb of God? Can this be a revelation given to the disciple whom Jesus loved, and who had entered so deeply into his Master's spirit of tenderness and compassion for the sinner?

1. Let us consider that the words are addressed, not directly to sinners, but to the Church of Christ, which is safe from the threatened doom; not to the former that they may be led to repentance, but to the latter that through the thought of what she has escaped she may be filled with eternal gratitude and joy 2. Let us notice the degree to which sin is here supposed to have developed; that it is not the sin of Mary in the house of Simon, of the penitent thief, of the Philippian gaoler, or of the publicans and harlots who gathered around our Lord in the days of His flesh to listen to Him, but sin bold, determined, loved, and clung to as the sinner's self-chosen good, the sin of sinners who will die for sin as martyrs die for Christ and holiness. 3. Let us observe that, whatever the angel may mean, he certainly does not speak of never-ending existence in never-ending torment, for the words of the original unhappily translated both in the Authorised and Revised Versions "for ever and ever" ought properly to be rendered "unto ages of ages;" [400] and, distinguished as they are on this occasion alone in the Apocalypse from the first of these expressions by the absence of the Greek articles, they ought not to be translated in the same way. 4. Let us recall the strong figures of speech in which the inhabitants of the East were wont to give utterance to their feelings, figures illustrated in the present instance by the mention of that "fire and brimstone" which no man will interpret literally, as well as by the language of St. Jude when he describes Sodom and Gomorrah as "an example of eternal fire." [401] 5. Let us remember that hatred of sin is the correlative of love of goodness, and that the kingdom of God cannot be fully established in the world until sin has been completely banished from it. 6. Above all, let us mark carefully the distinction, so often forced upon us in the writings of St. John, between sinners in the ordinary sense and the system of sin to which other sinners cling in deadliest enmity to God and righteousness; and, as we do all this, the words of the third angel will produce on us another than their first impression. So far as the human being is before us we shall be moved only to compassion and eagerness to save. But his sin, the sin which has mastered the Divinely implanted elements of his nature, which has fouled what God made

pure and embittered what God made sweet, the sin which has subjected one created in the nobility of the image of God to the miserable thraldom of the devil, the sin the thought of which we can separate, like the Apostle Paul, from the "I" of man's true nature [402] --of that sin we can only say, Let the wrath of God be poured out upon it unmingled with mercy; let it be destroyed with a destruction the memory of which shall last "unto ages of ages" and even take its place amidst the verities sustaining the throne of the Eternal and securing the obedience and the happiness of His creatures. [403] If a minister of Christ thinks that he may gather from this passage, or others similar to it, a commission to go to sinners rather than to sin with "tidings of damnation," he mistakes alike the Master whom he serves and the commission with which he has been entrusted.

At this point, after the thought of that spirit of allegiance to the beast which draws down such terrors upon itself, and before we reach the central figure of the whole movement, we have some words of comfort interposed. The meaning of the first part of them is similar to that of chap. xiii. 10, and need not be further spoken of. The meaning of their second part, conveying to us the contents of the "voice from heaven," demands a moment's notice. Blessed, exclaims the heavenly voice (at the same time prefixing the command Write), are the dead which die in the Lord from henceforth. It is difficult to determine the precise point of time referred to in the word "henceforth." If it be the moment of the end, the moment of the Second Coming of the Lord, then the promise must express the glory of the resurrection. But, to say nothing of the fact that "resting from labours" is too weak to bring out the glory of the resurrection state, there is at that instant no more time to die in the Lord. The living shall be "changed." It seems better, therefore, to understand the words as a voice of consolation running throughout the whole Christian age. In the view of "heaven" the lapse of time is hardly thought of. All is Now. The meaning of "dying in the Lord," again, must not be regarded as equivalent to the Scriptural expression "falling asleep in Jesus." Not the thought of "falling asleep" in a quiet Christian home, but of "dying" as Jesus died, is in the Seer's mind; and not the thought of rest from work, but of rest from toils, an entirely different and far stronger word, is in the answer of the Spirit. Thus are believers blessed. Their life is a life of toil, of hardship, of trial, of persecution, of death; but when they die, they "rest." And their "works"--that is, their Christian character and life--are not lost. They follow with them, and meet them again in the heavenly mansions as the record of all that they have done and suffered in their Master's cause.

The first three angels have accomplished their task. We now reach the fourth and chief member in this series of seven, and meet with the Lord as He comes to take His people to Himself, that where He is, there they may also be. That it is the Lord who is here before us we cannot for a moment doubt. The designation like unto a Son of man, the same as that of chap. i. 13, itself establishes the fact, which is again confirmed by the mention of the white cloud and of the golden crown. In His hand He holds a sharp sickle, with which to reap. Thus also in different passages of the New Testament our Lord speaks of the harvest of His people, although in them He acts by His angels and Apostles. [404] In one passage of the Gospel of St. John He acts by Himself. [405] The glorified Redeemer is thus ready to complete His work.

Another angel now appears, the first of the second series of three, and styled "another," not by comparison with Him who sat on the white cloud, and who is exalted far above all angels, but by comparison with the angels previously spoken of at the sixth, eighth, and ninth verses of the chapter. This angel is said to come out from the temple--that is, out of the naos, out of the innermost shrine of the temple--and the notice is important, for it shows that he comes from the immediate presence of God, and is a messenger from Him. Therefore it is that he can say to the Son, Send forth Thy sickle, and reap. "The Son can do nothing of Himself, but what He seeth the Father doing." [406] Until the Father gives the sign His "hour is not yet come;" and more especially of the hour now arrived Jesus had Himself said, "But of that day or that hour knoweth no one, not even the angels in heaven, neither the Son, but the Father." [407] The day, the hour, the moment, has now arrived; and, as usual in this book, the message of the Father is communicated by an angel. The intimation that the hour is come is grounded upon the fact that the harvest about to be gathered in is fully ripe. The Revised Version translates "overripe;" but the translation, though literal, is unhappy, and so far false as it unquestionably suggests a false idea. God's time for working is always right, not wrong; and it is perfectly legitimate to understand the word of the original as meaning simply dry, hard, the soft juices of its ripening state absorbed, and the time of its firmness come. [408] Thus summoned by the message of the Father to the work, the Son enters upon it without delay. "As He hears, He judges." [409] He that sat on the cloud cast His sickle upon the earth; and the earth was reaped.

The second angel of the second group of three next appears, having, like Him that sat upon the cloud, "a sharp sickle;" and he too waits for the summons to use it.

This summons is given by the third angel of the second group, of whom it is said that he came out from the altar, he that hath power over fire. The altar of this verse must be that already spoken of in chap. viii. 3, where we were told that "another angel came and stood over the altar, having a golden censer," an altar which we have been led to identify with the brazen altar of chap. v. 9, beneath which were found the souls of the Old Testament saints; and the "fire" over which this angel has power must be the "fire" of chap. viii. 5, the fire taken from that altar to kindle the incense of the prayers of the saints. The angel is thus a messenger of judgment, about to command a final and full answer to be given to the prayer that the Almighty will finish His work and vindicate His cause. To this character, accordingly, his message corresponds, for he called with a great voice to him (that is, to the second angel) that had the sharp sickle, saying, Send forth thy sharp sickle, and gather the clusters of the vine of the earth; for her bunches of grapes are ripe. A vintage, not a harvest of grain, is here before us; and it is impossible to doubt that it is the purpose of the Seer to draw a broad line of distinction between the two. The latter is the harvest of the good; the former is the vintage of the evil: and the propriety of the figure thus used for the evil is easily perceived when we remember that grapes were gathered to be trodden in the winefat, and that the juice when trodden out had the colour of blood. The figure was indeed one already familiar to the prophets: "Let the nations bestir themselves, and come up to the valley of Jehoshaphat" (that is, The Lord judges): "for there will I sit to judge all the nations round about. Put ye in the sickle, for the vintage is ripe: come, tread ye; for the winepress is full, the fats overflow; for their wickedness is great;" [410] "Wherefore art Thou red in Thine apparel, and Thy garments like him that treadeth in the winefat? I have trodden the winepress alone; and of the people there was no man with Me: yea, I trod them in Mine anger, and trampled them in My fury; and their life-blood is sprinkled upon My garments, and I have stained all My raiment. For the day of vengeance is in Mine heart, and My year of redemption is come." [411] The figure is here employed in a similar manner, for the angel gathered the vine (not "the vintage," the whole vine being plucked up by the roots) of the earth, and cast it into the winepress, the great winepress, of the wrath of God. And the winepress was trodden without the city, and there came out blood from the winepress, even unto the bridles of the horses, as far as a thousand and six hundred furlongs. In these words we have undoubtedly the judgment of the wicked, and the last portion of them alone need detain us for a moment.

1. What is meant by the statement that the sea of blood thus created by the slaughter spoken of reached "even unto the bridles of the horses"? The horses are those of chap. xix. 11-16, where we have again a description of the final victory of Christ over all His enemies, and where it is again said of Him that "He treadeth the winepress of the fierceness of the wrath of Almighty God." [412] The same winepress which meets us here meets us there. The battle and the victory are the same; and the horses here are therefore those upon which He that is called Faithful and True, together with His armies that are in heaven, rides forth to conquest. The mention of "the bridles" of the horses is more uncertain and more difficult to explain, but one passage of the Old Testament helps us. In speaking of the glories of the latter day, the prophet Zechariah says, "In that day shall there be upon the bells of the horses (the bells strung along the bridles) Holy unto the Lord." [413] The sea of blood reached to, but could not be allowed to touch, these sacred words.

2. What is meant by the space of "a thousand and six hundred furlongs," over which the sea extended? To resolve it simply into a large space is at variance with the spirit of the Apocalypse; and to imagine that it marks the extent of the Holy Land from Dan to Beersheba is both to introduce an incorrect calculation and to forget who constitute the hosts of wickedness that had been engaged in the battle. These were not the inhabitants of Palestine only, but of "the earth," three times mentioned in the description. They were "all the nations" spoken of by the second angel of the first group, all that worship the beast and his image and receive a mark on their forehead or their hand, referred to by the third angel of the same group. They are thus the wicked gathered from every corner of the earth. With this idea the figures 1,600 agree--four, the number of the world, multiplied by itself to express intensity, and then by a hundred, the number so often associated with evil in this book. Whether "furlongs," literally "stadia," are chosen as the measure of space because, as suggested by Cornelius a Lapide, the arena or circus in which the martyrs suffered was called "The Stadium," [414] it may be vain to conjecture. Enough that the sixteen hundred furlongs represent the whole surface of the earth upon which the wicked "sit" at ease, the universal efficacy of the sickle by which they are gathered to their doom.

One other point ought to be more particularly noticed before we close the consideration of this chapter. The harvest of the good is gathered in by the Lord Himself, that of the wicked by His angel. The same lesson appears to be read in the parables of the tares and of the drawnet. In the former (although allusions in each parable may seem to imply that angels take part in both acts) it is said that "at the end of the world the Son of man shall send forth His angels, and they shall gather out of His kingdom all things that cause stumbling, and them that do iniquity." [415] In the latter we read, "So shall it be in the end of the world: the angels shall come forth, and sever the wicked from among the righteous, and shall cast them into the furnace of fire." [416] In like manner here. The Son of man Himself gathers His own to their eternal rest. It is an angel, though commissioned by Him, who gathers the wicked to their fate. "And is there not a beauty and tenderness in this contrast? It is as though that Son of man and Son of God who is the Judge of quick and dead, the Judge alike of the righteous and of the wicked, loved one half of His office, and loved not the other. It is as though He cherished as His own prerogative the harvest of the earth, and were glad to delegate to other hands the vintage. It is as though the ministry of mercy were His chosen office, and the ministry of wrath His stern necessity. One like unto the Son of man puts forth the sickle of the ingathering; one of created, though it be of angelic, nature is employed to send forth the sickle of destruction." [417]

Footnotes:

375. John xii. 36-38.
376. Vers. 42, 50.
377. Ps. cxxxiii. 3.
378. Ps. ix. 11.
379. Ps. lxxviii. 68.
380. Ps. xiv. 7.
381. Ps. ii. 6, 7.
382. Isa. xxxv. 10.
383. Heb. xii. 22-24.
384. Ps. xlviii. 2.
385. Comp. Lee in Speaker's Commentary in loc. The distinction between the two references is there wrongly given.
386. 2 Cor. xi. 2.
387. 1 John v. 20, 21.
388. John xxi. 22.
389. Chaps. xxi. 27; xxii. 15.
390. Heb. ix. 14; 1 Pet. i. 19.
391. Rom. xi. 16; xvi. 5; 1 Cor. xv. 20; xvi. 15.
392. James i. 18.
393. Rom. viii. 21.
394. Isa. lv. 12.
395. Ps. xcvi. 13.
396. Chaps. xvii. 1; xviii. 7.
397. Comp. chaps. xi. 9; xiii. 7.
398. Comp. James ii. 19.
399. Chaps. viii., xv.
400. They are so rendered in the margin of the Revised Version.
401. Jude 7 (margin of R.V.).
402. Rom. vii.
403. Comp. p. 108.
404. Matt. ix. 37, 38; xiii. 29, 30.
405. John xiv. 3.
406. John v. 19.
407. Mark xiii. 32.
408. Comp. the "dried up" of the margin of the Revised Version.
409. John v. 30.
410. Joel iii. 12, 13.
411. Isa. lxiii. 2-4.
412. Ver. 15.
413. Zech. xiv. 20.
414. Comp. 1 Cor. ix. 24.
415. Matt. xiii. 41.
416. Matt. xiii. 49, 50.
417. Vaughan, u. s., p. 378.

CHAPTER XII - THE SEVEN BOWLS

Rev. xv., xvi.

Nothing can more clearly prove that the Revelation of St. John is not written upon chronological principles than the scenes to which we are introduced in the fifteenth and sixteenth chapters of the book. We have already been taken to the end. We have seen in chap. xiv. the Son of man upon the throne of judgment, the harvest of the righteous, and the vintage of the wicked. Yet we are now met by another series of visions setting before us judgments that must take place before the final issue. This is not chronology; it is apocalyptic vision, which again and again turns round the kaleidoscope of the future, and delights to behold under different aspects the same great principles of the Almighty's government, leading always to the same glorious results.

One other preliminary observation may be made. The third series of judgments does not really begin till we reach chap. xvi. Chap. xv. is introductory, and we are thus reminded that the series of the Trumpets had a similar introduction in chap. viii. 1-6. It is the manner of St. John, who thus in his Gospel introduces his account of our Lord's conversation with Nicodemus in chap. iii. by the last three verses of chap. ii., which ought to be connected with the third chapter; and who also introduces his narrative regarding the woman of Samaria by the first three verses of chap. iv.

To introduce chap. xvi. is the object of chap. xv.

And I saw another sign in heaven, great and marvellous, seven angels having seven plagues, which are the last, for in them is finished the wrath of God (xv. 1).

The plagues about to be spoken of are "the last," and in them the final judgments of God upon evil are contained. What they are, and who are the special objects of them, will afterwards appear. Meanwhile, another vision is presented to our view:--

And I saw as it were a glassy sea mingled with fire; and them that come victorious out of the beast, and out of his image, and out of the number of his name, standing upon the glassy sea, having harps of God. And they sing the song of Moses the servant of God, and the song of the Lamb, saying, Great and marvellous are Thy works, O Lord God the Almighty; righteous and true are Thy ways, Thou King of the nations. Who shall not fear, O Lord, and glorify Thy name? for Thou only art holy: for all the nations shall come and worship before Thee; for Thy righteous acts have been made manifest (xv. 2-4).

It can hardly be doubted that the glassy sea spoken of in these words is the same as that already met with at chap. iv. 6. Yet again, as in the case of the hundred and forty and four thousand of chap. xiv. 1, the definite article is wanting; and, in all probability, for the same reason. The aspect in which the object is viewed, though not the object itself, is different. The glassy sea is here mingled with fire, a point of which no mention was made in chap. iv. The difference may be explained if we remember that the "fire" spoken of can only be that of the judgments by which the Almighty vindicates His cause, or of the trials by which He purifies His people. As these, therefore, now stand upon the sea, delivered from every adversary, we are reminded of the troubles which by Divine grace they have been enabled to surmount. It was otherwise in chap. iv. No persons were there connected with the sea, and it stretched away, clear as crystal, before Him all whose dealings with His people are "right." The sea itself is in both cases the same, but in the latter it is beheld from the Divine point of view, in the former from the human.

The vision as a whole takes us back to the exodus of Israel from Egypt, and hence the mention of the song of Moses, the servant of God. The enemies of the Church have their type in Pharaoh and his host as they pursue Israel across the sands which had been laid bare for the passage of the chosen people; the waters, driven back for a time, return to their ancient bed; the hostile force, with its chariots and its chosen captains, "goes down into the depths like a stone;" and Israel raises its song of victory, "I will sing unto the Lord, for He hath triumphed gloriously, the horse and his rider hath He thrown into the sea." [418]

The song now sung, however, is not that of Moses only, the great centre of the Old Testament

Dispensation; it is also the Song of the Lamb, the centre and the sum of the New Testament. Both Dispensations are in the Seer's thoughts, and in the number of those who sing are included the saints of each, the members of the one Universal Church. No disciple of Jesus either before or after His first coming is omitted. Every one is there from whose hands the bonds of the world have fallen off, and who has cast in his lot with the followers of the Lamb. Hence also the song is wider in its range than that by which the thought of it appears to have been suggested. It celebrates the great and marvellous works of the Almighty in general. It speaks of Him as the King of the nations, that is, as the King who subdues the nations under Him. It rejoices in the fact that His righteous acts have been made manifest. And it anticipates the time when all the nations shall come and worship before Him, shall bow themselves at His feet, and shall acknowledge that His judgments against sin are not only just in themselves, but are allowed to be so by the very persons on whom they fall.

A second vision follows:--

And after these things I saw, and the temple of the tabernacle of the testimony in heaven was opened; and there came out from the temple the seven angels that had the seven plagues, clothed with a precious stone pure and lustrous, and girt about their breasts with golden girdles. And one of the four living creatures gave unto the seven angels seven golden bowls full of the wrath of God, who liveth for ever and ever. And the temple was filled with smoke from the glory of God, and from His power: and none was able to enter into the temple, till the seven plagues of the seven angels should be finished (xv. 5-8).

The temple spoken of is, as upon every occasion when the word is used, the shrine or innermost sanctuary, the Holy of holies, the peculiar dwelling-place of the Most High; so that the seven angels with the seven last plagues come from God's immediate presence. But this sanctuary is now beheld in a different light from that in which it was seen in chap. xi. 19. There it contained the ark of God's covenant, the symbol of His grace. Here the eye is directed to the testimony, to the two tables of the law which were kept in the ark, and were God's witness both to the holiness of His character and the justice of His government. The giving of the law then was in the Seer's mind, and that fact will explain the allusions to the Old Testament found in his words. The description of the seven angels, as clothed with a precious stone pure and lustrous (not with "fine linen" as in the Authorised Version) may be explained, when we attend to the second characteristic of their appearance, girt about their breasts with golden girdles. These words take us back to the vision of the Son of man in chap. i., where the same expression occurs, and where we have already seen that it points to the priests of Israel, when engaged in the active service of the sanctuary. The angels now spoken of are thus priestly after the fashion of the Lord Himself, who is not merely the Priest but also the High Priest of His people. The high priest, however, wore a jewelled breastplate; and in correspondence with the nobler functions of the New Testament priesthood, these jewels are now extended to the whole clothing of the angels spoken of. A similar figure for the clothing of the glorified Church meets us in the prophecies of Isaiah: "I will greatly rejoice in the Lord, my soul shall be joyful in my God; for He hath clothed me with the garments of salvation, He hath covered me with the robe of righteousness; as a bridegroom decketh himself (the margin of the Revised Version calling attention to the fact that the meaning of the original is "decketh himself as a priest") with a garland, and as a bride adorneth herself with her jewels;" [419] while the same figure, though applied to Tyre, is employed by Ezekiel: "Every precious stone was thy covering." [420] The seven angels are thus about to engage in a priestly work.

This work is pointed out to them by one of the four living creatures, the representatives of redeemed creation. All creation owns the propriety of the judgments now about to be fulfilled. [421]

These judgments are contained, not in seven "vials," as in the Authorised Version, but in seven golden bowls, vessels probably of a saucer shape, of no great depth, and their circumference largest at the rim. They are the "basins" of the Old Testament, used for carrying into the sanctuary the incense which had been lighted by fire from the brazen altar. They were thus much better adapted than "vials" for the execution of a final judgment. Their contents could be poured out at once and suddenly.

The bowls have been delivered to the angels, and nothing remains but to pour them out. The moment is one of terror, and it is fitting that even all outward things shall correspond. Smoke, therefore, filled the sanctuary, and none was able to enter into it. Thus, when Moses reared up the tabernacle, and the glory of the Lord filled it, "Moses was not able to enter into the tent of meeting:" [422] thus, when Solomon dedicated the temple and the cloud filled the house of the Lord, "The priests could not stand to minister by reason of the cloud." [423] Thus, when Isaiah beheld the glory of the Lord in His temple, and heard the cry of the Seraphim, "Holy, holy, holy is the Lord of Hosts," "the foundations of the thresholds were moved at the voice of him that cried, and the house was filled with smoke;" [424] and thus, above all, when the law was given, "Mount Sinai was altogether on smoke, because the Lord descended upon it in fire: and the smoke thereof ascended as the smoke of a furnace, and the whole mount quaked greatly." [425]

All due preparation having been made, the Seven Bowls are now poured out in rapid and uninterrupted succession. As in the case of the Seals and of the Trumpets, they are divided into two groups of four and three; and those of the first group may be taken together:--

And I heard a great voice out of the temple, saying to the seven angels, Go ye, and pour out the seven bowls of the wrath of God into the earth. And the first went, and poured out his bowl into the earth; and it became a noisome and grievous sore upon the men which had the mark of the beast, and which worshipped his image. And the second poured out his bowl into the sea; and it became blood as of a dead man, and every living soul died, even the things that were in the sea. And the third poured out his bowl into the rivers and the fountains of the waters; and it became blood. And I heard the angel of the waters saying, Righteous art Thou which art and which wast, Thou holy one, because Thou didst thus judge: for they poured out the blood of saints and prophets, and blood hast Thou given them to drink: they are worthy. And I heard the altar saying, Yea, O Lord, God, the Almighty, true and righteous are Thy judgments. And the fourth poured out his bowl upon the sun; and it was given unto it to scorch men with fire. And men were scorched with great heat: and they blasphemed the name of the God which hath the power over these plagues; and they repented not to give Him glory (xvi. 1-9).

Upon the particulars of these plagues it is unnecessary to dwell. No attempt to determine the special meaning of the objects thus visited by the wrath of God--the land, the sea, the rivers and fountains of the waters, and the sun--has yet been, or is ever perhaps likely to be, successful; and the general effect alone appears to be important. The chief point claiming attention is the singular closeness of the parallelism between them and the Trumpet plagues, a parallelism which extends also to the fifth, sixth, and seventh members of the series. Close, however, as it is, there is also a marked climax in the later plagues, corresponding to the fact that they are "the last," and that in them "the wrath of God is finished." [426] Thus the first Trumpet affects only the third part of the earth, and the trees, and all green grass: the first Bowl affects men. [427] Under the second Trumpet the "third part" of the sea becomes blood, and the third part of the creatures which are in the sea die, and the third part of the ships are destroyed: under the second Bowl, the "third part" of the sea is exchanged for the whole; the blood assumes its most offensive form, blood as of a dead man; and not the third part only, but every living soul died, even the things that were in the sea." [428] Under the third Trumpet the great star falls only upon the "third part" of the rivers and fountains, and they become wormwood: under the third Bowl all the waters are visited by the plague, and they become blood. [429] Lastly, under the fourth Trumpet only the "third part" of sun and moon and stars is smitten: under the fourth Bowl the whole sun is affected, and it is given unto it to scorch men with fire. [430] With this climactic character of the Bowls as compared with the Trumpets may also be connected a striking addition made to the details of the third Bowl, to which in the Trumpet series there is nothing to correspond. The angel of the waters, not an angel to whom the smiting of the waters had been entrusted, but the waters themselves speaking through their angel, and the altar, that is, the brazen altar of chap. vi. 9, respond to the judgments executed. They recognise the true and righteous character of the Almighty, and they welcome this manifestation of Himself to men.

Another feature of these Bowls will at once strike the reader,--their correspondence to some of the plagues of Egypt: for in the first we see a repetition, as it were, of that sixth plague by which Pharaoh and his people were visited, when Moses sprinkled ashes of the furnace towards heaven, and they became "a boil breaking forth with blains upon man and beast," [431] and in the second and third a repetition of the first plague, when Moses lifted up his rod and smote the waters that were in the river, "and all the waters that were in the river were turned to blood." [432] The fourth Bowl reminds us of the terror of the appearance of the Son of man in chap. i. 16, when "His countenance was as the sun shineth in his strength."

One other characteristic of these plagues ought to be noticed. It comes to view no doubt only under the fourth, yet, as we shall immediately see, it is not to be confined to it. The plagues had no softening or converting power. On the contrary, as at chap. ix. 20, 21, the impiety of the worshippers of the beast was only aggravated by their sufferings; and, instead of turning to Him who had power over the plagues, they blasphemed His name.

From the first group of Bowls we turn to the second, embracing the last three in the series of seven:--

And the fifth poured out his bowl upon the throne of the beast; and his kingdom was darkened; and they gnawed their tongues for pain, and they blasphemed the God of heaven because of their pains and their sores; and they repented not of their works (xvi. 10, 11).

The transition from the realm of nature to the spiritual world, already marked at the introduction of the fifth Seal and of the fifth Trumpet, is here again observable; but, as in the case of the sixth Trumpet, the spiritual world alluded to is that of the prince of darkness. With darkness he is smitten. That there is a reference to the darkness which, at the word of Moses, fell upon the land of Egypt when visited by its plagues can hardly be doubted, for the darkness of that plague was not ordinary darkness; it was "a darkness that might be felt." [433] More than darkness, however, is alluded to. We are told of their pains and of their sores. But pains and sores are not an effect produced by darkness. They can, therefore, be only those of the first Bowl, a conclusion confirmed by the use of the word "plagues" instead of plague. The inference to be drawn from this is important, for we thus learn that the effects of any earlier Bowl are not exhausted before the contents of one following are discharged. Each Bowl rather adds fresh punishment to that of its predecessors, and all of them go on accumulating their terrors to the end. Nothing could more clearly show how impossible it is to interpret such plagues literally, and how mistaken is any effort to apply them to the particular events of history.

The sixth Bowl follows:--

And the sixth poured out his bowl upon the great river, the river Euphrates, and the water thereof was dried up, that the way might be made ready for the kings that come from the sun-rising. And I saw coming out of the mouth of the dragon, and out of the mouth of the beast, and out of the mouth of the false prophet, three unclean spirits, as it were frogs: for they are spirits of devils, working signs, which go forth unto the kings of the whole inhabited earth, to gather them together unto the war of the great day of God, the Almighty. (Behold, I come as a thief. Blessed is he that watcheth, and keepeth his garments, lest he walk naked, and they see his shame.) And they gathered them together into the place which is called in Hebrew Har-Magedon (xvi. 12-16).

Probably no part of the Apocalypse has received more varied interpretation than the first statement of this Bowl. Who are these kings that come from the sun-rising is the point to be determined; and the answer usually given is, that they are part of the anti-christian host, part of those afterwards spoken of as the kings of the whole inhabited earth, before whom God dries up the Euphrates in order that they may pursue an uninterrupted march to the spot on which they are to be overwhelmed with a final and complete destruction. Something may certainly be said on behalf of such a view; yet it is exposed to serious objections.

1. We have already at chap. ix. 14, at the sounding of the sixth Trumpet, been made acquainted with the river Euphrates; and, so far from being a hindrance to the progress of Christ's enemies, it is rather the symbol of their overflowing and destructive might. 2. We have also met at chap. vii. 2 with the expression "from the sun-rising," and it is there applied to the quarter from which the angel comes by whom the people of God are sealed. In a book so carefully written as the Apocalypse, it is not easy to think of anti-christian foes coming from a quarter described in the same terms. 3. These kings "from the sun-rising" are not said to be a part of "the kings of the whole inhabited earth" immediately afterwards referred to. They are rather distinguished from them. 4. The "preparing of the way" connects itself with the thought of Him whose way was prepared by the coming of the Baptist. 5. The type of drying up the waters of a river takes us back, alike in the historical and prophetic writings of the Old Testament, to the means by which the Almighty secures the deliverance of His people, not the destruction of His enemies. Thus the waters of the Red Sea were dried up, not for the overthrow of the Egyptians, but for the safety of Israel, and the bed of the river Jordan was dried up for a similar purpose. Thus, too, the prophet Isaiah speaks: "And the Lord shall utterly destroy the tongue of the Egyptian sea, and with His scorching wind shall He shake His hand over the river, and shall smite it into seven streams, and cause men to march over dryshod. And there shall be an highway for the remnant of His people, which shall return, from Assyria; like as there was for Israel in the day that he came up out of the land of Egypt." [434] Again the same prophet celebrates the great deeds of the arm of the Lord in the following words: "Art thou not it which dried up the sea, the waters of the great deep; that made the depths of the sea a way for the redeemed to pass over?" [435] And, once more, to a similar effect the prophet Zechariah: "I will bring them again also out of the land of Egypt, and gather them out of Assyria.... And He shall pass through the sea of affliction, and shall smite the waves of the sea, and all the depths of the Nile shall dry up.... And I will strengthen them in the Lord; and they shall walk up and down in His name, saith the Lord." [436] It is unnecessary to say more. In these "kings from the sun-rising" we have an emblem of the remnant of the Israel of God as they return from all the places whither they have been led captive, and as God makes their way plain before them.

Nor is this all. In the fate of these foes a striking incident of Old Testament history is repeated, in order that they may be led to the destruction which awaits them. When Micaiah warned Ahab of his approaching fate, and told him of the lying spirit by which his own prophets were urging him to the battle, he said, "I saw the Lord sitting on His throne, and all the host of heaven standing by Him on His right hand and on His left. And the Lord said, Who shall entice Ahab that he may go up and fall at

Ramoth-gilead? And one said on this manner; and another said on that manner. And there came forth a spirit, and stood before the Lord, and said, I will entice him. And the Lord said unto him, Wherewith? And he said, I will go forth, and be a lying spirit in the mouth of all his prophets. And He said, Thou shalt entice him, and shalt prevail also; go forth and do so." [437] In that incident of Ahab's reign is found the type of the three lying spirits or demons which, like frogs, unclean, noisy, and loquacious, go forth from the three great enemies of the Church, the dragon, the first beast, and the second beast, now first called the false prophet, that they may entice the "kings of the whole inhabited earth" to their overthrow. And they succeed. All unknowing of what is before them, proud of their strength, and flushed with hope of victory, these kings listen to the demons and gather themselves together unto the war of the great day of God, the Almighty. It is a supreme moment in the history of the Church and of the world; and, before he names the battlefield which shall, in its very name, be prophetic of the fate of the wicked, the Seer pauses to behold the assembled armies. Upon the one side is a little flock, but they are all "kings," and before them is He by whom, like David before the host of Israel and over against the Philistines, the battle shall be fought and the victory won. On the other side are the hosts of earth in all their multitudes, gathered together by the deceitful promise of success. The Seer hears the voice of the Captain of salvation, Behold I come as a thief, to break up and to destroy. He hears further the promise of blessing to all who are faithful to the Redeemer's cause: and then, with mind at rest as to the result, he names the place where the final battle is to be fought, Har-Magedon.

Why Har-Magedon? There was, we have every reason to believe, no such place. The name is symbolical. It is a compound word derived from the Hebrew, and signifying the mountain of Megiddo. We are thus again taken back to Old Testament history, in which the great plain of Megiddo, the most extensive in Palestine, plays on more than one occasion a notable part. In particular, that plain was famous for two great slaughters, that of the Canaanitish host by Barak, celebrated in the song of Deborah, [438] and that in which King Josiah fell. [439] The former is probably alluded to, for the enemies of Israel were there completely routed. For a similar though still more terrible destruction the hosts of evil are assembled at Har-Magedon. The Seer thinks it enough to assemble them, and to name the place. He does not need to go further or to describe the victory.

The seventh Bowl now follows:--

And the seventh poured out his bowl upon the air; and there came forth a great voice out of the temple, from the throne, saying, It is done; and there were lightnings, and voices, and thunders; and there was a great earthquake, such as was not since there were men upon the earth, so great an earthquake, so mighty. And the great city was divided into three parts, and the cities of the nations fell: and Babylon the great was remembered in the sight of God, to give unto her the cup of the wine of the fierceness of His wrath. And every island fled away, and the mountains were not found. And great hail, every stone about the weight of a talent, cometh down out of heaven upon men: and men blasphemed God because of the plague of the hail; for the plague thereof is exceeding great (xvi. 17-21).

The seventh or last Bowl is poured out into the air, here thought of as the realm of that prince of this world who is also "the prince of the power of the air." [440] All else, land and sea and waters and sun and the throne of the beast, has now been smitten so that evil has only to suffer its final blow. It has been searched out everywhere; and therefore the end may come. That end comes, and is spoken of in figures more strongly coloured than those of either the sixth Seal or the seventh Trumpet. First of all a great voice is heard out of the (sanctuary of the) temple, from the throne, saying, It is done, God's plan is executed. His last manifestation of Himself in judgment has been made. This voice is then accompanied by a more terrible shaking of the heavens and the earth than we have as yet been called to witness, the earthquake in particular being such as was not since there were men upon the earth, so great an earthquake, so mighty.

Some of the effects of the earthquake are next spoken of. More especially, The great city was divided into three parts, and the cities of the nations fell. As to the meaning of "the cities of the nations" there can be no doubt. They are the strongholds of the world's sin, the places from which ungodliness and impiety have ruled. Under the shaking of the earthquake they fall in ruins. The first words as to "the great city" must be considered in connexion with the words which follow regarding Babylon, and they are more difficult to interpret. By some it is contended that the "great city" is Jerusalem, by others that it is Babylon. The expression is one which the Apocalypse must itself explain, and in seeking the explanation we must proceed upon the principle that in this book, as much as in any other of the New Testament, the rules of all good writing are followed, and that the meaning of the same words is not arbitrarily changed. When this rule, accordingly, is observed, we find that the epithet is, in chap. xi. 8, distinctly applied to Jerusalem, the words "the great city, where also their Lord was crucified" leaving no doubt upon the point. But, in chap. xviii. 10, 16, 18, 19, 21, the same epithet is not less distinctly applied to Babylon. The only legitimate conclusion is, that there is a sense in which Jerusalem and Babylon are one. This corresponds exactly to what we otherwise learn of the light in which the metropolis of Israel appeared to St. John. To him as an Apostle of the Lord, and during the time that he followed Jesus in the flesh, Jerusalem presented itself in a twofold aspect. It was the city of God's solemnities, the centre of the old Divine theocracy, the "holy city," the "beloved city." [441] But it was also the city of "the Jews," the city which scorned and rejected and crucified its rightful King. When in later life he beheld, in the picture once exhibited around him and graven upon his memory, the type of the future history and fortunes of the Church, the two Jerusalems again rose before his view, the one the emblem of all that was most precious, the other of all that was most repulsive, in the eyes both of God and of spiritually enlightened men. The first of these Jerusalems is the true Church of Christ, the faithful remnant, the little flock that knew the Good Shepherd's voice and followed Him. The second is the degenerate Church, the mass of those who misinterpreted the aim and spirit of their calling, and who by their worldliness and sin "crucified their Lord afresh, and put Him to an open shame." In the latter aspect Jerusalem becomes Babylon. As in chap. xi. 8 it became "spiritually," that is mystically, "Sodom and Egypt," so it becomes also the mystical Babylon, partaker of that city's sins, and doomed to its fate. This thought we shall find fully expanded in the following chapter. The question may indeed be asked, how it comes to pass that, if this representation be correct, we should read, immediately after the words now under consideration, that Babylon the great was remembered in the sight of God, to give unto her the cup of the wine of the fierceness of His wrath. But the answer is substantially contained in what has been said. When Jerusalem is first thought of as "the great city," it is as the city of "the Jews," as the centre and essence of those principles by which spiritual is transformed into formal religion, and all sins are permitted to hide and multiply under the cloak of a merely outward piety. When it is next thought of as Babylon, the conception is extended so as to embrace, not a false Judaism only, but a similar falseness in the bosom of the universal Church. Just as "the great city where also our Lord was crucified" widened in chap. xi. 8 to the thought of Sodom and Egypt, so here it widens to the thought of Babylon. May it not be added that we have thus in the mention of Jerusalem and Babylon a counterpart to the mention in chap. xv. 3 of "the song of Moses and the Lamb"? These two expressions, as we have seen, comprehend a song of universal victory. Thus also the two expressions, "the great city" and "Babylon," having one and the same idea at their root, comprehend all who in the professing Church of the whole world are faithless to Christian truth.

Further effects of the last judgment follow. Every island fled away, and the mountains were not found. Effects similar, though not so terrible, had been connected with the sixth Seal. Mountains and islands had then been simply "moved out of their places." [442] Now they "flee away." Similar effects will again meet us, but in an enhanced degree. [443] As yet, while mountains and islands flee away, the earth and the heavens remain. In the last description of the judgment of the wicked the heavens and the earth themselves flee away from the face of Him that sitteth upon the throne, and no place is found for them. The climax in the different accounts of what is substantially the same event cannot be mistaken.

The same climax appears in the statement of the next effect, the great hail, every stone about the weight of a talent, that is, fully more than fifty pounds. No such weight had been spoken of at the close of the seventh Trumpet in chap. xi. 19.

Again, however, there is no repentance and no conversion. Those who suffer are the deliberate and determined followers of the beast. As under the fourth Bowl, therefore, so under the seventh they rather blaspheme God amidst their sufferings, because of the plague of the hail, for the plague thereof is exceeding great.

Footnotes:

418. Exod. xv. 1.
419. Isa. lxi. 10.
420. Ezek. xxviii. 13.
421. Comp. chap. vi.
422. Exod. xl. 35.
423. 1 Kings viii. 11.
424. Isa. vi. 4.
425. Exod. xix. 18; Heb. xii. 18.
426. Chap. xv. 1.
427. Comp. chap. viii. 7 and xvi. 2.
428. Comp. chap. viii. 8, 9 and xvi. 3.
429. Comp. chap. viii. 10, 11 and xvi. 4.
430. Comp. chap. viii. 12 and xvi. 8.
431. Exod. ix. 10.
432. Exod. vii. 20.
433. Exod. x. 21.
434. Isa. xi. 15, 16.

435. Isa. li. 10.
436. Zech. x. 10-12.
437. 1 Kings xxii. 19-22.
438. Judges v.
439. 2 Chron. xxxv. 22.
440. Ephes. ii. 2.
441. Chap. xi. 2; xx. 9.
442. Chap. vi. 14.
443. Chap. xx. 11.

CHAPTER XIII – THE BEAST AND BABYLON

Rev. xvii.

At the close of chap. xvi. we reached the end of the three great series of judgments which constitute the chief contents of the Revelation of St. John,--the series of the Seals, the Trumpets, and the Bowls. It cannot surprise us, however, that at this point other visions of judgment are to follow. Already we had reached the end at chap. vi. 17, and again at chap. xi. 18; yet on both occasions the same general subject was immediately afterwards renewed, and the same truths were again presented to us, though in a different aspect and with heightened colouring. We are prepared therefore to meet something of the same kind now. Yet it is not the whole history of that "little season" with which the Apocalypse deals that is brought under our notice in fresh and striking vision. One great topic, the greatest that has hitherto been spoken of, is selected for fuller treatment,--the fall of Babylon. Twice before we have heard of Babylon and of her doom,--at chap. xiv. 8, when the second angel of the first group gathered around the Lord as He came to judgment exclaimed, "Fallen, fallen, is Babylon the great, which hath made all the nations to drink of the wine of the wrath of her fornication;" and again at chap. xvi. 19, when under the seventh Bowl we were told that "Babylon the great was remembered in the sight of God, to give unto her the cup of the wine of the fierceness of His wrath." So much importance, however, is attached by the Seer to the fortunes of this city that two chapters of his book--the seventeenth and the eighteenth--are devoted to the more detailed descriptions of her and of her fate. These two chapters form one of the most striking, if at the same time one of the most difficult, portions of his book. We have first to listen to the language of St. John; and, long as the passage is, it will be necessary to take the whole of chap. xvii. at once:--

And there came one of the seven angels that had the seven bowls, and spake with me, saying, Come hither; I will show thee the judgment of the great harlot that sitteth upon many waters: with whom the kings of the earth committed fornication, and they that dwell in the earth were made drunken with the wine of her fornication. And he carried me away in the Spirit into a wilderness: and I saw a woman sitting upon a scarlet-coloured beast, full of names of blasphemy, having seven heads and ten horns. And the woman was arrayed in purple and scarlet, and decked with gold and precious stone and pearls, having in her hand a golden cup full of abominations, even the unclean things of her fornication, and upon her forehead a name written, Mystery, Babylon the great, the mother of the harlots and of the abominations of the earth. And I saw the woman drunken with the blood of the saints, and with the blood of the martyrs of Jesus: and when I saw her, I marvelled with a great marvelling. And the angel said unto me, Wherefore didst thou marvel? I will tell thee the mystery of the woman, and of the beast that carrieth her, which hath the seven heads and the ten horns. The beast that thou sawest was, and is not, and is about to come up out of the abyss: and he goeth into perdition. And they that dwell on the earth shall marvel, they whose name hath not been written in the book of life from the foundation of the world, when they behold the beast, how that he was, and is not, and shall be present. Here is the mind that hath wisdom. The seven heads are seven mountains, on which the woman sitteth. And they are seven kings: the five are fallen, the one is the other is not yet come; and when he cometh, he must continue a little while. And the beast that was, and is not, is himself also an eighth, and is of the seven; and he goeth into perdition. And the ten horns that thou sawest are ten kings, which have received no kingdom as yet; but they receive authority as kings with the beast for one hour. These have one mind, and they give their power and authority unto the beast. These shall war against the Lamb, and the Lamb shall overcome them: for He is Lord of lords, and King of kings: and they also shall overcome that are with Him called, and chosen, and faithful. And he saith unto me, The waters which thou sawest, where the harlot sitteth, are peoples, and multitudes, and nations, and tongues. And the ten horns which thou sawest, and the beast, these shall hate the harlot, and shall make her desolate and naked, and shall eat her flesh, and shall burn her utterly with fire. For God did put in their hearts to do His mind, and to come to one mind, and to give their kingdom unto the beast, until the words of God should be accomplished. And the woman whom thou sawest is the great city, which reigneth over the kings of the earth (xvii.).

The main questions connected with the interpretation of this chapter are, What are we to understand by the beast spoken of, and what by Babylon? The Seer is summoned by one of the angels that had the seven Bowls to behold a spectacle which fills him with a great marvelling. Thus summoned, he obeys; and he is immediately carried away into a wilderness, where he sees a woman sitting upon a scarlet-coloured beast, full of names of blasphemy, having seven heads and ten horns.

1. What is this beast, and what in particular is his relation to the beast of chap. xiii.?

At first sight the points of difference appear to be neither few nor unimportant. The order of the heads and of the horns is different, the horns taking precedence of the heads in the earlier, the heads of the horns in the later, of the two. [444] The first is said to have had upon "his heads" names of blasphemy; the second is "full of" such names. [445] There are diadems on the horns of the former, but not of the latter. [446] Of the first we are told that he comes up "out of the sea," of the second that he is about to come up "out of the abyss." [447] In addition to these particulars, it will be observed that several traits of the first beast are not mentioned in connexion with the second. These last points of difference may be easily set aside. They create no inconsistency between the descriptions given; and we have already had occasion for the remark, that it is the manner of the Seer to enlarge in one part of his book his account of an object also referred to in another part. His readers are expected to combine the different particulars in order to form a complete conception of the object.

The more positive points of difference, again, may be simply and naturally explained. In chap. xiii. 1 the horns take precedence of the heads because the beast is beheld rising up out of the sea, the horns in this case appearing before the heads. In the second case, when the beast is seen in the wilderness, the order of nature is preserved. The distribution of the names of blasphemy is in all probability to be accounted for in a similar manner. At the moment when the Seer beholds them in chap. xiii. his attention has been arrested by the heads of the beast, and he has not yet seen the whole body. When he beholds them in chap. xvii., the entire beast is before him, and is "full of" such names. The presence of diadems upon the ten horns in the first, and their absence in the second, beast depends upon the consideration that it is a common method of St. John to dwell upon an object presented to him ideally before he treats it historically. [448] We know that the ten horns are ten kings or kingdoms [449] ; and the diadem is the appropriate symbol of royalty. When therefore we think of the beast in his ideal or ultimate manifestation in the ten kings of whom we are shortly to read, we think of the horns as crowned with diadems; and it is thus accordingly that we see the beast in chap. xiii. On the other hand, at the point immediately before us "the ten kings have received no kingdom as yet;" [450] and the diadems are wanting. The application of this principle further explains the difference between what are apparently two origins for these beasts,--"the sea" and "the abyss." The former is mentioned in chap. xiii., because there we have the beast before us in himself, and in the source from which he springs. The latter is mentioned in chap. xvii., because the beast has now reached a definite period of his history to which the coming up out of "the abyss" belongs. The "sea" is his real source; the "abyss" has been only his temporary abode. The monster springs out of the sea, lives, dies, goes into the abyss, rises from the dead, is roused to his last paroxysm of rage, is defeated, and passes into perdition. [451] This last is his history in chap. xvii., and that history is in perfect harmony with what is stated of him in chap. xiii.,-- that by nature he comes up out of the sea.

While the points of difference between the beasts of chap. xiii. and chap. xvii. may thus without difficulty be reconciled, the points of agreement are such as to lead directly to the identification of the two. Some of these have already come under our notice in speaking of the differences. Others are still more striking. Thus the beast of chap. xiii. is described as the vicegerent of the dragon [452] ; and the object of the dragon is to make war upon the remnant of the woman's seed. [453] When therefore we find the beast of chap. xvii. engaged in the same work, [454] we must either resort to the most unlikely of all conclusions--that the dragon has two vicegerents--or we must admit that the two beasts are one. Again, the characteristic of a rising from the dead is so unexpected and mysterious that it is extremely difficult to assign it to two different agencies; yet we formerly saw that this characteristic belongs to the beast of chap. xiii., and we shall immediately see that it belongs also to that of chap. xvii. Nay more, it is to be noticed that both in chap. xiii. and in chap. xvii. the marvelling of the world after the beast is connected with his resurrection state. [455] This was undoubtedly the case in chap. xiii.; and in the present chapter the cause of the world's astonishment is not less expressly said to be its beholding in the beast how that he was, and is not, and shall be present. [456] Let us add to what has been said that the figures of the Apocalypse are the product of so rich and fertile an imagination that, had a difference between the two beasts been intended, it would, we may believe, have been more distinctly marked; and the conclusion is inevitable that the beast before us is that also of the thirteenth chapter.

Turning then to the beast as here represented, we have to note one or two particulars regarding him, either new or stated with greater fulness and precision than before; while, at the same time, we have the explanation of the angel to help us in interpreting the vision.

(1) The beast was, and is not, and is about to come up out of the abyss: and he goeth into perdition. The words are a travesty of what we read of the Son of man in chap. i.: "I am the first and the

last, and the living One; and I became dead: and, behold, I am alive for evermore." [457] An antichrist is before us, who has been slaughtered unto death, and the stroke of whose death shall be healed. [458] Still further we seem entitled to infer that when this beast appears he shall have the marks of his death upon him. They that dwell on the earth shall marvel when they behold the beast, how that he was, and is not, and shall be present. The inference is fair that there must be something visible upon him by which these different states may be distinguished. In other words, the beast exhibits marks which show that he had both died and passed through death. He is the counterpart of "the Lamb standing as though it had been slaughtered." [459]

(2) The seven heads are seven mountains, on which the woman sitteth. And they are seven kings: the five are fallen, the one is, the other is not yet come; and when he cometh, he must continue a little while. Notwithstanding all that has been said to the contrary by numerous and able expositors, these words cannot be applied directly to any seven emperors of Rome. It may be granted that the Seer had the thought of Rome sitting upon its seven hills in his eye as one of the manifestations of the beast, but the whole tenor of his language is too wide and comprehensive to permit the thought that the beast itself is Rome. Besides this, the heads are spoken of as being also "mountains;" and we cannot say of any five of the seven hills of Rome that they "are fallen," or of any one of them that it is "not yet come." Nor could even any five successive kings of Rome be described as "fallen," for that word denotes passing away, not simply by death, but by violent and conspicuous overthrow; [460] and no series of five emperors in other respects suitable to the circumstances can be mentioned some of whom at least did not die peaceably in their beds. Finally, the word "kings" in the language of prophecy denotes, not personal kings, but kingdoms. [461] These seven "mountains" or seven "kings," therefore, are the manifestations of the beast in successive eras of oppression suffered by the people of God. Egypt, Assyria, Babylonia, Persia, and Greece are the first five; and they are "fallen"--fallen in the open ruin which they brought upon themselves by wickedness. Rome is the sixth, and "it is" in the Apostle's days. The seventh will come when Rome, beheld by the Seer as on the brink of destruction, has perished, and when its mighty empire has been rent in pieces. These pieces will then be the ten horns which occupy the place of the seventh head. They will be even more wicked and more oppressive to the true followers of Christ than the great single empires which preceded them. In them the antichristian might of the beast will culminate. They are "ten" in number. They cover the whole "earth." That universality of dominion which was always the beast's ideal will then become his actual possession. They receive authority as kings with the beast for one hour; and together with him they shall rage against the Lamb. Hence--

(3) And the beast that was, and is not, is himself also an eighth, and is of the seven. The reader will notice that the expression of the eighth verse of the chapter "and is about to come up out of the abyss," as also another expression of the same verse, "and shall be present," are here dropped. We have met with a similar omission in the case of the Lord Himself at chap. xi. 17, and the explanation now is the same as then. The beast can no more be thought of as "about to come up out of the abyss," because he is viewed as come, or as about "to be present," because he is present. In other words, the beast has attained the highest point of his history and action. He has reached a position analogous to that of our Lord after His resurrection and exaltation, when all authority was given Him both in heaven and on earth, and when He began the dispensation of the Spirit, founding His Church, strengthening her for the execution of her mission, and perfecting her for her glorious future. In like manner at the time here spoken of the beast is at the summit of his evil influence. In one sense he is the same beast as he was in Egypt, in Assyria, in Babylonia, in Persia, in Greece, and in Rome. In another sense he is not the same, for the wickedness of all these earlier stages has been concentrated into one. He has "great wrath, knowing that he has but a short season." [462] At the last moment he rages with the keen and determined energy of despair. Thus he may be spoken of as "an eighth;" and thus he is also "of the seven," not one of the seven, but the highest, and fiercest, and most cruel embodiment of them all. Thus also he is identified with the "Little Horn" of Daniel, which has "eyes like the eyes of a man, and a mouth speaking great things." [463] That Little Horn takes the place of three out of the ten horns which are plucked up by the roots; that is, of the eighth, ninth, and tenth horns. It is thus itself an eighth; and we have already had occasion to notice that in the science of numbers the number eight marks the beginning of a new life, with quickened and heightened powers. Thus also fresh light is thrown upon the statement which so closely follows the description of the beast,--that he goeth into perdition. As in the case of Belshazzar, of Nebuchadnezzar, and of the traitor Judas, the instant when he reaches the summit of his guilty ambition is also the instant of his fall.

Before proceeding to consider the meaning of the "Babylon" spoken of in this chapter, it may be well to recall for a moment the principle lying at the bottom of the exposition now given of the "beast." That principle is that St. John sees in the world-power, or power of the world, the contrast, or travesty, or mocking counterpart of the true Christ, of the world's rightful King. The latter lived, died, was buried, rose from the grave, and returned to His Father to work with quickened energy and to enjoy everlasting glory; the former lived, was brought to nought by Christ, was plunged into the abyss, came up out of the abyss, reached his highest point of influence, and went into perdition. Such is the form in which the

Seer's visions take possession of his mind; and it will be seen that the mould of thought is precisely the same as that of chap. xx. The fact that it is so may be regarded as a proof that the interpretation yet to be offered of that chapter is correct.

It may be further noticed that the beast's being brought to nought and being sent into the abyss takes place under the sixth, or Roman, head. We know that this was actually the case, because it was under the Roman government that our Lord gained His victory. The history of the beast, however, does not close with this defeat. He must rise again; and he does this as the seventh head, which is associated with the ten horns. In them and "with" them he assumes a greater power than ever, gaining all the additional force which is connected with a resurrection life. The objection may indeed be made that such an exposition is not in correspondence either with the view taken in this commentary that the beast is active from the very beginning of the Christian era, or with those facts of history which show that, instead of falling, Rome continued to exist for a lengthened period after the completion of the Redeemer's victory.

But, as to the first of these difficulties, it is not necessary to think that the beast rages in his highest and ultimate form from the very instant when Jesus rose from the dead and ascended to His Father. That was rather the moment of the beast's destruction, the moment when, under the sixth head, he "is and is not;" and a certain extent of time must be interposed before he rises in his new, or seventh, head. The Seer, too, deals largely in climax; and, although in doing so he is always occupied with the climactic idea rather than with the time needed for its manifestation, the element of time, if our attention is called to it, must be allowed its place. Now in the development of the beast there is climax. In chap. xi. 7 it is said that "the beast that cometh up out of the abyss shall make war with" the two faithful witnesses "when they shall have finished their testimony," and this finishing of their testimony implies time. Again, in chap. xii. 17 the increased wrath of the dragon against the remnant of the woman's seed appears to be subsequent to the persecution of the woman in the same chapter. [464] No doubt the thought of the increased wrath of the dragon is the main point, but it may be quite truly said that some time at least is needed for the increase. The view, therefore, that the beast rages from the beginning of the Christian era, from the moment when he rises after his fall, or, in other words, is loosed after having been shut up into the abyss, is not inconsistent with the view that his rage goes on augmenting until it attains its culminating point.

The answer to the second difficulty is to be found in the consideration that to the Seer the whole Christian era appears no more than "a little season," in which events must follow closely on one another, so closely that the time required for their evolution passes almost entirely, if not indeed entirely, out of his field of vision. He has no thought that Rome will last for centuries. "The times or the seasons the Father hath set within His own authority." [465] The guilt of Rome is so dark and frightful that the Seer can fix his mind upon nothing but that overthrow which shall be the just punishment of her crimes. She is not to be doomed; she is doomed. She is not to perish; she is perishing. Divine vengeance has already overtaken her. Her last hour is come; and the ten kings who are to follow her are already upon their thrones. Thus these kings come into immediate juxtaposition with the beast in that last stage of his history which had begun, but had not reached its greatest intensity, before Rome is supposed to fall.

2. The second figure of this chapter now meets us; and we have to ask, Who is the woman that sits on the beast? or, What is meant by Babylon?

No more important question can be asked in connexion with the interpretation of the Apocalypse. The thought of Babylon is evidently one by which the writer is moved to a greater than ordinary degree. Twice already have we had premonitions of her doom, and that in language which shows how deeply it was felt. [466] In the passage before us he is awed by the contemplation of her splendour and her guilt. And in chap. xviii. he describes the lamentation of the world over her fate in language of almost unparalleled sublimity and pathos. What is Babylon? We must make up our minds upon the point, or the effort to interpret one of the most important parts of the Revelation of St. John can result in nothing but defeat.

Very various opinions have been entertained as to the meaning of Babylon, of which the most famous are that the word is a name for papal Rome, pagan Rome, or a great world-city of the future which shall stand to the whole earth in a relation similar to that occupied by Rome towards the world of its day. These opinions cannot be discussed here; and no more can be attempted than to show, with as much brevity as possible, that by Babylon is to be understood the degenerate Church, or that principle of degenerate religion which allies itself with the world, and more than all else brings dishonour upon the name and the cause of Christ.

(1) Babylon is the representative of religious, not civil, degeneracy and wickedness. She is a harlot, and her name is associated with the most reckless and unrestrained fornication. But fornication and adultery are throughout the Old Testament the emblem of religious degeneracy, and not of civil misrule. In numerous passages familiar to every reader of Scripture both terms are employed to describe the departure of Israel from the worship of Jehovah and a holy life to the worship of idols and the degrading sensuality by which such worship was everywhere accompanied. Nor ought we to imagine

that adultery, not fornication, is the most suitable expression for religious degeneracy. In some important respects the latter is the more suitable of the two. It brings out more strongly the ideas of playing the harlot with "many lovers" [467] and of sinning for "hire." [468] In this sense then it seems proper to understand the charge of fornication brought in so many passages of the Apocalypse against Babylon. Not in their civil, but in their religious, aspect have the kings of the earth committed fornication with her, and they that dwell on the earth been made drunk with the wine of her fornication. Her sin has been that of leading men astray from the worship of the true God, and of substituting for the purity and unworldliness of Christian living the irreligious and worldly spirit of the "earth." To this it may be added that, had Babylon not been the symbol of religious declension, she could hardly have borne upon her forehead the term mystery. St. John could not have used a word connected only with religious associations to express anything but a religious state awakening the awe, and wonder, and perplexity of a religious mind. Babylon, therefore, represents persons who are not only sinful, but who have fallen into sin by treachery to a high and holy standard formerly acknowledged by them.

(2) We have already had occasion to allude to a fact which must immediately receive further notice,--that to the eye of St. John there is an aspect of Jerusalem different from that in which she is regarded as the holy and beloved city of God. Jerusalem in that aspect and Babylon are one. Each is "the great city," and the same epithet could not be applied to both were they not to be identified. Not only so. The words here used of Babylon lead us directly to what our Lord once said of Jerusalem. "Therefore," said Jesus, "behold, I send unto you prophets, and wise men, and scribes: some of them shall ye kill and crucify; and some of them shall ye scourge in your synagogues, and persecute from city to city: that upon you may come all the righteous blood shed on the earth, from the blood of Abel the righteous unto the blood of Zachariah son of Barachiah, whom ye slew between the sanctuary and the altar. Verily I say unto you, All these things shall come upon this generation." [469] Precisely similar to this is the language of the Seer, And I saw the woman drunken with the blood of the saints, and with the blood of the martyrs of Jesus.

It may indeed be thought impossible that under any circumstances whatever St. John could have applied an epithet like that of Babylon, steeped in so many associations of lust, and bloodshed, and oppression, to the metropolis of Israel, the city of God. But in this very book he has illustrated the reverse. He has already spoken of Jerusalem as represented by names felt by a pious Jew to be the most terrible of the Old Testament,--"Sodom and Egypt." [470] The prophets before him had employed language no less severe. "Hear the word of the Lord," said Isaiah, addressing the inhabitants of the holy city, "ye rulers of Sodom; give ear unto the law of our God, ye people of Gomorrah," [471] and again, "How is the faithful city become an harlot, she that was full of judgment! righteousness lodged in her; but now murderers;" [472] whilst the degenerate metropolis of Israel is not unfrequently painted by Jeremiah and Ezekiel and other prophets in colours than which none more dark or repulsive can be conceived.

In forming a conclusion upon this point, it is necessary to bear in mind that to the eye of the faithful in Israel, and certainly of St. John, there were two Jerusalems, the one true, the other false, to its heavenly King; and that in exact proportion to the feelings of admiration, love, and devotion with which they turned to the one were those of pain, indignation, and alienation with which they turned from the other. The latter Jerusalem, the city of "the Jews," is that of which the Apocalyptist thinks when he speaks of it as Babylon; and, looking upon the city in this aspect as he did, the whole language of the Old Testament fully justifies him in applying to it the opprobrious name.

(3) The contrast between the new Jerusalem and Babylon leads to the same conclusion. We have already more than once had occasion to allude to the principle of antithesis, or contrast, as affording an important rule of interpretation in many passages of this book. Nowhere is it more distinctly marked or more applicable than in the case before us. The contrast has been drawn out by a recent writer in the following words:--

"These prophecies present two broadly contrasted women, identified with two broadly contrasted cities, one reality being in each case doubly represented: as a woman and as a city. The harlot and Babylon are one; the bride and the heavenly Jerusalem are one.

"The two women are contrasted in every particular that is mentioned about them: the one is pure as purity itself, 'made ready' and fit for heaven's unsullied holiness, the other foul as corruption could make her, fit only for the fires of destruction.

"The one belongs to the Lamb, who loves her as the bridegroom loves the bride; the other is associated with a wild beast, and with the kings of the earth, who ultimately hate and destroy her.

"The one is clothed with fine linen, and in another place is said to be clothed with the sun and crowned with a coronet of stars: that is, robed in Divine righteousness and resplendent with heavenly glory; the other is attired in scarlet and gold, in jewels and pearls, gorgeous indeed, but with earthly splendour only. The one is represented as a chaste virgin, espoused to Christ; the other is mother of harlots and abominations of the earth.

"The one is persecuted, pressed hard by the dragon, driven into the wilderness, and well-nigh overwhelmed; the other is drunken with martyr blood, and seated on a beast which has received its power from the persecuting dragon.

"The one sojourns in solitude in the wilderness; the other reigns 'in the wilderness' over peoples, and nations, and kindreds, and tongues.

"The one goes in with the Lamb to the marriage supper, amid the glad hallelujahs; the other is stripped, insulted, torn, and destroyed by her guilty paramours.

"We lose sight of the bride amid the effulgence of heavenly glory and joy, and of the harlot amid the gloom and darkness of the smoke that 'rose up for ever and ever.'" [473]

A contrast presented in so many striking particulars leaves only one conclusion possible. The two cities are the counterparts of one another. But we know that by the first is represented the bride, the Lamb's wife, or the true Church of Christ as, separated from the world, she remains faithful to her Lord, is purified from sin, and is made meet for that eternal home into which there enters nothing that defiles. What can the other be but the representative of a false and degenerate Church, of a Church that has yielded to the temptations of the world, and has turned back in heart from the trials of the wilderness to the flesh-pots of Egypt? Every feature of the description answers, although with the heightened colour of ideal portraiture, to what such a professing but degenerate Church becomes,--the pride, the show, the love of luxury, the subordination of the future to the present. Even her very cruelty to the poor saints of God is drawn from actual reality, and has been depicted upon many a page of history. With the meek and lowly followers of Jesus, whose life is a constant protest that the things of time are nothing in comparison with those of eternity, none have less sympathy than those who have a name to live while they are dead. The world may admire, even while it cannot understand, these little ones, these lambs of the flock; but to those who seek the life that now is by the help of the life that is to come they are a perpetual reproach, and they are felt to be so. Therefore they are persecuted in such manner and to such degree as the times will tolerate.

One other remark has to be made upon the identification of Jerusalem and Babylon by the Seer. It has been said that he has one special aspect of the metropolis of Israel in his eye. Yet we are not to suppose that he confines himself to that metropolis. As on so many other occasions, he starts from what is limited and local only to pass in thought to what is unlimited and universal. His Jerusalem, his Babylon, is not the literal city. She is "the great harlot that sitteth upon many waters;" and "the waters which thou sawest," says the angel to the Seer, "are peoples, and multitudes, and nations, and tongues." [474] The fourfold division guides us, as usual, to the thought of dominion over the whole earth. Babylon is not the Jerusalem only of "the Jews." She is the great Church of God throughout the world when that Church becomes faithless to her true Lord and King.

Babylon then is not pagan Rome. No doubt seven mountains are spoken of on which the woman sitteth. But this was not peculiar to Rome. Both Babylon and Jerusalem are also said to have been situated upon seven hills; and even if we had before us, as we certainly may have, a distinct reference to Rome, it would be only because Rome was one of the manifestations of the beast, and because the city afforded a suitable point of departure for a wider survey. The very closing words of the chapter, upon which so much stress is laid by those who find the harlot in pagan Rome, negative, instead of justifying, the supposition: And the woman whom thou sawest is the great city, which reigneth over the kings of the earth. Rome never possessed such universal dominion as is here referred to. She may illustrate, but she cannot exhaust, that subtler, more penetrating, and more widespread spirit which is in the Seer's view.

Again, Babylon cannot be papal Rome. As in the last case, there may indeed be a most intimate connexion between her and one of the manifestations of Babylon. But it is impossible to speak of the papal Church as the guide, the counsellor, and the inspirer of anti-christian efforts to dethrone the Redeemer, and to substitute the world or the devil in His stead. The papal Church has toiled, and suffered, and died for Christ. Babylon never did so.

Nor, finally, can we think of Babylon as a great city of the future which shall stand to the kings and kingdoms of the earth in a relation similar to that in which ancient Rome stood to the kings and kingdoms of her day. Wholly apart from the impossibility of our forming any clear conception of such a city, the want of the religious or spiritual element is fatal to the theory.

One explanation alone seems to meet the conditions of the case. Babylon is the world in the Church. In whatever section of the Church, or in whatever age of her history, an unspiritual and earthly element prevails, there is Babylon.

We have spoken of the two great figures of this chapter separately. We have still to speak of their relation to one another, and of the manner in which it is brought suddenly and for ever to a close.

This relation appears in the words, I saw a woman sitting upon a scarlet-coloured beast, and in later words of the chapter: the beast that carrieth her. The woman then is not subordinate to the beast, but is rather his controller and guide. And this relation is precisely what we should expect. The beast is before us in his final stage, in that immediately preceding his own destruction. He is no longer in the form of Egypt, or Assyria, or Babylonia, or Persia, or Greece, or Rome. These six forms of his manifestation have passed away. The restrainer has been withdrawn, [475] and the beast has stepped forth in the plenitude of his power. He has been revealed as the "ten horns" which occupy the place of the seventh head; and these ten horns are ten kings who, having now received their kingdoms and with their kingdoms their diadems, are the actual manifestation in history of the beast as he had been seen in his ideal form in chap. xiii. The beast is therefore the spirit of the world, partly in its secularising influence, partly in its brute force, in that tyranny and oppression which it exercises against the children of God. The woman, again, is the spirit of false religion and religious zeal, which had shown itself under all previous forms of worldly domination, and which was destined to show itself more than ever under the last. To the eye of St. John this spirit was not confined to Christian times. The woman, considered in herself, is not simply the false Christian Church. She is so at the moment when we behold her on the field of history. But St. John did not believe that saving truth, the truth which unites us to Christ, the truth which is "of God," was to be found in Christianity alone. It had existed in Judaism. It had existed even in Heathenism, for in his Gospel he remembers and quotes the words of our Lord in which Jesus says, "And other sheep I have, which are not of this fold: them also I must bring, and they shall hear My voice; and they shall become one flock, one Shepherd." [476] As then Divine truth, the light which never ceases to contend with the darkness, had been present in the world under every one of its successive kingdoms, so also perversions of that truth had never failed to be present by its side. All along the line of past history, in Heathenism as well as in Judaism, the ideal bride of Christ had been putting on her ornaments to meet the Bridegroom; and not less all along the same line had the harlot been arraying herself in purple and scarlet and decking herself with gold and precious stones and jewels, that she might tempt men to resist the influence of their rightful King. The harlot had been always thus superior to the beast. The beast had only the powers of this world at his command; the harlot wielded the powers of another and a higher world. The one dealt only with the seen and temporal, the other with the unseen and eternal, the one with material forces, the other with those spiritual forces which reach the profoundest depths of the human heart and give rise to the greatest movements of human history. The woman is therefore superior to the beast. She inspires and animates him. The beast only lends her the material strength needed for the execution of her plans. In the war, accordingly, which is carried on by the ten kings who have one mind, and who give their power and authority unto the beast, in the war which the beast and they, with their combined power, wage for one hour against the Lamb, it would be a great mistake to suppose that the woman, although she is not mentioned, takes no part and exerts no influence. She is really there, the prime mover in all its horrors. The "one mind" comes from her. The beast can do nothing of himself. The ten kings who are the form in which he appears are not less weak and helpless. They have the outward power, but they cannot regulate it. They want the skill, the subtlety, the wisdom, which are found only in the spiritual domain. But the great harlot, who at this point of history is the perversion of Christian truth, is with them; and they depend on her. Such is the first part of the relation between the beast and the harlot.

A second, most unexpected and most startling, follows.

We have seen that in the war between the ten kings and the Lamb the woman is present. That war ends in disaster to her and to those whom she inspires. The Lamb shall overcome them: for He is Lord of lords, and King of kings. The name is the same as that which we shall afterwards meet in chap. xix. 16, though the order of the clauses is different. This Lamb, therefore, is here the Conqueror described in chap. xix. 11-16; and many particulars of these latter verses take us back to the Son of man as He appeared in chap. i., or, in other words, to the risen and glorified Redeemer. The thought of the risen Christ is thus in the mind of St. John when he speaks of the Lamb who shall overcome. The leaders of the Jewish Church had believed that they had for ever rid themselves of the Prophet who "tormenteth them that dwell on the earth." [477] They had sealed the stone, and set a watch, and returned to their homes for joy and merriment. But on the third morning there was a great earthquake, and the stone was rolled away from the door of the sepulchre; and the Crucified came forth, the Conqueror of death and Hades. Then the Lamb overcame. Then He began His victorious progress as King of kings and Lord of lords. Then the power and the wisdom of the world were alike put to shame. Was not this enough? No, for now follow the words which come upon us in a way so wholly unexpected: And the ten horns which thou sawest, and the beast, these shall hate the harlot, and shall make her desolate and naked, and shall eat her flesh, and shall burn her utterly with fire.

What is the meaning of these words? Surely not that Rome was to be attacked and overthrown by the barbaric hordes that burst upon her from the North: for, in the first place, the Roman manifestation of the world-power had passed away before the ten kings came to their kingdom; and, in the second place, when Rome fell, she fell as the beast, not as the harlot. Surely also not that a great world-city, concentrating in itself all the resources of the world-power, is to be hated and burned by its subjects, for we have already seen that this whole notion of a great world-city of the end is groundless; and the resources of the world-power are always in this book concentrated in the beast, and not in the harlot who directs their use. There seems only one method of explaining the words, but it is one in perfect consonance with the method and purpose of the Apocalypse as a whole. As on many other occasions, the fortunes of the Church of Christ are modelled upon the fortunes of her Master. With that Master the Church was one. He had always identified His people with Himself, in life and death, in time and in eternity. Could the beloved disciple do otherwise? He looked round upon the suffering Church of his day. He was a "companion with it in the tribulation, and kingdom, and patience which are in Jesus." [478] He felt all its wounds and shared all its sorrows, just as he felt and shared the wounds and sorrows of that Lord who lived in him, and in whom he lived. Here, therefore, was the mould in which the fortunes of the Church appeared to him. He went back to well-remembered scenes in the life of Christ; and he beheld these repeating themselves, in principle at least, in the members of His Body.

Now there was one scene of the past--how well does he remember it, for he was present at the time!--when the Roman power and a degenerate Judaism, the beast and the harlot of the day, combined to make war upon the Lamb. For a moment they seemed to succeed, yet only for a moment. They nailed the Lamb to the cross; but the Lamb overcame them, and rose in triumph from the grave. But the Seer did not pause there. He looked a few more years onward, and what did he next behold? That wicked partnership was dissolved. These companions in crime had turned round upon one another. The harlot had counselled the beast, and the beast had given the harlot power, to execute the darkest deed which had stained the pages of human history. But the alliance did not last. The alienation of the two from each other, restrained for a little by co-operation in common crime, burst forth afresh, and deepened with each passing year, until it ended in the march of the Roman armies into Palestine, their investment of the Jewish capital, and that sack and burning of the city which still remain the most awful spectacle of bloodshed and of ruin that the world has seen. Even this is not all. St. John looks still further into the future, and the tragedy is repeated in the darker deeds of the last "hour." There will again be a "beast" in the brute power of the ten kings of the world, and a harlot in a degenerate Jerusalem, animating and controlling it. The two will again direct their united energies against the true Church of Christ, the "called, and chosen, and faithful." They may succeed; it will be only for a moment. Again the Lamb will overcome them; and in the hour of defeat the sinful league between them will be broken, and the world-power will hate the harlot, and make her desolate and naked, and eat her flesh, and burn her utterly with fire.

This is the prospect set before us in these words, and this the consolation of the Church under the trials that await her at the end of the age. "When the wicked spring as the grass, and all the workers of iniquity do flourish; it is that they shall be destroyed for ever: but Thou, O Lord, art on high for evermore. For, lo, Thine enemies, O Lord, for, lo, Thine enemies shall perish; all the workers of iniquity shall be scattered." [479]

Babylon is fallen, not indeed in a strictly chronological narrative, for she will again be spoken of as if she still existed upon earth. But for the time her overthrow has been consummated, her destruction is complete, and all that is good can only rejoice at the spectacle of her fate. Hence the opening verses of the next chapter.

Footnotes:

444. Comp. chaps. xiii. 1 and xvii. 3, 7.
445. Comp. chaps. xiii. 1 and xvii. 3.
446. Comp. chaps. xiii. 1 and xvii. 3, 12.
447. Comp. chaps. xiii. 1 and xvii. 8.
448. Comp. pp. 75, 199.
449. Chap. xvii. 12.
450. Chap. xvii. 12.
451. Chap. xvii. 11.
452. Chap. xiii. 2.
453. Chap. xii. 17.
454. Chap. xvii. 14.
455. Comp. p. 222.
456. Ver. 8.
457. Chap. i. 18.
458. Comp. chap. xiii. 3.
459. Chap. v. 6.
460. Comp. chaps. vi. 13; viii. 10; ix. 1; xi. 13; xiv. 8; xvi. 19; xviii. 2.
461. Comp. Dan. vii. 17, 23; Rev. xviii. 3.
462. Chap. xii. 12.
463. Dan. vii. 7, 8.
464. Chap. xii. 13.
465. Acts i. 7.
466. Chaps. xiv. 8; xvi. 19.

467. Jer. iii. 1.
468. Micah i. 7.
469. Matt. xxiii. 34-36.
470. Chap. xi. 8.
471. Isa. i. 10.
472. Isa. i. 21.
473. Guinness, The Approaching End of the Age, p. 143.
474. Chap. xvii. 15.
475. Comp. 2 Thess. ii. 7.
476. John x. 16.
477. Comp. chap. xi. 10.
478. Chap. i. 9.
479. Ps. xcii. 7-9.

CHAPTER XIV – THE FALL OF BABYLON

Rev. xviii.

Babylon has fallen. We have now the Divine proclamation of her fate, and the lamentation of the world over the doom to which she has been consigned:--

After these things I saw another angel coming down out of heaven, having great authority; and the earth was lightened with his glory. And he cried with a mighty voice, saying, Fallen, fallen is Babylon the great, and is become a habitation of devils, and a hold of every unclean spirit, and a hold of every unclean and hateful bird. For by the wine of the wrath of her fornication all the nations are fallen and the kings of the earth committed fornication with her, and the merchants of the earth waxed rich by the power of her wantonness (xviii. 1-3).

At chap. xvii. 1 we read of one of the angels that had the seven Bowls. The angel now introduced is another, or a second. We shall find as we proceed that we have entered upon a new series of seven parts, similar to that in chap. xiv., where six angels and their actions, three on either side, are grouped around One higher than angels, and forming the central figure of the movement. [480] The series is a long one, extending from chap. xvii. 1 to chap. xxii. 5, the central figure meeting us at chap. xix. 11; and again, as before, the fact ought to be carefully noticed, for it has a bearing on the interpretation of some of the most difficult sections of this book. Meanwhile we have to do with the second angel, whose action extends to ver. 20 of the present chapter.

The description given of this angel is proportioned to the importance of his message. He has great authority; the earth is lightened with his glory; the voice with which he cries is mighty. It could hardly be otherwise than that, with such joyful tidings as he bears to men, the "glory of the Lord should shine round about him, and a light from heaven above the brightness of the sun." [481] The tidings themselves follow, taken from the Old Testament accounts of the desolation that was to come upon Babylon: "And Babylon, the glory of kingdoms, the beauty of the Chaldeans' pride, shall be as when God overthrew Sodom and Gomorrah. It shall never be inhabited, neither shall it be dwelt in from generation to generation: neither shall the Arabian pitch tent there; neither shall shepherds make their flocks to lie down there. But wild beasts of the desert shall lie there; and their houses shall be full of doleful creatures; and ostriches shall dwell there, and satyrs shall dance there. And wolves shall cry in their castles, and jackals in the pleasant palaces." [482] In words such as these, though combined throughout both the present and following descriptions with expressions taken from the ruin of other famous and guilty cities of the Old Testament, we have the source whence the powerful and pathetic words of this chapter are drawn. The most terrible disasters of bygone times are but types of that wreck of all the grandeur of earth which we are now invited to behold, while Babylon's sinfulness is referred to that her fate may appear to be no more than her appropriate punishment.

At this point we are met by one of those sudden transitions, common in the Apocalypse, which so completely negative the idea of chronological arrangement. A cry is heard which seems to imply that Babylon has not yet fallen:--

And I heard another voice from heaven, saying, Come forth, My people, out of her, that ye have no fellowship with her sins, and that ye receive not of her plagues. For her sins have reached even unto heaven, and God hath remembered her iniquities. Render unto her even as she rendered, and double unto her the double according to her works: in the cup which she hath mingled mingle unto her double. How much soever she glorified herself, and waxed wanton, so much give her of torment and mourning: for she saith in her heart, I sit a queen, and am no widow, and shall in no wise see mourning. Therefore in one day shall her plagues come, death, and mourning, and famine; and she shall be utterly burned with fire: for strong is the Lord God which judged her (xviii. 4-8).

The first words of this voice from heaven deserve peculiar attention: Come forth, My people, out of her; that is, out of Babylon, the degenerate Church. We are at once reminded of the striking teaching of our Lord in chap. x. of the fourth Gospel, where He compares Himself to the "door" of the fold, not the door by which the sheep enter into, but by which they come out of, the fold. [483] We are also reminded of the blind man of chap. ix. of the same Gospel, whom our Lord "found" only after he had been "cast out" of the synagogue. [484] In the midst of the blinded theocracy of Israel in the days of Jesus there was a faithful, though small, remnant. It had been betrayed by the religious guides of the people, who had become "thieves and robbers," whom the true sheep did not know, and to whom they ought not to listen. Jesus came to call it out of the theocracy to Himself. Such was the spectacle which St. John had witnessed when his Master was in the world, and that experience is now repeated. The Church as a whole degenerates. Called to prepare men for the Second Coming of the Lord, and to teach them to live, not for the present, but the future, she becomes herself the victim of the present. She forgets that, in the absence of the Bridegroom, her days are days of fasting. She fails to realize the fact that until her Lord comes again her state is one of widowhood. And, instead of mourning, she sits as a queen, at ease and satisfied, proud of her pomp and jewellery. What is all this but a recurrence of the old events of history? The Apostle sees the future mirrored in the past; and he can only follow in his Master's footsteps, and call His Christian remnant out of Babylon.

The words are in the highest degree important for the interpretation and understanding of the Apocalypse. We have already found in more than one passage distinct traces of this double Church, of the true Church within the false, of the few living ones within the Body which had a name to live, but was dead. Here the distinction meets us in all its sharpness, and fresh light is cast upon passages that may have formerly seemed dark. "Many are called," "many" constituting the outward Church; but "few are chosen," "few" constituting the real Church, the Church which consists of the poor, and meek, and lowly. The two parts may keep together for a time, but the union cannot last; and the day comes when, as Christ called His sheep out of the Jewish, so He will again call His sheep out of the Christian "fold," that they may hear His voice, and follow Him.

Having summoned the true disciples of Jesus out of Babylon, the voice from heaven again proclaims in a double form, as sins and as iniquities, the guilt of the doomed city, and invites the ministers of judgment, according to the lex talionis, to render unto her double. The command may also be founded upon the law of the theocracy by which thieves and violent aggressors of the poor were required to make a double repayment to those whom they had injured, [485] or it may rest upon the remembrance of such threatenings as those by the prophet Jeremiah, "I will recompense their iniquity and their sin double." [486]

Judgment is next supposed to have been executed upon Babylon; and the Seer proceeds to describe in language of unexampled eloquence the lamentation of the world over the city's fall:--

And the kings of the earth, who committed fornication and lived wantonly with her, shall weep and wail over her, when they look upon the smoke of her burning, standing afar off for the fear of her torment, saying, Woe, woe, the great city Babylon, the strong city! for in one hour is thy judgment come. And the merchants of the earth weep and mourn over her; for no man buyeth their merchandise any more: merchandise of gold, and silver, and precious stone, and pearls, and fine linen, and purple, and silk, and scarlet, and all thyine wood, and every vessel of ivory, and every vessel made of most precious wood, and of brass, and iron, and marble, and cinnamon, and spice, and incense, and ointment, and frankincense, and wine, and oil, and fine flour, and wheat, and cattle, and sheep, and merchandise of horses, and chariots, and slaves, and souls of men. And the fruits which thy soul lusted after are gone from thee, and all things that were dainty and sumptuous are perished from thee, and men shall find them no more at all. The merchants of these things, who were made rich by her, shall stand afar off for the fear of her torment, weeping and mourning, saying, Woe, woe, the great city, she that was arrayed in fine linen, and purple, and scarlet, and decked with gold, and precious stone, and pearl! for in one hour so great riches is made desolate. And every shipmaster, and every one that saileth anywhither, and mariners, and as many as gain their living by sea, stood afar off, and cried out as they looked upon the smoke of her burning, saying, What city is like the great city? And they cast dust on their heads, and cried, weeping and mourning, saying, Woe, woe, the great city, wherein were made rich all that had their ships in the sea by reason of her costliness! for in one hour is she made desolate. Rejoice with her, thou heaven, and ye saints, and ye apostles, and ye prophets; for God hath judged your judgment on her (xviii. 9-20).

Three classes of persons are introduced to us: Kings, Merchants, and Sailors. All are of the earth; and each class, in its own strain, swells the voice of lamentation. The words are largely taken from the Old Testament, and more particularly from the description of the overthrow of Tyre in Ezekiel (chaps. xxvi., xxvii.). There is even a peculiar propriety in this latter reference, for Tyre was known by the prophets as another Babylon. In describing the "Burden of Tyre," Isaiah uses in one part of his description the words, "The city of confusion" (the meaning of the word Babylon) "is broken down." [487]

It is unnecessary to enter into any examination clause by clause of the passage before us. We shall better catch its spirit and be made sensible of its effect by attending to a few general observations upon the description as a whole.

1. Not without interest may we mark that the classes selected to mourn over the burning of the city are three in number. We have thus another illustration of the manner in which that number penetrates the structure of all the writings of St. John.

2. Emphasis is laid upon the fact that the city is burned. Her destruction by fire has indeed been more than once alluded to. Of the beast and the ten horns it had been said that "they shall burn her utterly with fire;" [488] and, again, it had been proclaimed by the voice from heaven that "she shall be utterly burned with fire." [489] We shall not venture to say with any measure of positiveness that the type of this "burning" is taken from the burning of Jerusalem by the Romans. It may have been taken from the burning of other cities by victorious enemies. But this much at least is obvious: that, in conjunction with the fact that Babylon is a harlot, destruction by fire leads us directly to the thought of the spiritual, and not simply the civil, or political, or commercial, character of the city. According to the law of Moses, burning appears to have been the punishment of fornication only in the case of a priest's daughter: "And the daughter of any priest, if she profane herself by playing the harlot, she shall be burnt with fire." [490]

3. Whether there is any other allusion to spiritual traffic in the lamentations before us it is not easy to say. Of one at least which may be quoted in this connexion the interpretation is uncertain. When the merchants of the earth weep and mourn over the loss of that merchandise which they now miss, they extend it, not only to articles of commerce bought and sold in an ordinary market, but to souls of men. It may be that, as often suggested, slavery alone is thought of. Yet it is highly improbable that such is the case. Rather may it be supposed to refer to that spiritual life which is destroyed by too much occupation with, and too engrossing interest in, the world. "The characteristic of this fornication is the selling themselves for gold, as the Greek word signifies. Therefore with such wonderful force and emphasis of accumulation is every species of this merchandise mentioned, running up all into one head: the souls of men. Like that in the prophet: 'Their land is full of silver and gold, neither is there any end of their treasures; their land also is full of horses, neither is there any end of their chariots; their land also is full of idols.' And it must be observed that all these things which are so minutely particularized as expressive of the meshes of that net by which men's souls are taken have also their place in the new Jerusalem, where every jewel is specified by name, and the gold of its streets, and the fine linen, and the incense, and the wine, and the oil, its white horses also. In both alike must they stand for spiritual merchandise of good and evil, the false riches and the true." [491]

The conclusion to be drawn is that Babylon is a spiritual city. That, as such, she is Jerusalem is further confirmed by the fact that, at the close of the chapter, it is said, And in her was found the blood of prophets, and of saints, and of all that have been slain upon the earth. Similar words met us in chap. xvii. 6; and here, as there, they unmistakeably remind us of the words already quoted in which our Lord describes the great city of the Jews. [492]

4. From all that has been said, it must be obvious that nothing is here spoken of Babylon inapplicable to Jerusalem when we think of this latter city in the light in which the Seer specially regards it. Jerusalem was indeed neither a commercial nor a maritime city, but Rome also was no city on the sea. A large part, therefore, of the details of St. John's description is not less destitute of force when applied, if applied literally, to the latter than to the former. On the other hand, these details are more applicable to Jerusalem than to Rome, if we remember that Jerusalem supplies, in a way impossible to Rome, the groundwork for a delineation of those religious forces which are far more wide-spreading in their reach, and far more crushing in their power, than the legions of the imperial metropolis.

Babylon then is fallen, and that with a sudden and swift destruction, a destruction indeed so sudden and so swift that each of the three companies that lament takes particular notice of the fact that in one hour did her judgment come. [493]

More, however, so important is the subject, has to be said; and we are introduced to the action of the third angel of the first group:--

And a strong angel took up a stone, as it were a great millstone, and cast it into the sea, saying, Thus with a mighty fall shall Babylon, the great city, be cast down, and shall be found no more at all. And the voice of harpers, and minstrels, and flute-players, and trumpeters, shall be heard no more at all in thee; and no craftsman, of whatsoever craft, shall be found any more at all in thee; and the voice of a millstone shall be heard no more at all in thee; and the voice of the bridegroom and of the bride shall be heard no more at all in thee: for with thy sorcery were all the nations deceived. And in her was found the blood of prophets, and of saints, and of all that have been slain upon the earth (xviii. 21-24).

Yet once again, it would seem, must we think of Babylon as to be destroyed rather than as destroyed already. So great is her guiltiness that the Seer again and again approaches it, and dwells, though from different points of view, upon the thought of her disastrous fate. In the present case it is less the method than the effect of her destruction that is before his eye, and nothing can be more touching than the light in which he presents it. At one moment we behold the city in her brightness, her gaiety, her rich and varied life. We hear the voice of her harpers, and minstrels, and flute-players, and trumpeters, all that can delight the ear accompanying all that can please the eye. Her craftsmen of every craft are busy at their work; and each shop in the great city resounds with the noise of the hammer, or the shuttle, or the other instruments of prosperous industry. The cheering sound of the millstone tells that there is food in her humbler dwellings. Her merchants, too, are the princes of the earth; innumerable lamps glitter in their halls and gardens; and the voice of the bridegroom and the bride is the pledge of her well-being and joy. The next moment the proud city is cast like a millstone into the sea; and all is silence, desolation, and ruin. The resources of language appear as if they had been exhausted to supply the description of so great a fall.

***

We have now reached the close of the longest and most important section of the Apocalypse, beginning, as has been already pointed out, with chap. vi. It is the fourth in that series of seven of which the book is composed; and the main purpose of St. John in writing finds expression in it. As the writer of the fourth Gospel describes in the fourth section of that book, extending from chap. v. to chap. xii., the conflict between the Son of God and "the Jews," so he describes in the corresponding section of the Apocalypse the conflict between the glorified Son of man as He lives and reigns in His Church and the evil of the world. Throughout the conflict we are not once permitted to forget that, although Christ and the true members of His Body may be the objects of attack, and may even have to retire for security from the field, God is on their side, and will never suffer His faithfulness to fail or forget His promises. In a threefold series of judgments the guilty world and the guilty Church are visited with the terrors of His wrath. These three series of judgments, too, go on in an ascending line. The climactic character of their contents has already been pointed out, and nothing more need be said of it. But it may be worth while to notice that the element of climax appears not less in the nature of the instruments employed. Comparing the Trumpets with the Seals, the simple fact that they are Trumpets indicates a higher, more exciting, more terrible unfolding of wrath. The Trumpet is peculiarly the warlike instrument, summoning the hosts to battle: "Thou hast heard, O my soul, the sound of the trumpet, the alarm of war;" "That day is a day of wrath, a day of trouble and distress, a day of wasteness and desolation, a day of darkness and gloominess, a day of clouds and thick darkness, a day of the trumpet and alarm against the fenced cities." [494] That the Bowls, again, are still more potent than the Trumpets, appears from the language in which they are described, from their mode of introduction, and from the vessels made use of for the plagues. They are "the last" plagues; in them is "finished" the wrath of God; they are called for by a "great voice out of the sanctuary;" and they proceed, not from a secular instrument, however warlike, but from a sacred vessel, not from one which must be sounded for a length of time before it produces its effect, but from one which, inverted in a moment, pours out with a sudden gush its terrors upon men. Similar though they thus are, the three series of judgments lose what might otherwise be their sameness; and the mind is invited to rest upon that most instructive lesson of the providence of God, that in proportion to privilege misused is the severity with which sin is punished. Throughout all these judgments the righteous are kept safe.

It will thus be observed that there is no strict chronological succession in the visions of this book. There is succession of a certain kind, succession in intensity of punishment. But we cannot assign one series of judgments to one period in the history of the Church or limit another to another. All the three series may continually fulfil themselves wherever persons are found of the character and disposition to which they severally apply.

But while these three series constitute the chief substance of the fourth, or leading, section of the seven into which the Apocalypse is divided, they do not exhaust the subject. The last series, in particular--that of the Bowls--has proceeded upon a supposition the most startling and pathetic by which the history of the Church is marked,--that "they are not all Israel which are of Israel," that tares have mingled with the wheat, and that the spirit of Babylon has found its way into the heart of the city of God. A phenomenon so unexpected and so melancholy stands in need of particular examination, and that examination is given in the description of the character and fate of Babylon. The remarks already made upon this point need not be repeated. It may be enough to remind the reader that in no part of his whole book is the Seer more deeply moved, and that in none does he rise to strains of more powerful and touching eloquence. Yet what is chiefly required of us is to open our minds to the full impression of the fact that Babylon does fall, deep in ruin as in guilt, and that with her fall the conflict ends.

Footnotes:

480. Kliefoth seems to have been the first to point this out.
481. Luke ii. 9; Acts xxvi. 13.
482. Isa. xiii. 19-22.
483. John x. 7.
484. John ix. 35.
485. Exod. xxii. 4, 7, 9.
486. Jer. xvi. 18.
487. Isa. xxiv. 10.
488. Chap. xvii. 16.
489. Chap. xviii. 8.
490. Lev. xxi. 9.
491. Isaac Williams, The Apocalypse, with Notes, etc., p. 360.
492. Matt. xxiii. 35. Comp. p. 291.
493. Vers. 10, 17, 19.
494. Jer. iv. 19; Zeph. i. 15, 16.

CHAPTER XV – THE PAUSE OF VICTORY AND JUDGMENT OF THE BEAST AND THE FALSE PROPHET

Rev. xix.

Those who have followed with attention the course of this commentary can hardly fail to have observed its leading conception of the book with which it deals. That conception is that the Revelation of St. John presents to us in visions the history of the Church moulded upon the history of her Lord whilst He tabernacled among men. It is the invariable lesson of the New Testament that Christ and His people are one. He is the Vine; they are the branches. He is in them; they are in Him. With equal uniformity the sacred writers teach us that just as Christ suffered during the course of His earthly ministry, so also His people suffer. They have to endure the struggle before they enjoy the victory, and to bear the cross before they win the crown. But the peculiarity of the Apocalypse is, that it carries out this thought much more fully than the other New Testament books. St. John does not merely see the Church suffer. He sees her suffer in a way precisely as her Lord did. He lives in the thought of those words spoken by Jesus to Salome at a striking moment of his life with regard to his brother and himself, "The cup that I drink ye shall drink; and with the baptism that I am baptized withal shall ye be baptized." [495] That very cup is put into his hands and into the hands of his brethren, who are "partakers with him in the tribulation, and kingdom, and patience which are in Jesus;" [496] with that very baptism they are all baptized.

Now we know from the fourth Gospel what the light was in which St. John looked back, at a distance of more than half a century, upon the life of Jesus. Nothing therefore was more natural than that, dealing only with the great principles at work in God's government of the world and guidance of His Church, and seeing these principles embodied in visions, the visions should present to him a course of things precisely similar to that which had been followed in the case of the Forerunner of the Church and the Captain of her salvation.

Turning then to the fourth Gospel, it has long been acknowledged by every inquirer of importance that the struggle of Jesus with the world, which the Evangelist chiefly intends to relate, ends with the close of chap. xii. It is equally undeniable that with the beginning of chap. xviii. the struggle breaks out afresh. Between these two points lie chaps. xiii. to xvii., five chapters altogether different from those that either precede or follow them, marked by a different tone, and centring around that institution of the Last Supper in which, Judas having now "gone out," the love of Jesus to His disciples is poured forth with a tenderness previously unexampled. In these chapters we have first a narrative in which the love of Jesus is related as it appears in the foot-washing and in the institution of the Supper, and then, immediately afterwards, a pause. This pause--chaps. xiii. 31-xvii.--together with the narrative preceding it, occurs at the close of a struggle substantially finished--"I glorified Thee on the earth, having accomplished the work which Thou hast given Me to do" [497] --and only yet again to burst forth in one final and unsuccessful effort against the Prince of life.

It would seem as if we had a similar structure at the point of the Apocalypse now reached by us. There is a transition narrative which, so far as the thought in it is concerned, may be regarded either as closing the fourth or as beginning the fifth section of the book. It is probably better to understand it as the latter, because the mould of the Gospel is thus better preserved; and, where so much else speaks distinctly of that mould, there is no impropriety in giving the benefit of a doubt to what is otherwise sufficiently established. Although therefore the fifth section of the Apocalypse, the Pause, begins properly with ver. 11 of the present chapter, the first ten verses may be taken along with these as a preparatory narrative standing to what follows as John xiii. 1-30 stands to chap. xiii. 31-chap. xvii. The probability, too, that this is the light in which we are to look at the passage before us, is rendered greater when we notice, first, that there is in the midst of the preliminary narrative, and for the first time mention made of a "supper," the marriage supper of the Lamb, [498] and, secondly, that at a later point in the book there is a final outburst of evil against the Church, which, notwithstanding the powerful forces ranged against her, is unsuccessful. [499]

What we have now to do with is thus not a continuation of the struggle. It is a pause in which the fall of Babylon is celebrated, and the great enemies of the Church are consigned to their merited fate:--

After these things I heard as it were a great voice of a great multitude in heaven, saying, Hallelujah; Salvation, and glory, and power, belong to our God: for true and righteous are His judgments: for He hath judged the great harlot, which did corrupt the earth with her fornication, and He hath avenged the blood of His servants at her hand. And a second time they say, Hallelujah. And her smoke goeth up for ever and ever. And the four-and-twenty elders and the four living creatures fell down and worshipped God that sitteth on the throne, saying, Amen; Hallelujah. And a voice came forth from the throne, saying, Give praise to our God, all ye His servants, ye that fear Him, the small and the great. And I heard as it were the voice of a great multitude, and as the voice of many waters, and as the voice of mighty thunders, saying, Hallelujah: for the Lord our God, the Almighty, reigneth. Let us rejoice and be exceeding glad, and let us give the glory unto Him: for the marriage of the Lamb is come, and His wife hath made herself ready. And it was given unto her that she should clothe herself in fine linen, bright and pure: for the fine linen is the righteous acts of the saints. And he saith unto me, Write, Blessed are they which are bidden unto the marriage supper of the Lamb. And he saith unto me, These are true words of God. And I fell down before his feet to worship him. And he saith unto me, See thou do it not: I am a fellow-servant with thee and with thy brethren that hold the testimony of Jesus: worship God: for the testimony of Jesus is the spirit of prophecy (xix. 1-10).

Babylon has fallen; and the world, represented by three classes of its inhabitants--kings, merchants, and sailors--has poured out its lamentations over her fall. Very different are the feelings of the good, and these feelings appear in the narrative before us. A great multitude is heard in heaven, not necessarily in the region beyond the grave, but in that of the righteous, of the unworldly, of the spiritual, whether in time or in eternity. This "multitude" is probably to be identified with that of chap. vii. 9. The definite article, which would render the identification complete, is indeed wanting; but we have already found instances of the same method of speech with regard to the one hundred and forty and four thousand of chap. xiv. 1, and with regard to the glassy sea of chap. xv. 2. The whole ransomed Church of God is therefore included in the expression. They sing first; and the burden of their song is Hallelujah, or Praise to God, because He has inflicted upon the harlot the due punishment of her sins and crimes. Nor do they sing only once; they sing the same ascription of praise a second time. The meaning is not simply that they do this twice, the "second time" having more than its numerical force, and being designed to bring out the intensity of their feelings and their song. [500] Then the four-and-twenty elders, the representatives of the glorified Church, and the four living creatures, the representatives of redeemed creation, answer, Amen, and take up the same song: Hallelujah. All creation, animate and inanimate, swells the voice of joy and praise.

Meanwhile the smoke of the harlot's torment goeth up for ever and ever. Again, as once before, [501] we have here no right to fasten our thoughts upon immortal spirits of men deceived and led astray. Such may be included. If they have identified themselves with the harlot, we need not hesitate to say that they are induced. But what is mainly brought under our notice is the overthrow, complete and final, of sin itself. Babylon has been utterly overthrown, and her punishment shall never be forgotten. Her fate shall remain a monument of the righteous judgment of God, and shall illustrate unto the ages of the ages the character of Him who, for creation's sake, will "by no means clear the guilty." [502]

A voice from heaven is then heard calling upon all the servants of God to praise Him; and this is followed by another voice, as it were the voice of a great multitude, and as the voice of many waters, and as the voice of mighty thunders, saying, Hallelujah: for the Lord our God, the Almighty, reigneth. He always indeed really reigned, but now He has taken to Himself His great power, and everything acknowledges its King.

Thus a new moment is reached in the history of God's saints. The Lamb is come to claim His bride, and His wife hath made herself ready. She has been long betrothed, and has been waiting for the Bridegroom. Through storm and calm, through sorrow and joy, through darkness and light, she has waited for Him, crying ever and again, "Come quickly." At last He comes, and the marriage and the marriage supper are to take place. For the first time in the Apocalypse we read of this marriage, and for the first time, although the general idea of supping with the Lord had been once alluded to, [503] of this marriage supper. The figure indeed is far from being new. The writers both of the Old and of the New Testament use it with remarkable frequency. [504] But no sacred writer appears to have felt more the power and beauty of the similitude than St. John. In the first miracle which he records, and in which he sees the whole glory of the New Testament dispensation mirrored forth, He who changed the water into wine is the Bridegroom of His Church [505] ; and, when the Baptist passes out of view in the presence of Him for whom he had prepared the way, he records the swan-like song in which the great prophet terminated his mission in order that another and a higher than himself might have sole possession of the field: "Ye yourselves bear me witness, that I said, I am not the Christ, but that I am sent before Him. He that hath the bride is the bridegroom: but the friend of the bridegroom, which standeth and heareth him, rejoiceth greatly because of the bridegroom's voice: this my joy therefore is fulfilled." [506]

Such is the moment that has now arrived, and the bride is ready for it. Her raiment is worthy of our notice. It is fine linen, bright and pure; and then it is immediately added, for the fine linen is the righteous acts of the saints. These acts are not the imputed righteousness of Christ, although only in Christ are the acts performed. They express the moral and religious condition of those who constitute the bride. No outward righteousness alone, with which we might be clothed as with a garment, is a sufficient preparation for future blessedness. An inward change is not less necessary, a personal and spiritual meetness for the inheritance of the saints in light. Christ must not only be on us as a robe, but in us as a life, if we are to have the hope of glory. [507] Let us not be afraid of words like these. Rightly viewed, they in no way interfere with our completeness in the Beloved alone, or with the fact that not by works of righteousness that we have done, but by grace, are we saved through faith, and that not of ourselves; it is the gift of God. [508] All our salvation is of Christ, but the change upon us must be internal as well as external. The elect are foreordained to be conformed to the image of God's Son [509] ; and the Christian condition is expressed in the words which say, not only "Ye were justified," but also "ye were washed, ye were sanctified in the name of the Lord Jesus Christ, and in the Spirit of our God." [510]

Thus "made ready," the bride now enters with the Bridegroom into the marriage feast; and, as the whole of her future rises before the view of the heavenly visitant who converses with the Seer, he says to him, Write, Blessed are they which are bidden to the marriage supper of the Lamb.

Once before St. John had heard a similar, perhaps the same, voice from heaven, saying, "Blessed are the dead which die in the Lord from henceforth." [511] Then we believed; now we see. The clouds are dispelled; the veil is rent asunder; we enter into the palace of the great King. There is music, and festivity, and joy. There is neither sin nor sorrow, no privilege abused, no cloud upon any countenance, no burden upon any heart, no shadow from the future to darken the rapture of the present. Here is life, and life abundantly; the peace that passeth understanding; the joy unspeakable and glorified; the inheritance incorruptible, undefiled, and unfading.

In particular, when we think of this marriage supper of the Lamb, we cannot but return to that supper in the upper chamber of Jerusalem which occupies so strikingly similar a position in the life of Jesus. There Jesus said, "Take, eat: this is My body, which is for you;" "This cup is the new covenant in My blood: drink ye all of it." [512] That was a feast, in which He gave Himself to be for ever the nourishment of His Church. And in like manner in the marriage supper of the Lamb the Lord who became dead and is alive for evermore is not only the Bridegroom, but the substance of the feast. In Him and by Him His people lived on earth; in Him and by Him they live for ever.

All this St. John saw. All this, too, he heard confirmed by the statement that, wonderful and glorious as was the spectacle, it was yet true words of God. He was overwhelmed, and would have worshipped his angelic visitant. But he was interrupted by the declaration on the angel's part, See thou do it not: I am a fellow-servant with thee and with thy brethren that hold the testimony of Jesus: worship God. These fellow-servants are first the prophets, but then also all true members of Christ's Body. The last not less than the first hold the testimony of Jesus [513] ; and because they do so, they too are prophets, for prophecy, whether in Old or in New Testament times, testifies to Him. In Him all revelation centres. He is the expression of the God whom no man hath seen. He is thus the Alpha and the Omega, "over all, God blessed for ever." [514]

By so contemplating Him we are prepared for the next following vision:--

And I saw the heavens opened, and behold a white horse, and He that sat thereon, called Faithful and True; and in righteousness He doth judge and make war. And His eyes are a flame of fire, and upon His head are many diadems; and He hath a name written, which no man knoweth, but He Himself. And He is arrayed in a garment sprinkled with blood: and His name is called The Word of God. And the armies which are in heaven followed Him upon white horses, clothed in fine linen, white and pure. And out of His mouth proceedeth a sharp sword, that with it He should smite the nations and He shall rule them with a rod of iron: and He treadeth the winepress of the fierceness of the wrath of Almighty God. And He hath on His garment and on His thigh a name written, King of kings, and Lord of lords (xix. 11-16).

Of the position of this passage in the structure of the Apocalypse we have already spoken; and, looked at in that its true light, it may be called the Pause of Victory. There is no renewal of the struggle. A Warrior is indeed presented to us; but He is a Warrior who has already conquered, and who comes forth not so much to subdue His enemies as to inflict upon them their final punishment.

Heaven is open, and our attention is first of all directed to a rider upon a white horse. The description given of this rider leaves no doubt as to who He is. The "whiteness" of the horse is the emblem of a purity that can be connected with the kingdom of God alone. The description of the Rider--Faithful, who will not suffer one word that He has promised to fail; True, not true as opposed to false, but real as opposed to shadowy--corresponds only to something essentially Divine; while the particulars of His appearance afterwards mentioned take us back to the glorified Son of man of chap. i., and to other passages of this and other books of the Bible which speak of the same glorious Person. There are the eyes like a flame of fire of chap. i. 14 and chap. ii. 18. There are upon His head many diadems, a fact not previously mentioned, but corresponding to the many royalties which belong to Him whom all things obey. There is the name which none but He Himself knoweth, for "no one knoweth the Son save the Father." [515] There is the garment sprinkled with blood, of which we read in the prophet Isaiah, [516] the blood, not that of the Conqueror shed for us, but the blood of His enemies staining His raiment as He returns victorious from the field. There is the name The Word of God, with which St. John alone has made us familiar in the opening of his Gospel. There are the armies which are in heaven, following Him upon white horses, and clothed in fine linen, white and pure, to which our attention is directed, not for their sake, but for His, for He has made them partakers of His victory. There is the sharp sword proceeding out of His mouth of chap. i. 16 and chap. ii. 12. There is the smiting of the nations, of which we have already heard in chap. ii. 27 and chap. xii. 5. There is the treading of the winepress of the fierceness of the wrath of Almighty God, spoken of in chap. xiv. 19, 20. Finally, there is on His garment and on His thigh the name King of kings, and Lord of lords. All these traits leave no doubt who this Captain of salvation is; and all are noted that we may better understand both the glory of His person, and the nature of His accomplished work.

One thing therefore alone remains: that the great adversaries of His people shall be consigned to their doom; and to this the Seer proceeds:--

And I saw an angel standing in the sun; and he cried with a loud voice, saying to all the birds that fly in mid-heaven, Come and be gathered together unto the great supper of God; that ye may eat the flesh of kings, and the flesh of captains, and the flesh of mighty men, and the flesh of horses, and of them that sit thereon, and the flesh of all men, both free and bond, and small and great. And I saw the beast, and the kings of the earth, and their armies, gathered together to make war against Him that sat upon the horse, and against His army. And the beast was taken, and he that was with him, the false prophet that wrought the signs in his sight, wherewith he deceived them that had received the mark of the beast, and them that worshipped his image. They twain were cast alive into the lake of fire that burneth with brimstone. And the rest were killed with the sword of Him that sat upon the horse, even the sword which came forth out of His mouth: and all the birds were filled with their flesh (xix. 17-21).

The angel beheld at the beginning of this scene is the first of the three forming the second group of that series of seven parts of which the triumphing Conqueror was the centre. He stood in the sun, which is to be thought of as in the zenith of its daily path, in order that he may be seen and heard by all. It is to the birds that fly in mid-heaven that he calls; that is, to those strong and fierce birds of prey, such as the eagle and the vulture, which fly in the highest regions of the atmosphere. His cry is that they shall come to the great supper of God, that they may feast upon the flesh of all the enemies of the Lamb. The idea of such a feast is found in the prophecies of Ezekiel; and there can be no doubt, from the many accompanying circumstances of similarity between the description of it there and here, that St. John has the language of the prophet in his eye: "And, thou son of man, thus saith the Lord God; Speak unto the birds of every sort, and to every beast of the field, Assemble yourselves, and come; gather yourselves on every side to My sacrifice that I do sacrifice for you, even a great sacrifice upon the mountains of Israel, that ye may eat flesh, and drink blood. Ye shall eat the flesh of the mighty, and drink the blood of the princes of the earth, of rams, of lambs, and of goats, of bullocks, all of them fatlings of Bashan. And ye shall eat fat till ye be full, and drink blood till ye be drunken, of My sacrifice which I have sacrificed for you. And ye shall be filled at My table with horses and chariots, with mighty men, and with all men of war, saith the Lord God." [517] Yet, while the picture of the prophet is unquestionably before the Seer's mind, it is impossible to doubt that we have in this supper a travesty of that marriage supper of the Lamb which had been spoken of in the previous part of the chapter. [518] In contrast with the joyful banquet at which the children of God shall be nourished by Him whose flesh is meat indeed and whose blood is drink indeed, the wicked, to whatever rank or station they belong, shall themselves be a meal for all foul and ravenous birds. The whole passage reminds us of the spectacle at Calvary, as it is set before us in the fourth Gospel, and may be accepted as one of the innumerable proofs of the similarity between two books--that Gospel and the Apocalypse--at first sight so different from each other. On the Cross Jesus is the true Paschal Lamb, not so much in the moment of its death as at a subsequent stage, when it was prepared for, and eaten at, the paschal meal. In the conduct of the Jews on that occasion St. John appears to behold an inverted and contorted Passover. The enemies of Jesus had not entered into the judgment-hall of Pilate, "lest they should be defiled; but that they might eat the passover." [519] They had not eaten it then Amidst the tumult and stormy passions of that dreadful morning, when had they an opportunity of eating it? St. John does not tell us that they found one. Rather is the whole narrative so constructed, so full of close, rapid, passionate action, that it is impossible to fix upon any point at which we can insert their eating until it was too late to make it legal. May it not be that they found no opportunity for eating it? They lost their passover. Lost it? Nay; the Evangelist seems to say, they found a passover. Go with me to the Cross; mark there their cruel mockeries of the Lamb of God; and you shall see the righteous dealings of the Almighty as He makes these mockeries take the shape of a passover of judgment, a passover of added sin and deepened shame. [520]

The punishment of the wicked, and especially of the three great enemies of the Church, now proceeds; and it ought still to be carefully observed that we have to do with punishment, not war or overthrow in war. It was so at ver. 17, where, after the triumphing Conqueror had ridden forth, followed by His armies, there is no mention of any battle. There is only the angel's cry to the birds to gather themselves together unto the great supper of God. The battle had been already fought, and the victory already won. We are now told indeed of the gathering together of the beast and the kings of the earth and their armies, to make war against Him that sat upon the horse, and against His army. But, whatever may have been their design, it is not executed. No actual fighting is spoken of. The enemies referred to are at once taken, apparently without fighting, and are consigned to the fate which they have brought upon themselves.

Two of the three great enemies of the Lord and of His Church meet this fate,--the beast and the false prophet. The first of these is the beast so frequently mentioned in previous chapters. More particularly it is the beast of chap. xvii., the representative of the antichristian world in its last and highest form. The second is not less certainly the second beast of chap. xiii., of whom it is said that "he deceiveth them that dwell on the earth by reason of the signs which it was given him to do in the sight of the beast; saying to them that dwell upon the earth, that they should make an image to the beast." [521] The "signs," the "deception," and the "worship" of the beast now spoken of can be no other than those thus referred to.

One point may be noticed further. According to what seems to be the best reading of the original Greek, we are told here, not that "the beast was taken, and with him the false prophet," but "the beast was taken, and he that was with him, the false prophet." In other words, the language of St. John is designed to bring out the closeness of connexion between these two beasts, the fact that the one is always dependent on the other. They are never separated. The first cannot act without the second. Hence in all probability the reason why, in treating of the doom by which these enemies of the Church are overtaken, a separate paragraph is not assigned to each. They are taken together.

A more important question has been raised in connexion with the words before us; and it has been urged that they conclusively prove that both the beast and the false prophet are persons, not personifications. [522] We have already seen that in regard to the "beast" that conclusion is hasty. [523] It appears to be not less so in regard to the "false prophet." The simple fact that he deceiveth them--that is, all that had received the mark of the beast--is inconsistent with such an idea, unless we ascribe to him a ubiquity that is Divine; or unless we suppose, what Scripture gives us no warrant for believing, that there is in the realm of evil a personal trinity--the dragon, the beast, and the false prophet-- corresponding to the Trinity of Father, Son, and Holy Spirit. It is much more natural to think that St. John's statements upon this point spring from that general method of conception which distinguishes him, and by which everything existing in the realm of good is thought of as having its counterpart in the realm of evil. The question thus raised is wholly independent of any consideration of the fate by which the two beasts are overtaken. When principles are viewed as persons, they must be spoken of as persons; and it will surely not be urged that death and Hades are persons because it is said of them, in chap. xx. 14, that they "were cast into the lake of fire."

The beast and the false prophet then are cast together into the lake of fire that burneth with brimstone; and this lake of fire is further explained in chap. xx. 14 to be "the second death." It is impossible to avoid the questions, How are we to conceive of this "lake of fire"? and, What is its effect? Yet, so far as at present concerns us, the answer to these questions must be taken from St. John alone. In the first instance at least we have nothing to do with the general teaching of Scripture on what is called the doctrine of "eternal punishment." Our only inquiry must be, What impression is the language employed by the Seer in these visions intended to convey? Upon this point it would seem as if there can be little doubt. To St. John it is no matter of consequence to tell us what shall be the condition of the enemies of the Church throughout the ages of the future, or whether they shall be preserved everlastingly alive in torment and misery and woe. His one aim is to deal with the condition of the kingdom of God while it contends with its foes in this present scene. His one object is to tell us that these foes shall be destroyed for ever, and that the world shall be wholly purged from them. No further information is required to comfort us. We may leave them in the hands of God.

Looking at the matter in this light, we do not need to ask whether by "the lake of fire" we are to understand a lake in which the wicked are consumed or one in which they are upheld in undying flames. Either interpretation is consistent with the Apostle's course of thought, and with the impression which he wishes to produce.

No doubt it may be said that the principle of contrast, of which we have so often availed ourselves in interpreting this book, implies that, as the righteous shall be upheld amidst the joys of everlasting life, so the wicked shall be upheld amidst the torments of everlasting death. But it is precisely here that the peculiarity of St. John's mode of thought comes in. To him "life" is in the very nature of the case everlasting. Were it not so, it would not be life. Only therefore in so far as the conception of everlasting torment lies in the idea of "death" can it be truly said that the principle of contrast, so deeply rooted in St. John's mode of thought, demands the application of everlasting torment to the wicked. But the idea of torment everlastingly continued does not lie in the idea of "death." Death is privation; when inflicted by fire, capacity for torment is speedily destroyed; and death itself is cast into the lake of fire. The natural conclusion is that the idea of torment belongs to the mode by which the death spoken of is inflicted--fire--and that the words with which we are dealing may mean no more than this,--that the eternity of effect following the overthrow of the beast and the false prophet is the leading conception associated with the "fire that burneth with brimstone" to which these great enemies of God's people are consigned.

If what has been said be correct, the whole question of the everlasting suffering of the wicked is left open so far as these passages in the Apocalypse are concerned; and St. John's main lesson is that when the beast and the false prophet are cast into the lake of fire they shall no longer have power to war against the righteous or to disturb their peace.

When these two enemies of the Church had thus been destroyed, the rest were killed with the sword of Him that sat upon the horse, even the sword which came forth out of His mouth. The persons thus called "the rest" are those who stand to the beast and the false prophet in the same relation as that in which "the rest of the woman's seed," spoken of in chap. xii. 17, stand to the man-child "caught up unto God and unto His throne." The man-child exalted and glorified is the same as "He that sat upon the horse," and in that condition a sword proceedeth out of His mouth. [524] The Guardian and Protector of His own, who has kept their true life safe amidst all outward troubles, brings also these troubles to an end. Their enemies are "killed." They are not yet cast into the lake of fire, because their hour of judgment has not come. By-and-by it will come. [525] Meanwhile not only can they harm the righteous no more, but they afford a supper to the ravenous birds already spoken of; and the birds are more than satisfied: they are gorged with the unholy banquet. All the birds were filled with their flesh.

Footnotes:

495. Mark x. 39.
496. Rev. i. 9.
497. John xvii. 4.
498. Ver. 9.
499. Chap. xx. 7.
500. Comp.
501. Comp. p. 250.
502. Exod. xxxiv. 7.
503. Comp. chap. iii. 20.
504. Comp. Ps. xiv. 9-15; Isa. liv. 5; Hos. ii. 19; Matt. xxii. 2; Eph. v. 32, etc.
505. John ii. 1-11.
506. John iii. 28, 29.
507. Col. i. 27.
508. Eph. ii. 8.
509. Rom. viii. 29.
510. 1 Cor. vi. 11.
511. Chap. xiv. 13.
512. Matt. xxvi. 26, 27; 1 Cor. xi. 24, 25.
513. Comp. chaps. i. 3, 9, vi. 9, xi. 7, xii. 17, xx. 4.
514. Rom. ix. 5.
515. Matt. xi. 27.
516. Isa. lxiii. 3.
517. Ezek. xxxix. 17-20.
518. Ver. 9.
519. John xviii. 28.
520. The writer has endeavoured to unfold this view of Jesus on the Cross in two papers in The Expositor, first series, vol. vi., pp. 17, 129.
521. Chap. xiii. 14.
522. Burger in loc.
523. Comp. p. 297.
524. Chaps. i. 16; xix. 15.

CHAPTER XVI – JUDGMENT OF SATAN AND OF THE WICKED.

Rev. xx.

In now approaching chap. xx., with its yet unsolved difficulties of interpretation, it is of essential importance to observe, in the first place, the relation of the chapter to what immediately precedes. The Seer is not entering upon an entirely new subject. He distinctly continues, on the contrary, the prosecution of a theme he had before begun. In the previous portion of his book three great enemies of the saints of God had been introduced to us,--the dragon or the devil, the beast, and the false prophet. These were the main opponents of the Lamb, in one way or another stirring up all the efforts that had been made against Him by the kings of the earth, their armies, and their followers. For a time they had appeared to succeed. They had persecuted the saints, had compelled them to flee, had overcome them, and killed them. This, however, could not continue; and it was to be shown that the final triumph remains with those who have suffered for the sake of righteousness. In chap. xix. we have the beginning, but not the close, of this triumph. Of the three great enemies only two--the beast and the false prophet--perish in that chapter. The destruction of the third is reserved for chap. xx., and is effected at the tenth verse of the chapter. The verses following then describe the judgment of those who had listened to these enemies, but who, though defeated, or even killed, [526] or devoured by fire out of heaven when in their service, [527] had not yet been consigned to their doom. Thereafter nothing remains, in order to complete the triumph of Christ and His saints, but that death and Hades shall also be removed from the scene and cast into the lake of fire.

These considerations are of themselves sufficient to show that the overthrow of Satan, and not the reign of a thousand years, is the main theme of the first ten verses of the chapter. So far is the latter from being the culminating point of the whole book, that it is not even introduced at the beginning of any new and important section. It starts no new series of visions. It comes in in the midst of a section devoted to an entirely different matter:--

And I saw an angel coming down out of heaven, having the key of the abyss and a great chain in his hand. And he laid hold on the dragon, the old serpent, which is the devil, and Satan, and bound him for a thousand years, and cast him into the abyss, and shut it, and sealed it over him, that he should deceive the nations no more, until the thousand years should be finished: after this he must be loosed for a little time. And I saw thrones, and they sat upon them, and judgment was given unto them: and I saw the souls of them that had been beheaded for the testimony of Jesus, and for the word of God, and such as worshipped not the beast, neither his image, and received not the mark upon their forehead and upon their hand; and they lived and reigned with Christ a thousand years. The rest of the dead lived not until the thousand years should be finished. This is the first resurrection. Blessed and holy is he that hath part in the first resurrection: over these the second death hath no authority, but they shall be priests of God and of Christ, and shall reign with Him a thousand years. And when the thousand years are finished, Satan shall be loosed out of his prison, and shall come forth to deceive the nations which are in the four corners of the earth, Gog and Magog, to gather them together to the war: the number of whom is as the sand of the sea. And they went up over the breadth of the earth, and compassed the camp of the saints about, and the beloved city: and fire came down out of heaven, and devoured them. And the devil that deceived them was cast into the lake of fire and brimstone, where are also the beast and the false prophet; and they shall be tormented day and night for ever and ever (xx. 1-10).

It is impossible within the limits of a commentary such as the present to discuss the different interpretations that have been given to a passage so difficult and so much controverted as the above. Nothing more can be attempted than to state briefly what seems to be the true meaning of the sacred writer, together with the grounds upon which the interpretation to be suggested rests.

The fundamental principle of that interpretation, to be kept clearly and resolutely in view, is this: that the thousand years mentioned in the passage express no period of time. They are not a figure for the whole Christian era, now extending to nearly nineteen hundred years. Nor do they denote a certain space of time, longer or shorter, it may be, than the definite number of years spoken of, at the close of the present dispensation, and to be in the view of some preceded, in the view of others followed, by the second Advent of our Lord. They embody an idea; and that idea, whether applied to the subjugation of Satan or to the triumph of the saints, is the idea of completeness or perfection. Satan is bound for a thousand years; that is, he is completely bound. The saints reign for a thousand years; that is, they are introduced into a state of perfect and glorious victory. Before endeavouring to bring out this thought more fully, several preliminary considerations may be noticed.

1. Years may be understood in this sense. In Ezek. xxxix. 9 it is said that the inhabitants of the cities of Israel shall prevail against the enemies described, and "shall go forth, and shall make fires of the weapons and burn them, both the shields and the bucklers, the bows and the arrows, and the hand-staves, and the spears, and they shall make fires of them seven years." No one can suppose that the "seven years" here spoken of are to be literally understood, or even that the length of time which would be needed to burn the weapons is the thought upon which the prophet dwells. His meaning, in correspondence with the use of the number seven, can only be that these weapons shall be destroyed with a great and complete destruction. Again, in the same chapter, at ver. 12, after the defeat of "Gog and all his multitude," it is said, "And seven months shall the house of Israel be burying of them, that they may cleanse the land." A literal interpretation is here not less impossible than in the case of the burning of the weapons; nor can the meaning be exhausted by the thought that a long time would be necessary for the burying. The number "seven" must have its due force assigned to it, and the prophet can only mean that the land should be thoroughly cleansed from heathen impurity. The use of the term "years" in the vision before us seems to be exactly similar; and the probability that it is so rises almost to certainty when we observe that, as proved by the vision of Gog and Magog in the subsequent part of the chapter, the prophecy of Ezekiel is before the Seer's eye, and that it constitutes the foundation upon which his whole delineation rests.

The only difficulty connected with this view is that in the third verse of the chapter Satan is said to have been shut into the abyss until the thousand years should be finished, and that in the seventh verse we read, And when the thousand years are finished, Satan shall be loosed. But the difficulty is more specious than real. Let us familiarise ourselves with the thought that the thousand years may simply express completeness, thoroughness, either of defeat or victory; let us remember that the Seer had represented the defeat of Satan by the figure of being bound for a thousand years; finally, let us notice, as we have yet to see more fully, that Satan, although deprived of power over the righteous, is still to be the deceiver and ruler of the wicked: and it immediately follows that this latter thought could find no more appropriate form than in the statement that the deception took place, not "until," or "after," the thousand years should be finished. This is simply the carrying out of the symbolism already employed. To revert for a moment to the symbolism of Ezekiel, let us suppose that, after the prophet had described the burning of the weapons for "seven years," he had wished to mention also some other step by which the burning was to be followed. What more suitable words could he have used than that it took place either "after this," or "after the seven years were finished"? In point of fact, this is exactly what the prophet does. He has occasion to refer to further efforts made to secure the purity of the land; and the words employed by him are, "After the end of seven months shall they search." [528] The one expression is no more than the natural consequence of the other.

2. What is the meaning of the last words of the third verse of the chapter,--He (i.e., Satan) must be loosed for a little time? What is this "little time"? The words take us directly to that conception of the Christian age which is so intimately interwoven with the structure of the Apocalypse, and even of the whole New Testament,--that it is all "a little time." This is particularly apparent in the application of the very same words to the souls under the altar in chap. vi. 11: "And it was said unto them, that they should rest yet for a little time, until their fellow-servants also and their brethren, which should be killed even as they were, should be fulfilled." The "little time" there is undeniably that extending from the moment of the vision to the close of the present dispensation. But, if it be so there, we are entitled to suppose that the very same expression, when used in the passage before us, will be used in the same sense; and that, when it is said Satan shall be loosed "for a little time," the meaning is that he shall be loosed for the whole Christian age. Again, in chap. xii. 12 we read, "The devil is gone down unto you, having great wrath, knowing that he hath but a short time." The "short time" here referred to begins with the casting down of the devil out of heaven into the earth spoken of in the ninth verse of the same chapter. It must therefore include the whole period of his action in this world; and the manner in which that period is designated corresponds closely with the description of the time during which he is said, in chap. xx., to be loosed. Again, in chap. x. 6 the angel swears that there shall be "time" no longer, using the same word for time that we meet with in the verse now under consideration; so that it would appear as if to the author of the Apocalypse the word "time" were a kind of technical term by which he was accustomed to denote the period of the Church's probation in this world. Lastly, this conclusion is powerfully confirmed by the many passages of the Apocalypse in which it is clear that the Christian dispensation, from its beginning to its end, is looked upon as a "very little while," as hastening to its final issue, and as about to be closed by One who cometh quickly. [529] The "little time" therefore, of

the present chapter during which Satan is loosed, and which, when more fully dwelt upon, is the time of the war spoken of in vers. 7-9, is the historical period of the Christian dispensation, during which Satan is permitted to deceive the nations and to lead them against the camp of the saints and the beloved city. It is, in short, the time between the first and second coming of our Lord. The period so often sought in the thousand years of ver. 2 is really to be found in the "little time" of ver. 3.

3. Attention ought to be particularly directed to the condition of the saints during the thousand years spoken of. It is described in general terms as a first resurrection. Certain words of our Lord in the Gospel of St. John throw important light upon the meaning of this expression: "Verily, verily, I say unto you, The hour cometh, and now is, when the dead shall hear the voice of the Son of God: and they that have heard shall live," [530] and, again, a little later in the same discourse, "Marvel not at this: for the hour cometh, in which all that are in the tombs shall hear His voice, and shall come forth." [531] Let us compare these two verses with one another, and the presence of the clause "and now is" in the first, taken along with its omission in the second, leaves no doubt as to the principle on which they are to be interpreted. The first refers to a spiritual, the second to a bodily, resurrection. Here then in the words of our Lord Himself we have the source whence the idea of the "first resurrection" of the Apocalypse is derived. It is not an actual resurrection from the grave, although that resurrection is potentially involved in it. It is a spiritual resurrection in an hour "that now is;" and the fact that this is St. John's meaning is brought out still more clearly by the intimation that what he saw was souls, whose resurrection bodies had not yet been given them. [532]

The condition of the saints thought of in this vision is described, however, not only generally, but in various particulars, all of which, it will be seen, correspond with the apocalyptic idea of it even in a present world. And I saw thrones, and they sat upon them. But we have been already told that "they reign over the earth." [533] Judgment was given unto them, words which seem best understood in the sense, so peculiar to St. John, that for believers there is in the ordinary sense of the term no judgment. As they have passed through death, so also they have passed through judgment. [534] They lived with Christ. But Christ Himself had said in the Gospel, "Because I live, and ye shall live." [535] They reigned with Christ. But that is only another method of saying that they sat on thrones, with the added conception, so often associated with the word in the Apocalypse, that their enemies were bruised beneath their feet. Over these the second death hath no authority. But we have before been told of "him that overcometh" that "he shall not be hurt of the second death." [536] Finally, they shall be priests of God and of Christ. But it is needless to dwell upon the fact that from the opening of this book such has always been spoken of as the position of believers.

Nothing, in short, is said of the saints of God in this picture of millennial bliss that does not find a parallel in what the Seer has elsewhere written of their present life. On not a few different occasions their ideal condition in this world is set forth in as glowing terms as is their thousand years' glory and joy.

One expression may indeed startle us. What the Seer beheld is said to have been the souls of them that had been beheaded for the testimony of Jesus, and for the word of God. Is the word "beheaded" to be literally understood? Then a very small number of martyrs can be thought of. The great majority of those who have died for the faith of Jesus have been martyred in other and more dreadful ways. The word is the counterpart of "slaughtered" in the vision of the souls under the altar. [537] These were the saints of the Old Testament, whose death is described by a term characteristic to the Jewish mind of the mode in which offerings were presented to God. When the Seer passes to the thought of the great Gentile Church, he uses a term more appropriate to the Gentile method of terminating human life. "Beheaded" therefore expresses the same thing as "slaughtered." Both words refer to martyrdom; and both include all faithful ones in the dispensations to which they respectively belong, for in the eyes of St. John all the disciples of a martyred Lord are martyrs. [538]

4. The meaning of the doom inflicted upon Satan demands our notice. And the angel laid hold on the dragon, the old serpent, which is the devil, and Satan, and bound him for a thousand years, and cast him into the abyss, and shut it, and sealed it over him. It is hardly possible to read these words, at the same time remembering St. John's love of contrast or even travesty, and not to see in them a mocking counterpart of the death and burial of Jesus, when the stone was rolled to the door of the sepulchre and sealed. If so, it is not enough to say that by the infliction of this doom the power of Satan was restrained, and his influence lessened. Much more must be implied; and the language can only mean that, in one sense or another, Satan was rendered powerless and harmless, as unable to act his part as though he had been laid in the grave.

5. The use of numbers in the Apocalypse ought to be remembered. These numbers are invariably symbolical; and, if the number a thousand is to be here interpreted literally, it seems in that respect to stand alone. Nor is it a reply to this to say that, though not in the strict sense literal, it may signify a period of indefinite length. Such an interpretation would be not less opposed than the former to the genius and spirit of this book. The numbers of the Apocalypse have always a definite meaning. They express ideas, but the ideas are distinct. They may belong to a region of thought different from that with

which arithmetical numbers are concerned, but within that region we cannot change their value without at the same time changing the thought. We are not to imagine that numbers, in the allegorical or spiritual use made of them by the Jews, might be tossed about at their pleasure or shuffled like a pack of cards. They were a language; and the bond between them and the ideas that they involved was quite as close as it is between the words of ordinary speech and the speaker's thoughts. A thousand years cannot mean two, or ten, or twenty, or three hundred and sixty-five thousand years according as we please. If they are a measure of time, the measure must be fixed; and we ought to be able to explain the principle leading us to attach to the number one thousand a value different from that which it naturally possesses.

6. The teaching of Scripture elsewhere upon this subject has to be considered. Upon this point it is unnecessary to say much, for the difference between that teaching and any view commonly taken of the thousand years' reign is acknowledged. It ought to be observed, however, that this difference is not merely negative, as if the rest of the New Testament simply failed to fill in certain details of events more largely described in the Apocalypse, but upon the whole substantially the same. The difference is also positive, and in some respects irreconcilable with what we are taught by the other sacred writers. The New Testament, unless this passage be an exception, always brings the Parousia and the general judgment into the closest possible connexion. It nowhere interposes a lengthened period between the resurrection of believers and that of unbelievers. It knows only of one, and that a general, resurrection; and the passages, such as 1 Cor. xv. 23, 24, and 1 Thess. iv. 16, 17, usually quoted to support another conclusion, fail when correctly interpreted to do so. When our Lord comes again, He at once perfects the happiness of His saints and makes all His enemies His footstool. [539] One text alone may be quoted upon this point. While the "first resurrection" is assigned to a date a thousand or even thousands of years before the end, it is several times repeated in the discourse of Jesus in the sixth chapter of St. John that the resurrection of believers takes place at the "last day." [540]

7. One other consideration may be kept in view. It would appear that about the time of the Advent of our Lord there was a widely extended opinion among the Jews, traces of which are also to be found among the Gentiles, that a golden age of a thousand years' duration might be anticipated in the future as a happy close to all the sins and miseries of the world. [541] Here, it is sometimes urged, is the source of the apocalyptic figure of this chapter, which thus becomes only one of the wild chiliastic expectations of the time. But, even if it be allowed that St. John drew the particular figure employed by him from a general belief of his age, it by no means follows that he accepted the literal interpretation of that belief as the reality and substance of prophetic hope. In many a passage of his book he has undeniably spiritualised hopes of Israel founded on the language of the Old Testament in its outward form. He might easily do the same with what he recognised as a belief not less widely spread and not less deeply seated in both the Jewish and Gentile portions of the Church. To use the language of the late Archdeacon Lee, "a world-wide belief such as this naturally supplied St. John with symbols and with language wherein to clothe his revelation of the fortunes of the Church, just as he has employed for the same purpose the details of the theocracy, or the imagery of war, or the phenomena and the convulsions of nature." [542] In all such cases the determination of the point at issue really rests upon our view of the general tone of the writing in which the difficulty occurs, and on our perception of what will give the unity and harmony to his words for which every intelligent writer is entitled to expect credit at his reader's hands. This conclusion is in the present instance strengthened by the fact that St. John did not confine himself to the traditional belief he is said to have adopted. So far from doing so, he occupies himself chiefly with a picture of that overthrow of Satan which seems to have been no part of the belief, and the mould of which is taken from entirely different sources.

Putting together the different considerations now adduced, we can have but little difficulty in understanding either the binding of Satan or the reign of the saints for a thousand years. The vision describes no period of blessedness to be enjoyed by the Church at the close of the present dispensation. Alike negatively and positively we have simply an ideal picture of results effected by the Redeemer for His people, when for them He lived, and suffered, and died, and rose again. Thus He bound Satan for them; He cast him into the abyss; He shut him in; He sealed the abyss over him,--so that against them he can effect nothing. He is a bruised and conquered foe. He may war against them, afflict them, persecute them, kill them, but their true life is beyond his reach. Already they live a resurrection and ascended life, for it is a life hid with Christ in God, a life in that "heaven" from which the devil has been finally and for ever expelled. They rest upon, they live in, a risen and glorified Redeemer; and, whatever be the age, or country, or circumstances in which their lot is cast, they sit with their Lord in the heavenly places and share His victory. He has been always triumphant, and in His triumph His people even now have part. The glory which the Father gave the Son the Son has given them. [543] They cannot sin, because they are begotten of God. [544] He that was begotten of God keepeth them, and the evil one toucheth them not. [545] This is the reign of a thousand years, and it is the portion of every believer who in any age of the Church shares the life of his risen and exalted Lord.

Thus also we may comprehend what is meant by the loosing of Satan. There is no point in the future at which he is to be loosed. He has been already loosed. Hardly was he completely conquered for the saints before he was loosed for the world. He was loosed as a great adversary who, however he may persecute the children of God, cannot touch their inner life, and who can only "deceive the nations,"-- the nations that have despised and rejected Christ. He has never been really absent from the earth. He has gone about continually, "knowing that he hath but a short time." [546] But he is unable to hurt those who are kept in the hollow of the Lord's hand. No doubt he tries it. That is the meaning of the description extending from the seventh to the ninth verse of this chapter,--the meaning of the war which Satan carries on against the camp of the saints and the beloved city when the thousand years are finished. In other words, no sooner was Satan, as regards the saints, completely bound than, as regards the world, he was loosed; and from that hour, through all the past history of Christianity, he has been stirring up the world against the Church. He has been summoning the nations that are in the four corners of the earth, Gog and Magog, to gather them together to the war. They war, but they do not conquer, until at last fire comes down out of heaven and devours them. The devil that deceived them is cast into the lake of fire and brimstone, where are also the beast and the false prophet; and they shall be tormented day and night for ever and ever.

The whole picture of the thousand years is in its main features--in the binding of Satan, in the security and blessedness of the righteous, and in the loosing of Satan for the war--a striking parallel to the scenes in chap. xii. of this book. There Michael and his angels contended with the devil and his angels; and the latter "prevailed not," [547] but were cast out of heaven into the earth, so that the inhabitants of heaven are for ever safe from them. There the man-child who is to rule all the nations with a rod of iron, and from the thought of whom it is impossible to separate the thought of those who are one with Him, is caught up unto God and unto His throne. Finally, there also the dragon, though unable really to hurt the saints, "the rest of the woman's seed," makes war upon them, but without result. Of this scene the picture which we have been considering is at once a repetition and a fuller development; and, when we call to mind the peculiarities marking the structure of the Apocalypse, we seem in this fact alone to have no slight evidence of the correctness of the interpretation now proposed. [548]

The three great enemies of the Church have not only been overcome, but judged, and for ever removed from all possibility of troubling the righteous more. But the great mass of the wicked have not yet been overtaken by a similar fate. The time has now come to show us in vision what awaits them also:--

And I saw a great white throne, and Him that sat upon it, from whose face the earth and the heaven fled away; and there was found no place for them. And I saw the dead, the great and the small, standing before the throne; and books were opened: and another book was opened, which is the book of life: and the dead were judged out of the things which were written in the books, according to their works. And the sea gave up the dead which were in it; and death and Hades gave up the dead which were in them: and they were judged every man according to their works. And death and Hades were cast into the lake of fire. This is the second death, even the lake of fire. And if any was not found written in the book of life, he was cast into the lake of fire (xx. 11-15).

Upon various particulars mentioned in this passage it is unnecessary to say much. The throne beheld by the Seer is great, at once in contrast with the "thrones" of the millennial reign, and as befitting the majesty of Him who sits upon it. It is also white, as emblematic of His purity and holiness. The Judge is God, the Father in the Son, the Son in the Father; and thus the judgment is searching and complete, and is answered by the consciences of those upon whom it is executed. They see that the Judge's eye penetrates into the most secret recesses of their hearts, and that He is One who has been in the same position, has fought the same battle, and has endured the same trials as themselves. Thus His sentence finds an echo in their hearts, and they are speechless. [549] Thus also judgment becomes really judgment, and not merely the infliction of punishment by resistless power.

The effect of the Judge's taking His seat upon His throne was that from His face the earth and the heaven fled away, and there was found no place for them. Yet we are not to understand that after their flight there was neither an earth nor a heaven to be found. It is only the old earth and the old heaven that are spoken of; and almost immediately afterwards the Seer exclaims, "I saw a new heaven and a new earth: for the first heaven and the first earth are passed away." [550] The change is part of that "restoration of all things" of which St. Peter spoke to the multitude gathered together in Solomon's porch, [551] of which he then added, "Whereof God spake by the mouth of His holy prophets which have been since the world began," and upon which he dwelt more fully in his second Epistle when he said, "But the day of the Lord will come as a thief; in the which the heavens shall pass away with a great noise, and the elements shall melt with fervent heat, and the earth and the works that are therein shall be burned up. But, according to His promise, we look for new heavens and a new earth, wherein dwelleth righteousness." [552] In the Epistle to the Romans, too, "creation" longs, not for destruction, but for something akin to that "liberty of the glory of the children of God" which they shall obtain along with their "adoption, to wit, the redemption of their body." [553] In all these passages it is not the translation of God's saints to an immaterial sphere that lies at the bottom of the thought. It is rather the idea of change, of the transfiguration, of the glorification, of this present scene into a state corresponding with that of its redeemed inhabitants, when they shall "not be unclothed, but clothed upon," [554] and shall dwell in "spiritual bodies." [555] To St. John "heaven" is not an abode of bliss in a scene of which we can form no clear conception, but the spiritual atmosphere in which, alike on this side the grave and on the other, the saints live and move. The "dwellers upon earth" are not those who simply tread its firm soil and breathe its atmosphere, but those who are worldly in their spirit and whose views are bounded by the things of time. The kingdom which Christ establishes is the "kingdom of this world" in its cleansed and purified condition rather than one to which we travel by long and unknown paths. As the Seer looks forward to the future there is nothing to show that he thinks of any other residence for man than that which the Son consecrated by His tomb in Joseph's garden and by the glory of the resurrection morning; and even the new Jerusalem comes down out of heaven to be established upon earth.

Many may doubtless think that such a hope is too earthly, too material, to be suited to the spiritual nature of the Christian dispensation. They fear that it has a tendency to withdraw us from Him who is "spirit," and who must be worshipped, if He is to be worshipped acceptably, "in spirit and truth." [556] But any such apprehension is at variance with the fundamental fact of our Christian faith, the incarnation of our Lord, and is little less than the revival of the old Manichean heresy that matter is essentially evil. Two errors have existed, and may exist, in the Church upon this point. We may strip the Gospel of its spiritual element, and may reduce it to a system of outward and material forms, or we may strip it of its material element, and may resolve it into a vague and shadowy mysticism. Both are the errors of extremes, and it would be difficult to say which has wrought most havoc in the Church. If the one was disastrous in the days of the supremacy of Romanism, the other is hardly less disastrous now. To the false and spurious spiritualism which it engenders we owe not a few of the most serious misconceptions of the present time with regard to the person of Christ, the Church, the Sacraments, and the purpose of redemption as a whole. [557]

To return to the main question in connexion with the passage before us. Does it present us with the picture of a general judgment or of a judgment of the wicked alone? There is much in the passage that leads distinctly to the latter conclusion.

1. The whole vision is obviously an enlargement of what we have already met under the seventh Trumpet, when it was said that "the time of the dead to be judged came." [558] In both visions the persons spoken of as "the dead" must be the same; and they are clearly distinguished in the earlier vision from those called "Thy servants the prophets," the season of whose "reward" was come. With this corresponds the fact that in the writings of St. John the words "to judge" and "judgment" are always used, not in a neutral sense, but in one tending to condemnation. Without some qualifying term the Apostle could hardly have applied them to the acquittal of the righteous.

2. The sources whence the "dead" are gathered confirm this conclusion. These are three in number: the sea, death, and Hades. Looking first at the two last of these, it is plain that "death" cannot in this connexion be the neutral grave, for it is "cast into the lake of fire," where the devil, the beast, and the false prophet are. Similar remarks apply to "Hades," which in chap. vi. 8 is the coadjutor of death, and which in the New Testament always appears as a region of gloom, and punishment, and opposition to the truth: "And thou, Capernaum, shalt thou be exalted unto heaven? thou shalt go down unto Hades;" "And I also say unto thee that thou art Peter, and upon this rock I will build My Church; and the gates of Hades shall not prevail against it." [559] If such be the sense in which we are to understand death and Hades, light is thrown upon the manner in which we are to interpret the first of the three sources,--"the sea." This cannot be the ocean, because the number of those to be given up from its depths at the last day is comparatively small; because, as the literal sea, it is in no way suitably associated with death and Hades; and because, when we read in chap. xxi. 1, "And the sea is no more," it is impossible to think that the word is used in any other than a figurative sense. No reason can be imagined why, when the earth is renewed, there should be no more that sea which is one grand instrument of its present greatness and glory. Besides all this, we have hitherto found that in the Apocalypse the "sea" is the emblem of the unruly and troubled nations of the earth, and the source from which the first beast of chap. xiii. had his origin. In the same sense therefore we must understand it here. Like "death" and "Hades," "the sea" spoken of can give up none but ungodly dead to the judgment of the great day.

3. The "books" mentioned in the passage are clearly books containing the record of evil deeds alone. When it is said that "books" were opened, and that "another book was opened, which is the book of life," the "books" are distinguished from the "book." It harmonizes with this that the book of life is not opened in order to secure deliverance for those whose names are inscribed in it, but only to justify the sentence passed on any who are cast into the lake of fire.

4. The general teaching of St. John ought not to be lost sight of in considering this question. That teaching is that the eternal condition of the righteous is fully secured to them even in this life, and that in their glorified Head they have already passed through all those preparatory stages on their way to

everlasting blessedness at the thought of which they might otherwise have trembled. In Him they have lived, and overcome, and died. In Him they have been raised from the dead, and been seated in the heavenly places. All along they have followed the Lamb whithersoever He goeth, and everything that befell Him has in principle befallen them. We cannot say, in the Johannine sense of the word, that Christ has been "judged;" and therefore "judgment" cannot be predicated of the members of His Body. To these last "judgment," we have already seen, "was given" at the time when they entered on their millennial reign; and, with the result of this judgment (for that is the true meaning of the original) in their hands, it is impossible to think of them as judged again.

The judgment of these verses is therefore a judgment of the wicked; and, when it is closed, all Christ's enemies have not only been vanquished, but have been banished from the scene where He is to reign "before His ancients gloriously." [560] The first part of the final triumph has been accomplished.

Footnotes:

526. Chap. xix. 21.
527. Chap. xx. 9.
528. Ezek. xxxix. 14.
529. Chaps. i. 3, ii. 16, iii. 20, xxii. 20, etc.; 1 Cor. vii. 29; Heb. x. 37.
530. John v. 25.
531. John v. 28.
532. Comp. chap. vi. 9.
533. Chap. v. 10.
534. Comp. the teaching of our Lord in John xi. 25, 26, and v. 24.
535. John xiv. 19 (margin of R.V.).
536. Chap. ii. 11.
537. Chap. vi. 9.
538. Comp. p. 102.
539. Matt. xxv. 31-46; Rom. ii. 5, 7; 1 Thess. iv. 17; 2 Thess. i. 7, 10.
540. John vi. 39, 40, 44.
541. See authorities in Lee (Speaker's Commentary) on Rev. xx. 2, and his excursus on that chapter.
542. Speaker's Commentary, u.s.
543. John xvii. 22.
544. 1 John iii. 9.
545. 1 John v. 18.
546. Chap. xii. 12.
547. Comp. the remarkable parallel in John i. 5: "and the darkness overcame it not."
548. It is not to be denied that difficulties attend the interpretation of the thousand years suggested in the text. The writer would advert in a note to the two which appear to him to be the most formidable. 1. In ver. 3 we read that Satan was cast into the abyss, etc., "that he should deceive the nations no more, until the thousand years should be finished." Let it be granted that "the nations" here referred to can hardly be understood in any other sense than that common in the Apocalypse: the heathen, the ungodly, nations or the wicked in general. We then seem to read that there must be a time during which Satan does not "deceive the nations," while the explanation given above has been that he was no sooner subjugated for the righteous than he was let loose to deceive the unrighteous. In his Lectures on the Revelation of St. John (p. 224, note) the author was disposed to plead that the words in question may not have been intended to indicate that action on Satan's part was for a time to cease, but rather to bring out and express that aspect of Satan by which he is specially distinguished in the Apocalypse. In deference to the criticism of the Rev. H. W. Reynolds (Remarks on Dr. Milligan's Interpretation of the Apocalypse, pp. 9, 27), he would yield this point. Notwithstanding the irregular constructions of the Apocalypse, it is at least precarious; and it is better to leave a difficulty unsolved, especially in a case where difficulties surround every interpretation yet offered, than to propose solutions of the sufficiency of which even the proposer is doubtful. It may be asked, however, without resorting to the conjecture formerly thrown out, whether the words "that he should deceive," even when taken in what is said to be their only true sense, are irreconcilable with the view of the thousand years advocated in this commentary. That view is that the subjugation of Satan for a thousand years means his complete subjugation. When, therefore, it is said that he has been so shut up as "to deceive the nations no more, until the thousand years should be finished," the meaning may simply be that in the act of being subjected he was deprived alike of authority and opportunity to deceive the nations. It lay within the power of the Conqueror to grant or not to grant him fresh liberty to do so. The "strong man" was then bound, and "his goods were spoiled." He was completely subjected to Christ. When, therefore, we are told of the thousand years during which he was to deceive the nations no more, this language is only the

continuation of the figure used in the second verse of the chapter; and what the Seer intends to express is, that during the process of his subjection, and until he should be again loosed by Him who had subjected him, he could do nothing. Satan, in short, must be permitted to come up out of the abyss either in his own person or by his agents before he can disturb the earth (comp. chap. ix. 2); and it is the purpose of God that he shall not have power to disturb it until, having been really "brought to nought" by Christ (comp. Heb. ii. 14), he shall go forth to his evil work among the nations as one who, whatever may be the increase of his wrath (comp. chap. xii. 12), has yet been overcome by another far mightier than himself. 2. The second difficulty demanding notice is presented by the words of ver. 5, "The rest of the dead lived not until the thousand years should be finished." Who are these called "the rest of the dead," and in what sense did they "live"? The term "the rest," applied to persons, occurs in the following passages of the Apocalypse in addition to that before us: chaps. ii. 24, ix. 20, xi. 13, xii. 17, xix. 21. In every one of these cases it refers to the remaining portion of a class mentioned, but not exhausted; and it cannot be extended to any class beyond them. Here, however, no class has been spoken of except the righteous, or rather the "souls" of the righteous, described by various particulars both of their character and their state. "The rest" of the dead must therefore belong to that class, and to it alone. They cannot be the general body of mankind, both good and bad, with the exception of those previously mentioned. Again, what is meant when it is said that the rest of the dead "lived"? The same word had occurred in the immediately preceding verse, and it must now be understood in the same sense. "If," says Dean Alford, who has been quoted with great confidence against the present writer (Reynolds, u.s., p. 23), "in such a passage the first resurrection may be understood to mean spiritual rising with Christ, while the second means literal rising from the grave, then there is an end of all significance in language; and Scripture is wiped out as a definite testimony to anything. If the first resurrection is spiritual, then so is the second, which I suppose none will be hardy enough to maintain" (on Rev. xx. 4-6). Now that is exactly what is here maintained. The "lived" of ver. 4 is spiritual; the "lived" of ver. 5 is also spiritual. The "rest of the dead" then are the Old Testament saints of chap. vi. 9, who, by the completion of the Lord's redeeming work, were brought up to the level of the New Testament Church (comp. p. 101). The meaning of chap. xx. 5 may thus be said to be that, the New Testament Church having had first bestowed upon it a complete redemption, the same white robes were afterwards given to the Old Testament Church, the succession being again one of thought rather than time. In this way all the members of Christ's body are marked out as having been "dead" before they lived, thus identifying them with their Lord in chap. i. 18; the position of the words at the close of ver. 5, "this is the first resurrection," is rendered more natural by their thus following what is wholly a description of the condition of the blessed, instead of having a sentence interposed of an entirely different character; and, finally, to say nothing of the contextual considerations already referred to, the full Johannine force of the word "lived" is preserved. These answers to the two chief difficulties associated with the interpretation here suggested of the thousand years may not be satisfactory to all; but it is submitted that they go far at least to meet them, and that in themselves they are neither unfair nor strained. Against one thing only must the author of this commentary enter his most decided protest,--the allegation that the interpretation here offered is gained by dispensing with textual criticism (?) and by sacrificing grammar to an idea. If there be one ground more than another upon which it rests, it is upon the strictest principles of historical interpretation. It ought only to be remembered that the idiosyncrasies of an author are as much a part of such interpretation as the literal meaning of his words; and that to that interpretation, if honestly and thoroughly conducted, the most deeply ingrained prejudices will in due time be compelled to submit.

549. Comp. Matt. xxii. 12.
550. Chap. xxi. 1.
551. Acts iii. 21.
552. 2 Pet. iii. 10, 13.
553. Rom. viii. 21-23.
554. 2 Cor. v. 4.
555. Comp. 1 Cor. xv. 44.
556. John iv. 24.
557. In connexion with the point here spoken of, reference may be made to an interesting and instructive paper by Canon Dale Stewart, Rector of Coulsdon, in The Churchman for December, 1887.
558. Chap. xi. 18.
559. Matt. xi. 23, xvi. 18.
560. Isa. xxiv. 23.

CHAPTER XVII – THE NEW JERUSALEM

Rev. xxi. 1-xxii. 5.

The first part of the final triumph of the Lamb has been accomplished, but the second has still to be unfolded. We are introduced to it by one of those preparatory or transition passages which have already frequently met us in the Apocalypse, and which connect themselves both with what precedes and with what follows:--

And I saw a new heaven and a new earth: for the first heaven and the first earth are passed away; and the sea is no more. And I saw the holy city, new Jerusalem, coming down out of heaven from God, made ready as a bride adorned for her husband. And I heard a great voice out of the throne saying, Behold, the tabernacle of God is with men, and He shall dwell with them, and they shall be His peoples, and God Himself shall be with them, and be their God: and He shall wipe away every tear from their eyes; and death shall be no more, neither shall there be mourning, nor crying, nor pain any more: the first things are passed away. And He that sitteth on the throne said, Behold, I make all things new. And He saith, Write: for these words are faithful and true. And He said unto me, They are come to pass. I am the Alpha and the Omega, the beginning and the end. I will give unto him that is athirst of the fountain of the water of life freely. He that overcometh shall inherit these things; and I will be his God, and he shall be My son. But for the fearful, and unbelieving, and abominable, and murderers, and fornicators, and sorcerers, and idolaters, and all liars, their part shall be in the lake that burneth with fire and brimstone: which is the second death (xxi. 1-8).

These words, like many others that have already met us, throw light upon the principles on which the Apocalypse is composed. They show in the clearest possible manner that down to the very end of the book chronological considerations must be put out of view. Chronology cannot be thought of when we find, on the one hand, allusions to the new Jerusalem which are only amplified and extended in the next vision of the chapter, or when we find, on the other hand, a description of the exclusion from the new Jerusalem of certain classes that have already been consigned to "the second death." By the first-mentioned allusions the passage connects itself with what is yet to come, by the second with what has gone before. For the same reason it is unnecessary to dwell upon the passage at any length. It contains either nothing new, or nothing that will not again meet us in greater fulness of detail. One or two brief remarks alone seem called for.

The Seer beholds a new heaven and a new earth. Two words in the New Testament are translated "new," but there is a difference between them. The one contemplates the object spoken of under the aspect of something that has been recently brought into existence, the other under a fresh aspect given to what had previously existed, but been outworn. [561] The latter word is employed here, as it is also employed in the phrases a "new garment," that is, a garment not threadbare, like an old one; "new wine-skins," that is, skins not shrivelled and dried; a "new tomb," that is, not one recently hewn out of the rock, but one which had never been used as the last resting-place of the dead. The fact, therefore, that the heavens and the earth here spoken of are "new," does not imply that they are now first brought into being. They may be the old heavens and the old earth; but they have a new aspect, a new character, adapted to a new end. Of the sense in which the word "sea" is to be understood we have already spoken. [562] Another expression in the passage deserves notice. In saying that the time is come when the tabernacle of the Lord is with men, and He shall dwell with them, it is added, and they shall be His peoples. We are familiar with the Scripture use of the word "people" to denote the true Israel of God, and not less with the use of the word "peoples" to denote the nations of the earth alienated from Him. But here the word "peoples" is used instead of "people" for God's children; and the usage can only spring from this: that the Seer has entirely abandoned the idea that Israel according to the flesh can have the word "people" applied to it, and that all believers, to whatever race they belong, occupy the same ground in Christ, and are possessed of the same privileges. The "peoples" are the counterpart of the "many diadems" of chap. xix. 12.

    And there came one of the seven angels who had the seven bowls, who were laden with the seven last plagues; and he spake with me, saying, Come hither, I will show thee the bride, the wife of the Lamb. And he carried me away in the spirit to a mountain great and high, and showed me the holy city Jerusalem, coming down out of heaven from God, having the glory of God: her light was like unto a stone most precious, as it were a jasper stone, clear as crystal, having a wall great and high, having twelve gates, and at the gates twelve angels, and names written thereon, which are the names of the twelve tribes of the children of Israel. On the east were three gates, and on the north three gates, and on the south three gates, and on the west three gates. And the wall of the city had twelve foundations, and on them twelve names of the twelve apostles of the Lamb. And he that spake with me had for a measure a golden reed to measure the city, and the gates thereof, and the wall thereof. And the city lieth foursquare, and the length thereof is as great as the breadth: and he measured the city with the reed, twelve thousand furlongs: the length and the breadth and the height thereof are equal. And he measured the wall thereof, a hundred and forty and four cubits, according to the measure of a man, that is, of an angel. And the building of the wall thereof was jasper: and the city was pure gold, like unto pure glass. The foundations of the wall of the city were adorned with all manner of precious stones. The first foundation was jasper; the second, sapphire; the third, chalcedony; the fourth, emerald; the fifth, sardonyx; the sixth, sardius; the seventh, chrysolite; the eighth, beryl; the ninth, topaz; the tenth, chrysoprase; the eleventh, jacinth; the twelfth, amethyst. And the twelve gates were twelve pearls; each one of the several gates was of one pearl: and the street of the city was pure gold, as it were transparent glass. And I saw no temple therein: for the Lord God the Almighty, is the temple thereof, and the Lamb. And the city hath no need of the sun, neither of the moon, to shine upon it: for the glory of God did lighten it, and the lamp thereof is the Lamb. And the nations shall walk amidst the light thereof: and the kings of the earth do bring their glory into it. And the gates thereof shall in no wise be shut by day: for there shall be no night there. And they shall bring the glory and the honour of the nations into it. And there shall in no wise enter into it anything unclean, or he that maketh an abomination and a lie: but only they which are written in the Lamb's book of life. And he showed me a river of water of life, bright as crystal, proceeding out of the throne of God and of the Lamb, in the midst of the street thereof. And on this side of the river and on that was the tree of life, bearing twelve manner of fruits, yielding its fruit every month: and the leaves of the tree were for the healing of the nations. And there shall be no curse any more: and the throne of God and of the Lamb shall be therein; and His servants shall do Him service: and they shall see His face; and His name shall be on their foreheads. And there shall be night no more; and they need no light of lamp, neither light of sun; for the Lord God shall give them light: and they shall reign for ever and ever (xxi. 9-xxii. 5).

    The vision contained in these verses is shown the Seer by the angel forming the third of the second group associated with Him who had been described at chap. xix. 11 as the Rider upon the white horse, and who at that time rode forth to His final triumph. The first of this group of three had appeared at chap. xix. 17, and the second at chap. xx. 1. We have now the third; and it is not unimportant to observe this, for it helps to throw light upon the artificial structure of these chapters, while, at the same time, it connects the vision with Christ's victory upon earth rather than with any scene of splendour and glory in a region beyond the place of man's present abode. Thus it contributes something at least to the belief that there where the believer wars he also wears the crown of triumph.

    The substance of the vision is a description of the holy city, the new Jerusalem, the true Church of God wholly separated from the false Church, as she comes down from God, out of heaven, prepared as a bride adorned for her husband. Her marriage with the Lamb has taken place,--a marriage in which there shall be no unfaithfulness on the one side and no reproaches on the other, but in which, as the bridegroom rejoices over the bride, the Lord shall for ever rejoice in His people, and His people in Him. Then follows, to enhance the picture, a detailed account of the true Church under the figure of the city which had been already spoken of in the first vision of the chapter. The treasures of the Seer's imagination and language are exhausted in order that the thought of her beauty and her splendour may be suitably impressed upon our minds. Her light--that is, the light which she spreads abroad, for the word used in the original indicates that she is herself the luminary--is like that of the sun, only that it is of crystalline clearness and purity, as it were a jasper stone, the light of Him who sat upon the throne. [563] She is "the light of the world." [564] The city is also surrounded by a wall great and high. She is "a strong city." "Salvation has God appointed her for walls and bulwarks." [565] Her walls have twelve gates, and at the gates twelve angels, those to whom God gives charge over His people, to keep them in all their ways [566] ; while, as was the case with the new Jerusalem beheld by the prophet Ezekiel, names were written on the gates, which are the names of the twelve tribes of the children of Israel. [567] These gates are also harmoniously distributed, three on each side of the square which the city forms. The foundations of the city, a term under which we are not to think of foundations buried in the earth, but rather of courses of stones going round the city and rising one above another, are also twelve; and on them are twelve names of the twelve apostles of the Lamb.

The Seer, however, is not satisfied with this general picture of the greatness of the new Jerusalem. Like that in Ezekiel, the city must be measured. [568] When this is done, her proportions are found, in spite of the absence of all verisimilitude, to be those of a perfect cube. As in the Holy of holies of the Tabernacle, the thought of which lies at the bottom of the description, the length and the breadth and the height thereof are equal. Twelve thousand furlongs, or fifteen hundred miles, the city stretches along and across the plain, and rises into the sky,--twelve, the number of the people of God, multiplied by thousands, the heavenly number. The wall is also measured--it is difficult to say whether in height or in thickness, but most probably the latter--a hundred and forty and four cubits, or twelve multiplied by twelve.

The measuring is completed, and next follows an account of the material of which the city was composed. This was gold, the most precious metal, in its purest state, like unto pure glass. Precious stones formed, rather than ornamented, its twelve foundations. Its gates were of pearl: each one of the several gates was of one pearl; and the street of the city was pure gold, as it were transparent glass. In all these respects it is evident that the city is thought of as ideally perfect, and not according to the realities or possibilities of things.

Nor is this all. The glory of the city is still further illustrated by figures bearing more immediately upon its spiritual rather than its material aspect. The outward helps needed by men in leading the life of God in their present state of imperfection are dispensed with. There is no temple therein: for the Lord, God, the Almighty, is the temple thereof, and the Lamb. The city hath no need of the sun, neither of the moon, to shine upon it: for the glory of God lightens it by day, and the lamp thereof by night is the Lamb. There is in it no sin, and every positive element of happiness is provided in abundance for the blest inhabitants. A river of water of life, bright as crystal, flows there; and on this side of the river and on that side is the tree of life, not bearing fruit only once a year, but every month, not yielding one only, but twelve manner of fruits, so that all tastes may be gratified, having nothing about it useless or liable to decay. The very leaves of the tree were for the healing of the nations, and it is evidently implied that they are always green. Finally, there shall be no curse any more. The throne of God and of the Lamb is therein. His servants do Him service. They see His face. His name is in their foreheads. They are priests unto God in the service of the heavenly sanctuary. They reign for ever and ever.

One important question still remains: What aspect of the Church does the holy city Jerusalem, thus come down out of heaven from God, represent? Is it the Church as she shall be after the Judgment, when her three great enemies, together with all who have listened to them, have been for ever cast out? Or have we before us an ideal representation of the true Church of Christ as she exists now, and before a final separation has been made between the righteous and the wicked? Unquestionably the first aspect of the passage leads to the former view; and, if there be anything like a chronological statement of events in the Apocalypse, no other may be possible. But we have already seen that the thought of chronology must be banished from this book. The Apocalypse contains simply a series of visions intended to exhibit, with all the force of that inspiration under which the Seer wrote, certain great truths connected with the revelation in humanity of the Eternal Son. It is intended, too, to exhibit these in their ideal, and not merely in their historical, form. They are indeed to appear in history; but, inasmuch as they do not appear there in their ultimate and completed form, we are taken beyond the limited field of historical manifestation. We see them in their real and essential nature, and as they are, in themselves, whether we think of evil on the one hand, or of good on the other. In this treatment of them, however, chronology disappears. Such being the case, we are prepared to ask whether the vision of the new Jerusalem belongs to the end, or whether it expresses what, under the Christian dispensation, is always ideally true.

1. It must be borne in mind that the new Jerusalem, though described as a city, is really a figure, not of a place, but of a people. It is not the final home of the redeemed. It is the redeemed themselves. It is "the bride, the wife of the Lamb." [569] Whatever is said of it is said of the true followers of Jesus; and the great question, therefore, that has to be considered is, whether St. John's description is applicable to them in their present Christian condition, or whether it is suitable to them only when they have entered upon their state of glorification beyond the grave.

2. The vision is really an echo of Old Testament prophecy. We have already seen this in many particulars, and the correspondence might easily have been traced in many more. "It is all," says Isaac Williams, as he begins his comment upon the particular points of the description--"It is all from Ezekiel: 'The hand of the Lord was upon me, and brought me in the visions of God, and set me upon a very high mountain, by which was as the frame of a city;' [570] 'And the glory of the Lord came into the house by the gate toward the east;' [571] The Lord entered by the eastern gate; therefore shall it be shut, and opened for none but for the Prince. [572] Such was the coming of Christ's glory from the east into His Church, as so often alluded to before." [573] Other prophets, no doubt, who prophesied of the grace that should come unto us, who testified beforehand of the sufferings of Christ and the glories that should follow, are to be added to Ezekiel, but, whoever they were, it is undeniable that their highest and most glowing representations of that future for which they longed, and the advent of which they were commissioned to proclaim, are reproduced in St. John's description of the new Jerusalem. Of what was

it, then, that they spoke? Surely it was of the times of the Messiah upon earth, of that kingdom of God which He was to establish with the beginning, and not with the end, of the Christian dispensation. That they may have looked forward to the world beyond the grave is possible; but any distinction between the first and second coming of our Lord had not yet risen upon their minds. In the simple coming of the Hope of Israel into the world they beheld the accomplishment of every aspiration and longing of the heart of man. And they were right. The distinction which experience taught the New Testament writers to draw was not so much between a first and a second coming of the King as between a kingdom then hidden, but afterwards to be manifested in all its glory.

3. This ideal view of the Messianic age is also constantly brought before us in the New Testament. The character, the privileges, and the blessings of those who are partakers of the spirit of that time are always presented to us as irradiated with a heavenly and perfect glory. St. Paul addresses the various churches to which he wrote as, notwithstanding all their imperfections, "beloved of God," "sanctified in Christ Jesus," "saints and faithful brethren in Christ." [574] Christ is "in them," and they are "in Christ." [575] "Christ loved the Church, and gave Himself up for it; that He might present the Church to Himself a glorious Church, not having spot, or wrinkle, or any such thing; but that it should be holy and without blemish," [576] --the description evidently applying to the present world, where also the Church is seated, not in earthly, but in "the heavenly places" with her Lord. [577] Our "citizenship" is declared to be "in heaven;" [578] and we are even now "come unto Mount Zion, and unto the city of the living God, the heavenly Jerusalem, to innumerable hosts of angels, and to the general assembly and Church of the first-born, who are enrolled in heaven." [579] Our Lord Himself and St. John, following in His steps, are even more specific as to the present kingdom and the present glory. "In that day," says Jesus to His disciples, "ye shall know that I am in My Father, and ye in Me, and I in you," [580] and again, "And the glory which Thou hast given Me I have given unto them; that they may be one, even as We are one;" [581] while it is unnecessary to quote the passages meeting us everywhere in the writings of the beloved disciple in which he speaks of eternal life, and that, too, in the full greatness both of its privileges and of its results, as a possession enjoyed by the believer in this present world. The whole witness of the New Testament, in short, is to an ideal, to a perfect, kingdom of God even now established among men, in which sin is conquered, temptation overcome, strength substituted for weakness, death so deprived of its sting that it is no more death, and the Christian, though for a little put to grief in manifold temptations, made "to rejoice greatly with joy unspeakable and glorified." [582] From all this the representation of the new Jerusalem in the Apocalypse differs in no essential respect. It enters more into particulars. It illustrates the general thought by a greater variety of detail. But it contains nothing which is not found in principle in the other sacred writers, and which is not connected by them with the heavenly aspect of the Christian's pilgrimage to his eternal home.

4. There are distinct indications in the apocalyptic vision which leave no interpretation possible except one,--that the new Jerusalem has come, that it has been in the midst of us for more than eighteen hundred years, that it is now in the midst of us, and that it shall continue to be so wherever its King has those who love and serve Him, walk in His light, and share His peace and joy.

(1) Let us look at chap. xx. 9, where we read of "the camp of the saints and the beloved city." That city is none other than the new Jerusalem, about to be described in the following chapter. It is Jerusalem after the elements of the harlot character have been wholly expelled, and the call of chap. xviii. 4 has been heard and obeyed, "Come forth, My people, out of her." She is inhabited now by none but "saints," who, though they have still to war with the world, are themselves the "called, and chosen, and faithful." But this "beloved city" is spoken of as in the world, and as the object of attack by Satan and his hosts before the Judgment. [583]

(2) Let us look at chap. xxi. 24 and xxii. 2: "And the nations shall walk by the light thereof; and the kings of the earth do bring their glory into it;" "And the leaves of the tree were for the healing of the nations." Who are these "nations" and these "kings of the earth"? The constant use of the same expressions in other parts of this book, where there can be no doubt as to their meaning, compels us to understand them of nations and kings beyond the pale of the covenant. But if so, the difficulty of realizing the situation at a point of time beyond the Judgment appears to be insuperable, and may be well illustrated by the effort of Hengstenberg to overcome it. "Nations," says that commentator, "in the usage of the Revelation, are not nations generally, but always heathen nations in their natural or christianized state; compare at chap. xx. 3. That we are to think here only of converted heathen is as clear as day. No room for conversion can be found on the further side of chap. xx. 15, for every one who had not been found written in the book of life has already been cast into the lake of fire." [584] But the words "or christianized" in this comment have no countenance from any other passage in the Apocalypse, and in Hengstenberg's note at chap. xx. 3 we are referred to nothing but the texts before us. On every other occasion, too, where the word "nations" meets us, it means unconverted, not converted, nations; and here it can mean nothing else. Were the nations spoken of converted, they would be a part of that new Jerusalem which is not the residence of God's people, but His people themselves. They would be the light, and not such as walk "by the light" of others. They would be the healed, and not

those who stand in need of "healing." These "nations" must be the unconverted, these "kings of the earth" such as have not yet acknowledged Jesus to be their King; and nothing of this can be found beyond chap. xx. 15.

(3) Let us look at chap. xxi. 27, where we read, "And there shall in no wise enter into it anything unclean, or he that doeth an abomination and a lie." These words distinctly intimate that the time for final separation had not yet come. Persons of the wicked character described must be supposed to be alive upon the earth after the new Jerusalem has appeared.

5. Another consideration on the point under discussion may be noticed, which will have weight with those who admit the existence of that principle of structure in St. John's writings upon which it rests. Alike in the Gospel and in the Apocalypse the Apostle is marked by a tendency to return at the close of a section to what he had said at the beginning, and to shut up, as it were, between the two statements all he had to say. So here. In chap. i. 3 he introduces his Apocalypse with the words, "For the time is at hand." In chap. xxii. 10, immediately after closing it, he returns to the thought, "Seal not up the words of the prophecy of this book: for the time is at hand;" that is, the whole intervening revelation is enclosed between these two statements. All of it precedes the "time" spoken of. The new Jerusalem comes before the end.

In the new Jerusalem, therefore, we have essentially a picture, not of the future, but of the present; of the ideal condition of Christ's true people, of His "little flock" on earth, in every age. The picture may not yet be realized in fulness; but every blessing lined in upon its canvas is in principle the believer's now, and will be more and more his in actual experience as he opens his eyes to see and his heart to receive. We have been wrong in transferring the picture of the new Jerusalem to the future alone. It belongs also to the past and to the present. It is the heritage of the children of God at the very time when they are struggling with the world; and the thought of it ought to stimulate them to exertion and to console them under suffering.

Footnotes:

561. Trench, Synonyms, second series, p. 39.
562. Comp. pp. 227, 357.
563. Chap. iv. 3.
564. Matt. v. 14.
565. Ps. xxxi. 21; Isa. xxvi. 1.
566. Ps. xci. 11.
567. Comp. Ezek. xlviii. 31.
568. Comp. Ezek. xl. 2, 3.
569. Chap. xxi. 9.
570. Ezek. xl. 1, 2.
571. Ezek. xliii. 2.
572. Ezek. xliv. 1-3.
573. The Apocalypse, p. 438.
574. Rom. i. 7; 1 Cor. i. 2; Col. i. 2.
575. Col. i. 27; 1 Cor. i. 30; Phil. iii. 9.
576. Eph. v. 25-27.
577. Eph. i. 3.
578. Phil. iii. 20.
579. Heb. xii. 22, 23.
580. John xiv. 20.
581. John xvii. 22.
582. 1 Pet. i. 8.
583. Comp. Foxley, Hulsean Lectures, Lect. i.
584. Commentary in Clark's Foreign Theological Library, in loc.

CHAPTER XVIII - THE EPILOGUE.

Rev. xxii. 6-21.

The visions of the Seer have closed, and closed with a picture of the final and complete triumph of the Church over all her enemies. No more glorious representation of what her Lord has done for her could be set before us than that contained in the description of the new Jerusalem. Nothing further can be said when we know that in the garden of Paradise Restored into which she is introduced, in the Holy of holies of the Divine Tabernacle planted in the world, she shall eat of the fruit of the tree of life, drink of the water of life, and reign for ever and ever. Surely as these visions passed before the eye of St. John in the lonely isle of Patmos he would be gladdened with the light of heaven, and would need no more to strengthen him in the kingdom and patience of Jesus Christ. Was it not too much? The Epilogue of the book assures us that it was not; and that, although the natural eye of man had not seen, nor his ear heard, nor his heart conceived the things that had been spoken of, they had been revealed by the Spirit of God Himself, not one word of whose promises would fail.

And he said unto me, These words are faithful and true: and the Lord, the God of the spirits of the prophets, sent His angel to show unto His servants the things which must shortly come to pass. And, behold, I come quickly: blessed is he that keepeth the words of the prophecy of this book.
And I John am he that heard and saw these things. And when I heard and saw, I fell down to worship before the feet of the angel which showed me these things. And he saith unto me, See thou do it not: I am a fellow-servant with thee, and with thy brethren the prophets, and with them which keep the words of this book: worship God (xxii. 6-9).

Attention has been already called in this commentary both to that characteristic of St. John's style as a writer which leads him, at a longer or a shorter interval, to the point from which he started, and to the fact that light is thus frequently thrown on the interpretation of what he says. [585] Every illustration of such a point is therefore not only interesting, but important; and in the words before us it is illustrated with more than ordinary clearness.

The person introduced with the words He said unto me is not indeed named, but there can be little doubt that he is the angel spoken of in the Prologue as sent to "signify" the revelation that was to follow.[586]

Again, when the Seer is overwhelmed with what he has seen, and may be said to have almost feared that it was too wonderful for belief, the angel assures him that it was all faithful and true. A similar declaration had been made at chap. xix. 9 by the voice which there "came forth from the throne," [587] and likewise at chap. xxi. 5 by Him "that sitteth on the throne." The angel therefore who now speaks, like the angel of the Prologue, has the authority of this Divine Being for what he says. It is true that in the following words, which seem to come from the same speaker, the angel must thus be understood to refer to himself in the third person, and not, as we might have expected, in the first,--The Lord sent His angel, not The Lord sent me. But, to say nothing of the fact that such a method of address is met with in the prophetic style of the Old Testament, it appears to be characteristic of St. John in other passages of his writings. More particularly we mark it in the narrative in the fourth Gospel of the death of Jesus on the Cross: "And he that hath seen hath borne witness, and his witness is true: and he knoweth that he saith true, that ye may believe." [588]

Again, we read here that the Lord sent His angel to show unto His servants the things which must shortly come to pass; and the statement is the same as that of chap. i. 1.

The next words, And, behold, I come quickly, are probably words of our Lord Himself; but the blessing upon him that keepeth the words of the prophecy of this book again leads the Seer back to the Prologue, where a similar blessing is pronounced. [589]

Again, the remembrance of the Prologue is in the Apostle's mind when, naming himself, he proceeds, I John am he that heard and saw these things. In precisely the same manner, after the introductory verses of the Prologue, he had named himself as the writer of the book: "John to the seven Churches;" "I John, your brother." [590] Then he was about to write; now that he has written, he is the same John whom the Church knew and honoured, and whose consciousness of everything that had passed was undimmed and perfect. This going back upon the Prologue is also sufficient to prove, if proof be thought necessary, that the words "these things" are designed to include, not merely the vision of the new Jerusalem, but all the visions of the book.

That the Seer should have fallen down to worship before the feet of the angel which showed him these things has often caused surprise. He had already done so on a previous occasion, [591] and had been reproved in words almost exactly similar to those in which he is now addressed: See thou do it not: I am a fellow-servant with thee, and with thy brethren the prophets, and with them which keep the words of this book: worship God. How could he so soon forget the warning? We need not wonder. The thought of the one vision preceding his former mistake might easily be swallowed up by the thought of the whole revelation of which it was a part; and, as the splendour of all that he had witnessed passed once more before his view, he might imagine that the angel by whom it was communicated must be worthy of his worship. His mistake was corrected as before.

The prophecy is now in the Seer's hands, ideally, though not actually, written. He may easily speak of it, therefore, as written, and may relate the instructions which he received regarding it. He does this, and again it will be seen how closely he follows the lines of his Prologue:--

And he saith unto me, Seal not up the words of the prophecy of this book: for the time is at hand. He that is unrighteous, let him do unrighteousness still: and he that is filthy, let him be made filthy still: and he that is righteous, let him do righteousness still: and he that is holy, let him be made holy still. Behold, I come quickly; and My reward is with Me, to render to each man according as his work is. I am the Alpha and the Omega, the first and the last, the beginning and the end. Blessed are they that wash their robes, that they may have the right to come to the tree of life, and may enter in by the gates into the city. Without are the dogs, and the sorcerers, and the fornicators, and the murderers, and the idolaters, and every one that loveth and maketh a lie (xxii. 10-15).

To the prophet Daniel it had been said, "But thou, O Daniel, shut up the words, and seal the book, even to the time of the end." [592] The hour had not yet come for the full manifestation of that momentous future upon which he had been commissioned to dwell. The situation of St. John was wholly different, and the hour for winding up the history of this dispensation was about to strike. It was not a time then for sealing up, but for breaking seals, a time for prophecy, for the loudest, clearest, and most urgent proclamation of the truth. "Behold, I come quickly," had been a moment before the voice of the great Judge. Let the bride for whom He is to come be ready; and, that she may the more promptly be so, let her hear with earnest and immediate attention the words of the prophecy of this book.

It is by no means easy to say whether the following words, He that is unrighteous, let him do unrighteousness still: and he that is filthy, let him be made filthy still: and he that is righteous, let him do righteousness still: and he that is holy, let him be made holy still, are to be considered as coming from the Apostle or from the angel who has been speaking to him. This difficulty is the same as that experienced in the fourth Gospel at such passages as chap. iii. 16 and 31, where it is nearly impossible to tell the point at which in the one case the words of Jesus, at which in the other the words of the Baptist, end. It would appear as if St. John so sank himself in the person with whom he was occupied at the time that he often gave utterance to thoughts without being able to distinguish between the other's and his own. In the present instance it matters little to whom we directly refer the words, whether to St. John, or to the angel, or to Him who speaks by the angel. In any case they contain a striking and solemn view of the relation between the righteous Judge and His creatures, when that relation is looked at in its ultimate, in its final, form. One thing is clear: that the first two clauses cannot be regarded as a summons to the wicked telling them before the Judgment to go on in their wickedness even while the period of their probation lasts. Nor can the second two clauses be regarded as an assurance to the good that there is a point in the actual experience of life at which their perseverance in goodness is secured. The words can only be understood in the light of that idealism which is so characteristic alike of the Apocalypse and of the fourth Gospel. In both books the world of mankind is presented to us in exactly the same light. Men are divided into two great classes: those who are prepared to receive the truth and those who are obstinately opposed to it; and these classes are spoken of as if they had been formed, not merely after, but before, the work of Christ had tried and proved them. Not indeed that the salvation to be found in Jesus was not designed to be universal, that there was even one member of the human family doomed by eternal and irresistible decree to everlasting death, nor, again, that men are considered as so essentially identified with the two classes to which they respectively belong that they incur no moral responsibility in accepting or rejecting the Redeemer of the world. In that respect St. John occupied the same ground as his fellow-Apostles. Not less than they would he have declared that God willed all men to be saved; and not less than they would he have told them that, if they were not saved, it was because they "loved the darkness rather than the light." [593] Yet, notwithstanding this practical mode in which he would have dealt with men, such is his idealism, such his mode of looking at things in their ultimate, eternal, unchanging aspect, that he constantly presents the two classes as if they were divided from each other by a permanent wall of separation, and as if the work of Christ consisted not so much in bringing the one class over to the other as in making manifest the existing tendencies of each. The light of the one brightens, the darkness of the other deepens, as we proceed; but the light does not become darkness, and the darkness does not become light. [594]

Hence, accordingly, the conversion of Israel or of the heathen finds no place in the Apocalypse. The texts supposed to offer such a prospect will not bear the interpretation put upon them. It does not indeed follow that, according to the teaching of this book, neither Israel nor the heathen will be converted. St. John only sees the end in the beginning, and deals, not with the everyday practical, but with the ideal and everlasting, issues of God's kingdom. Hence, in interpreting the words before us, we must be careful to put into them the exact shade of meaning which the whole spirit and tone of the Apostle's writings prove to have been in his mind when they were written. The clauses "He that is unrighteous" and "He that is filthy" are to be understood as "He that has loved and chosen unrighteousness and filthiness:" the clauses "Let him do unrighteousness still" and "Let him be made filthy still" as "Let him sink deeper into the unrighteousness and filthiness which he has loved and chosen." A principle freely selected by himself is supposed to be in the breast of each, and that principle does not remain fixed and stationary. No principle does. It unfolds or develops itself according to its own nature, rising to greater heights of good if it be good, sinking to greater depths of evil if it be evil. Hence also we are not to imagine that the words under consideration are applicable only to the end, or are the record only of a final judgment. They are applicable to the Church and to the world throughout the whole course of their respective histories, and it is at this moment as true as it will ever be that, in so far as the heart and will of a man are really turned to evil or to good, the allegiance he has chosen has the tendency of continued progress towards the triumph of the one or of the other.

In connexion with thoughts like these, we see the peculiar propriety of that declaration as to Himself and His purposes next made by the Redeemer: Behold, I come quickly. He comes to wind up the history of the present dispensation. And My reward is with Me, to render to each man according as his work is. He comes to bestow "reward" [595] upon His own; and there is no mention of judgment, because for those who are to be rewarded judgment is past and gone. I am the Alpha and the Omega, the first and the last, the beginning and the end, the words again taking us back to the language of the Prologue, [596] upon which follows a blessing for such as wash their robes, for those otherwise described in the Prologue as "loosed from their sins in His blood," [597] and in chap. vii. 14 as having "washed their robes and made them white in the blood of the Lamb." These have the right to come to the tree of life, and they enter in by the gates into the city. A different order might have been expected, for the tree of life grows within the city, and it is the happy inhabitants of the city who eat its fruits. But this is the blessed paradox of faith. It is difficult to say which privilege enjoyed by the believer comes first, and which comes second. Rather may all that he enjoys be looked on as given at once, for the great gift to him is Christ Himself, and in Him everything is included. He is the gate of the city, and as such the way to the tree of life; He is the tree of life, and they who partake of Him have a right to enter into the city and dwell there. Why ask, Which comes first? At one moment we may think that it is one blessing, at another that it is another. The true description of our state is that we are "in Christ Jesus, who was made unto us wisdom from God, and righteousness, and sanctification, and redemption: that, according as it is written, He that glorieth, let him glory in the Lord." [598]

To enhance our estimate of the happiness of those who are within the city, there comes next a description of those who are without. They are first denoted by the general term the dogs, that animal, as we learn from many passages of Scripture, being to the Jew the emblem of all that was wild, unregulated, unclean, and offensive. [599] Then the general term is subdivided into various classes; and all of them are without, not put out. They were put out when judgment fell upon them. Now they are without; and the door once open to them "is shut." [600]

The last words follow:--

I Jesus have sent Mine angel to testify unto you these things for the Churches. I am the root and the offspring of David, the bright, the morning star.

And the Spirit and the bride say, Come. And he that heareth, let him say, Come. And he that is athirst, let him come. He that will, let him take the water of life freely. I testify unto every man that heareth the words of the prophecy of this book, If any man shall add unto them, God shall add unto him the plagues which are written in this book: and if any man shall take away from the words of the book of this prophecy, God shall take away his part from the tree of life, and out of the holy city, which are written in this book. He which testifieth these things saith, Yea: I come quickly. Amen, Come, Lord Jesus.

The grace of the Lord Jesus be with the saints. Amen (xxii. 16-21).

Once more in these words it will be seen that we return to the Prologue, in the opening words of which we read, "The Revelation of Jesus Christ, which God gave Him, to show unto His servants; ... and He sent and signified it by His angel unto His servant John." [601] The glorified Lord now takes up the same words Himself; and, connecting by the name "Jesus" all that He was on earth with all that belongs to His condition in heaven, He declares of the whole revelation contained in the visions of this book that the angel through whom it was communicated had been sent by Him. He Himself had given it--He, even Jesus,--Jesus the Saviour of His people from their sins, the Captain of their salvation, the Joshua who leads them out of the "wilderness" of this world, across the valley of the shadow of death, into that Promised Land which Canaan, with its milk and honey, its vines and olive trees, its rest after long wanderings, and its peace after hard warfare, only faintly pictured to their view. Well is He able to do this, for in Him earth meets heaven, and "the angels of God ascend and descend upon the Son of man." [602]

First, He is the root and the offspring of David, not the root out of which David springs, as if He would say that He is David's Lord as well as David's Son, [603] but the "shoot that comes out of the stock of Jesse and the branch out of his roots that bears fruit." [604] He is the "Son, who was born of the seed of David according to the flesh," [605] the substance of ancient prophecy, the long-promised and looked-for King. Secondly, He is the bright, the morning star, the star which shines in its greatest brilliancy when the darkness is about to disappear, and that day is about to break of which "the Sun of righteousness, with healing in His wings," shall be the everlasting light, [606] Himself "our Star, our Sun." Thus He is connected on the one side with earth, on the other with heaven, "Immanuel, God with us," [607] touched with a feeling of our infirmities, mighty to save. "What then shall we say to these things? If God is for us, who is against us? He that spared not His own Son, but delivered Him up for us all, how shall He not also with Him freely give us all things? Who shall say anything to the charge of God's elect? It is God that justifieth. Who is he that shall condemn? It is Christ Jesus that died, yea rather, that was raised from the dead, who is at the right hand of God, who also maketh intercession for us. Who shall separate us from the love of Christ? shall tribulation, or anguish, or persecution, or famine, or nakedness, or peril, or sword? Even as it is written,

For Thy sake we are killed all the day long; We were accounted as sheep for the slaughter.

Nay, in all these things we are more than conquerors through Him that loved us. For I am persuaded, that neither death, nor life, nor angels, nor principalities, nor things present, nor things to come, nor powers, nor height, nor depth, nor any other creature, shall be able to separate us from the love of God, which is in Christ Jesus our Lord." [608]

The Saviour had declared, "Behold, I come quickly," had spoken of the "reward" which He would bring with Him, and had used various images to set forth the happiness and joy which should be the everlasting portion of those for whom He came. These declarations could not fail to awaken in the breast of the Church a longing for His coming, and this longing now finds expression.

The Spirit and the bride say, Come. We are not to think of two separate voices: the voice of the Spirit and the voice of the bride. It is a characteristic of St. John's style that where there is combined action, action, having both an inward and invisible and an outward and visible side, he often separates the two agencies by which it is produced. Many illustrations of this may be found in his mention of the actions of the Father and the Son, but it will be enough to refer to one more strictly parallel to that met with here. In chap. xv. of the fourth Gospel we find Jesus saying to His disciples, "But when the Advocate is come, whom I will send unto you from the Father, even the Spirit of truth, which proceedeth from the Father, He shall bear witness of Me; and ye also bear witness, because ye have been with Me from the beginning." [609] In these words we have not two works of witnessing, the first that of the Advocate, the second that of the disciples. We have only one,--outwardly that of the disciples, inwardly that of the Advocate. In like manner now. The Spirit and the bride do not utter separate calls. The Spirit calls in the bride; the bride calls in the Spirit. The cry "Come" is therefore that of the spiritually enlightened Church as she answers the voice of her Lord and King. Her voice is the echo of His. He says, "I come;" she answers, "Come." St. John then adds the next clause himself: And let him that heareth say, Come; that is, let him that heareth with the hearing of faith; let him who has made his own the glorious prospects opened up in the visions of this book as to the Lord's Second Coming add his individual cry to the cry of the universal Church. To this the Saviour replies, And he that is athirst, let him come. He that will, let him take the water of life freely. The words appear to be addressed, not to the world, but to the Church. He that is "athirst" has already drunk of the living water, but he thirsts for deeper draughts from that river the streams whereof make glad the city of God. To partake more and more largely of these is the believer's longing; and fulness of blessing is within his reach. Let him never say, "It is enough." Let him drink and drink again; let him drink "freely," until the water that Christ shall give him becomes in him "a fountain of springing water unto eternal life." [610] The statements and replies contained in these words are those of the glorified Lord, of the Church speaking in the Spirit, and of the individual believer, as they hold converse with one another in that moment of highest rapture when evil has been extinguished, when the struggle is over, when the victory has been gained, and when the Lord of the Church is at the door. He in them and they in Him, what can they do but speak to and answer one another in strains expressive of mutual longing and affection and joy?

Once more the Seer--for it seems to be he that speaks--turns to the book which he has written.

In the Prologue he had said, "Blessed is he that readeth, and they that hear the words of the prophecy, and keep the things which are written therein." [611] In the same spirit he now denounces a woe upon him who adds to it: God shall add unto him the plagues which are written in the book; nor less upon him who takes from it: for God shall take away his part from the tree of life, and out of the holy city, which are written in this book. The book has come from Him who is the faithful and true Witness of God, and it has been written in obedience to His command and under the guidance of His Spirit. St. John himself is nothing; Christ is all: and St. John knows that the words of his great Master are fulfilled, "He that receiveth you receiveth Me, and he that receiveth Me receiveth Him that sent Me." [612] Therefore may he speak with all authority, for it is not he that speaks, but the Holy Spirit. [613]

Yet once again, before the parting salutation, Christ and the Church interchange their thoughts. The former speaks first: He which testifieth these things saith, Yea, I come quickly. It is the sum and substance of His message to His suffering people, for they can desire or need no more. The "I" is the Lord Himself as He is in glory, not in the feebleness of the flesh, not amidst the sins and sorrows of the world, not with the cup of trembling and astonishment in His hand, but in the unlimited fulness of His Divine power, clothed with the light of His heavenly abode, and anointed with the oil of gladness above His fellows. Especially is the Church told that this revelation is all she needs, because throughout the book she is supposed to be in the midst of trials. To the troubled heart the Apocalypse is given; and by such a heart is it best understood.

Jesus has spoken; and the Church replies, Amen. Come, Lord Jesus. Amen to all that the Lord has promised; Amen to the thought of sin and sorrow banished, of wounded hearts healed, of tears of affliction wiped away, of the sting taken from death and victory from the grave, of darkness dissipated for ever, of the light of the eternal day. Surely it cannot come too soon. "Why is His chariot so long in coming? Why tarry the wheels of His chariots?" [614] "Yea, I come quickly. Amen. Come, Lord Jesus."

The salutation of the writer to his readers alone remains. It ought to be read differently from its form in the authorised English version, not "The grace of our Lord Jesus Christ be with you all," but The grace of the Lord Jesus be with the saints. For the saints the book had been written; to them it had been spoken: they alone can keep it. Let no man who is not in Christ imagine that the Revelation of St. John is addressed to him. Let no man imagine that, if he has not found Christ already, he will find Him here. The book will rather perplex and puzzle, more probably offend, him. Only in that union with Christ which brings with it the hatred of sin and the love of holiness, which teaches us that we are "orphans" [615] in a present world, which makes us wait for the manifestation of the kingdom of God as they that wait for the morning, can we enter into the spirit of the Apocalypse, listen to its threatenings without thinking them too severe, or so embrace its promises that they shall heighten rather than lower the tone of our spiritual life. Here, if anywhere, faith and love are the key to knowledge, not knowledge the key to faith and love. It is in the very spirit of the book, therefore, not in a spirit hard, or narrow, or unsympathetic, that it closes with the words, "The grace of the Lord Jesus be with the saints."

***

We have reached the end of this singular, but at the same time most instructive, book of the New Testament. That the principles upon which it has been interpreted should be generally accepted were too much to hope for. Their acceptance, where they are received, must depend mainly upon the consideration that while, as scientific principles, they are thoroughly capable of defence, they give unity to the book and a meaning worthy of that Divine Spirit by whose influence upon the soul of the Apostle it was produced. On no other principles of interpretation does it seem possible to effect this; and the writer of these pages at least is compelled to think that, if they are rejected, there is only one conclusion possible,--that the Apocalypse, however interesting as a literary memorial of the early Christian age, must be regarded as a merely human production, and not entitled to a place in the canon of Scripture. Such a place, however, must in the present state of the argument be vindicated for it; and as an inspired book it has accordingly been treated here. What the reader, therefore, has to consider is whether, though some difficulties may not be completely overcome, he can accept in the main the principles upon which, in endeavouring to explain the book, the writer has proceeded. These principles the reader, whoever he be, undoubtedly applies to innumerable passages of Scripture. In so applying them to the prophets of the Old Testament, he follows the example of our Lord and His Apostles; and much of the New Testament itself equally demands their application. There is nothing new in them. All commentators in part apply them. They have only been followed out now with more consistency and uniformity than usual. Archdeacon Farrar has said that one of the two questions in New Testament criticism which have acquired new aspects during the last few years is, What is the key to the interpretation of the Apocalypse? [616] The question is certainly one urgently demanding the Church's answer, and one which will without doubt be answered in due time, either in the present or some other form. May the Spirit of God guide the Church and her students, and that speedily, into all the truth.

Footnotes:

585. Comp. p. 373.
586. Chap. i. 1.
587. Chap. xix. 5.
588. John xix. 35. Wider questions than can be here discussed would be opened up by an inquiry how far the same method of explanation may be applied to John xvii. 3.
589. Chap. i. 3.
590. Chap. i. 4, 9.
591. Chap. xix. 10.
592. Dan. xii. 4; comp. viii. 26.
593. Comp. John iii. 19.
594. See a fuller treatment of this important point by the author in his Lectures on the Revelation of St. John, p. 286, etc.
595. Comp. chap. xi. 18.
596. Chap. i. 8.
597. Chap. i. 5.
598. 1 Cor. i. 30.
599. Comp. Ps. xxii. 16, 20; Matt. vii. 6; Phil. iii. 2.
600. Comp. Matt. xxv. 10.
601. Chap. i. 1.
602. John i. 51.
603. Matt. xxii. 45.
604. Isa. xi. 1.
605. Rom. i. 3.
606. Mal. iv. 2.
607. Matt. i. 23.
608. Rom. viii. 31-39.
609. John xv. 26, 27.
610. John iv. 14.
611. Chap. i. 3.
612. Matt. x. 40.
613. Comp. Mark xiii. 11.
614. Judges v. 28.
615. John xiv. 18, R.V. (margin).
616. Expositor, July, 1888, p. 58.

www.ingramcontent.com/pod-product-compliance
Lightning Source LLC
Chambersburg PA
CBHW021238090426
42740CB00006B/583